Lecture Notes
in Business Information Processing

122

Series Editors

Wil van der Aalst
  Eindhoven Technical University, The Netherlands
John Mylopoulos
  University of Trento, Italy
Michael Rosemann
  Queensland University of Technology, Brisbane, Qld, Australia
Michael J. Shaw
  University of Illinois, Urbana-Champaign, IL, USA
Clemens Szyperski
  Microsoft Research, Redmond, WA, USA

Marten van Sinderen
Pontus Johnson
Xiaofei Xu
Guy Doumeingts (Eds.)

Enterprise Interoperability

4th International IFIP Working Conference, IWEI 2012
Harbin, China, September 6-7, 2012
Proceedings

 Springer

Volume Editors

Marten van Sinderen
University of Twente, The Netherlands
E-mail: m.j.vansinderen@utwente.nl

Pontus Johnson
KTH Royal Institute of Technology, Stockholm, Sweden
E-mail: pontus@ics.kth.se

Xiaofei Xu
Harbin Institute of Technology, China
E-mail: xiaofei@hit.edu.cn

Guy Doumeingts
Université Bordeaux1, Talence Cedex, France
E-mail: guy.doumeingts@interop-vlab.eu

ISSN 1865-1348   e-ISSN 1865-1356
ISBN 978-3-642-33067-4   e-ISBN 978-3-642-33068-1
DOI 10.1007/978-3-642-33068-1
Springer Heidelberg Dordrecht London New York

Library of Congress Control Number: 2012945076

ACM Computing Classification (1998): J.1, H.3.5, H.4, D.2.12

Typesetting: Camera-ready by author, data conversion by Scientific Publishing Services, Chennai, India

Printed on acid-free paper

Springer is part of Springer Science+Business Media (www.springer.com)

*The original version of the book was revised:
The copyright line was incorrect. The Erratum
to the book is available at
DOI: 10.1007/978-3-642-33068-1_20*

Preface

Several developments are expected to change the nature and affect the operation of enterprises in the near future. These developments are not new, and their influence when considered in isolation may not be decisive, but combined they represent important challenges as well as opportunities. Globalization, as one of the most important drivers of modern times, continues to influence enterprises and makes the boundaries for enterprise operation increasingly disappear. Constant and rapid change in technological capabilities, consumer demands, and legal/regulatory constraints push enterprises to become more agile and adaptive. The ability to create and offer value-added services by anyone to anyone has blurred the roles of consumer and producer, and of employee and employer. One conclusion to be drawn from these developments is that the success of an enterprise more and more depends on its ability to interoperate with other enterprises, of any size and in any place. Enterprises have to function in dynamic networks, with value being created in both directions in order to stay competitive and achieve their business goals.

Collaboration, interoperability, and services are essential for the networked enterprises of the future. A better understanding of these concepts and their relationships will help to face the challenges and exploit the opportunities ahead. In addition, it will foster appropriate architectural frameworks and IT solutions. For example, the technical development of the Future Internet should not only be driven by problems of the current Internet but also be guided and evaluated from the enterprise perspective regarding collaboration, interoperability, and services. This will ensure that the Future Internet really aims at empowering enterprises to create business value in competition and cooperation with other enterprises, based on relevant knowledge about each other and the market. Several enterprise-relevant aspects should be grounded in the Future Internet, meaning that collaboration is supported by IT services (to find information) for connecting partners and binding resources according to enterprise-defined performance indicators on top of a general interoperability infrastructure. Such IT services may require integration of physical sensing, business intelligence, and knowledge sharing

IWEI is an International IFIP Working Conference covering all aspects of enterprise interoperability with the purpose of achieving flexible cross-organizational collaboration through integrated support at business and technical levels. It provides a forum for discussing ideas and results among both researchers and practitioners. Contributions to the following areas are highlighted: scientific foundations for specifying, analyzing, and validating interoperability solutions; architectural frameworks for addressing interoperability challenges from different viewpoints and at different levels of abstraction; maturity models to evaluate and rank inter-operability solutions with respect to distinguished quality criteria; and practical solutions and tools that can be applied to interoperability problems to date.

This year's IWEI – IWEI 2012 – was held during September 6–7, 2012, in Harbin, China, following previous events in Stockholm, Sweden (2011), Valencia, Spain (2009), and Munich, Germany (2008). The theme of IWEI 2012 was "Collaboration, Interoperability and Services for Networked Enterprises," thus especially soliciting submissions and discussions related to the three previously mentioned interrelated areas for enterprise interoperability.

IWEI 2012 was organized by the IFIP Working Group 5.8 on Enterprise Interoperability in co-operation with InterOP-VLab. The objective of IFIP WG5.8 is to advance and disseminate research and development results in the area of enterprise interoperability. IWEI provides an excellent platform to discuss the ideas that have emerged from IFIP WG5.8 meetings, or, reversely, to transfer issues identified at the workshop to the IFIP community for further contemplation and investigation.

The proceedings of IWEI 2012 are contained in this volume. In total 14 full papers and three short papers were selected for oral presentation and publication. The selection was based on a thorough review process, in which each paper was reviewed by at least three experts in the field. The papers are representative of the current research activities in the area of enterprise interoperability. The papers cover a wide spectrum of enterprise interoperability issues, ranging from foundational theories, frameworks, architectures, methods and guidelines to applications and case studies.

The proceedings also include the abstracts of the invited talks of our two renowned keynote speakers: Sergio Gusmeroli (Director of TXT Labs Corporate Research Unit) and Lei Qin (Executive of Cloud Labs and Smarter Commerce Service Delivery, IBM China Development Laboratory).

We would like to take this opportunity to express our gratitude to all those who contributed to the IWEI 2012 working conference. We thank the authors for submitting content, which resulted in valuable information exchange and stimulating discussions; we thank the reviewers for providing useful feedback to the submitted content, which undoubtedly helped the authors to improve their work; and we thank the attendants for expressing interest in the content and initiating relevant discussions. We are indebted to IFIP TC5 as well as InterOP-VLab for recognizing the importance of enterprise interoperability as a research area with high economic impact, and acting accordingly with the establishment of WG5.8. Finally, we are grateful to HIT, the Harbin Institute of Technology, for hosting the working conference.

June 2012   Marten van Sinderen
                                                                  Pontus Johnson

Organization

IWEI 2011 was organized by IFIP Working Group 5.8 on Enterprise Interoperability, in cooperation with InterOP VLab.

General Chairs

Xiaofei Xu	Harbin Institute of Technology, China
Guy Doumeingts	InterOP-VLab/University of Bordeaux 1, France

Steering Committee

Degang Cui	AVIC, China
Guy Doumeingts	InterOP-VLab/University of Bordeaux 1, France
Tao Huang	Institute of Software, CAS, China
Pontus Johnson	Royal Institute of Technology, Sweden
Lea Kutvonen	University of Helsinki, Finland
Kai Mertins	Fraunhofer IPK, Germany
Marten van Sinderen	University of Twente, The Netherlands
Xiaofei Xu	Harbin Institute of Technology, China

Program Chairs

Marten van Sinderen	University of Twente, The Netherlands
Pontus Johnson	Royal Institute of Technology, Sweden

International Program Committee

Khalid Benali	LORIA - Nancy Université, France
Peter Bernus	University Griffith, Australia
Ricardo Chalmeta	University of Jaume I, Spain
David Chen	Université Bordeaux 1, France
Paul Davidsson	Malmö University, Sweden
Antonio De Nicola	ENEA, Italy
Yves Ducq	Université Bordeaux 1, France
Ip-Shing Fan	Cranfield University, UK
Ricardo Goncalves	New University of Lisbon, UNINOVA, Portugal
Claudia Guglielmina	TXT e-solutions, Italy
Sergio Gusmeroli	TXT e-solutions, Italy
Axel Hahn	University of Oldenburg, Germany
Jenny Harding	Loughborough University, UK
Roland Jochem	University of Kassel, Germany

Leonid Kalinichenko	Russian Academy of Sciences, Russian Federation
Bernhard Katzy	University of Munich, Germany
Kurt Kosanke	CIMOSA Association, Germany
Xiaoping Li	South-East University, China
Lanfen Lin	Zhejiang University, China
Shijun Liu	Shandong University, China
Jean-Pierre Lorre	PEtALS Link, France
Philippe Mahey	Blaise Pascal University, France
Michiko Matsuda	Kanagawa Institute of Technology, Japan
Lanshun Nie	Harbin Institute of Technology
Andreas Opdahl	University of Bergen, Norway
Angel Ortiz	Polytechnic University of Valencia, Spain
Hervé Panetto	UHP Nancy I, France
Hervé Pingaud	École des Mines d'Albi-Carmaux, France
Raul Poler	Polytechnic University of Valencia, Spain
Alain Quilliot	Blaise Pascal University, France
Raquel Sanchis	Polytechnic University of Valencia, Spain
Ulrike Stefefns	OFFIS, Germany
Raymond Slot	Hogeschool Utrecht, The Netherlands
Bruno Vallespir	Université Bordeaux 1, France
Nianbin Wang	Harbin Engineering University, China
Alain Wegmann	Ecole Polytechnique Federal de Lausanne, Switzerland
George Weichart	Johannes Kepler University Linz, Austria
Jun Wei	Institute of Software, CAS, China
Junfeng Zhan	Institute of Standardization, China
Li Zhang	BUAA, China
Cuilian Zhao	Shanghai University, China
Yunlong Zhu	Institute of Automation Shenyang, CAS, China

Local Organization Chairs

Dechen Zhan	Harbin Institute of Technology, China
Cathy Lieu	InterOP-VLab, Belgium

Local Organizing Committee

Shengchun Deng	Harbin Institute of Technology, China
Ting He	Harbin Institute of Technology, China
Quanglong Li	Harbin Institute of Technology, China
Xiaofeng Liu	Harbin Institute of Technology, China
HuiLuo	Harbin Institute of Technology, China
Lanshun Nie	Harbin Institute of Technology, China
Hanchuan Xu	Harbin Institute of Technology, China

Sponsoring Organizations

IFIP TC5, www.ifip.org
InterOP-VLab, www.interop-vlab.eu
InterOP-VLab, China Pole
Harbin Institute of Technology

Table of Contents

Session 3: Model Manipulation and Ontology Building

Session 4: Model-Driven Service Engineering in Enterprise Ecosystems

Short Papers

From Enterprise Interoperability to Service Innovation: European Research Activities in Future Internet Enterprise Systems

Sergio Gusmeroli

TXT e-solutions S.p.A., Via Frigia 27, 20126 Milan, Italy
sergio.gusmeroli@txtgroup.com

Abstract. The speech will describe the recent evolutionary paths of European research about Enterprise Interoperability. In 2006, the Enterprise Interoperability cluster of European projects coined the term ISU (Interoperability Service Utility) as the new IT infrastructure able to provide interoperability services to all SMEs, at low cost and under non-rivalry and non-discriminatory principles. This concept has been studied and developed further by the COIN flagship Integrated Project (COllaboration and INteroperability for networked enterprises), coordinated by TXT e-solutions, which started in 2008 and developed a first prototype of ISU by means of a dynamic federation of open and trusted Generic Service Delivery Platforms as well as envisaging a set of innovative business models for Enterprise Interoperability as a Service-Utility. More recently, the advent of EU 2020 Strategy and Digital Agenda for Europe confirmed the importance of having "interoperability and standards" as one of the most important pillars for a single digital market for European citizens and enterprises. This evident commoditization trend could induce readers to think that in 10 years time interoperability will not matter anymore (N. Carr "IT does not matter") and that it will soon be absorbed by Cloud Computing and Future Internet as one of the fundamental services of a so-called Universal Business System. However, more and more eminent scientists tend now to agree that it is when a technology really becomes a utility and apparently does not matter anymore (Z. Turk calls it sedimentation) that innovation could find the most fertile and promising ground to develop and grow. Based on the sound and solid base of Future Internet core platform and enterprise interoperability utility infrastructure, a new project, MSEE (Manufacturing SErvice Ecosystem), coordinated by TXT and started in October 2011, is now trying to explore how the commoditization and openness of IT could become an enabler for service innovation in the manufacturing industry, allowing virtual factories and enterprises to adopt a value co-creation and service dominant logic instead of a traditional perspective of producing and selling just physical goods. It is thanks to Enterprise Modelling and Interoperability as an integrated part of a Universal Business System that a milling machine industry could sell "holes per minute" or that an aircraft engine industry could sell "flying hours" or that a traditional car manufacturer could sell "mobility kilometers". As a future perspective, the speech will also address the key question whether technical-service-business

The original version of this chapter was revised: The copyright line was incorrect. This has been corrected. The Erratum to this chapter is available at DOI: 10.1007/978-3-642-33068-1_20

M. van Sinderen et al. (Eds.): IWEI 2012, LNBIP 122, pp. 1–2, 2012.
© IFIP International Federation for Information Processing 2012

innovation, implemented for instance by the Factories of the Future and the MSEE project, could be sufficient for European manufacturing industry to overcome the current economic crisis or, instead, a re-thinking of skills and competencies of employees is needed in order to implement and take up the changes imposed by innovation. In this perspective, a new research initiative, coordinated by TXT and called TELL ME (Technology Enhanced Learning Livinglab for Manufacturing Environments), is going to be launched in November 2012 with the aim of implementing human-centric manufacturing and innovative methods and solutions for blue collar workers lifelong training, via open innovation and participative creativity Living Labs.

Keywords: enterprise interoperability; service innovation; Future Internet; Universal Business System; manufacturing industry

Brief Biography

After several experiences in the research and software development domain, since July 2000, Sergio Gusmeroli is director of TXT Labs Corporate Research unit, counting now more than 20 researchers located in the TXT laboratories of Milano, Genoa and Bari. In the specific field of ICT infrastructures and architectures for enterprise interoperability and collaboration, his main research activities have been focusing on the following 3 major themes:

- Platforms and architectures for enterprise software and applications interoperability;
- Methodologies, models and software tools to support collaborative business in manufacturing;
- Methodologies, models and software tools to support the vision of the Internet of Things.

Sergio has been recently coordinating the European Commission FP7 ICT COIN (COllaboration and INteroperability for networked enterprises) Integrated Project, successfully concluded in December 2011 and he is currently the Technical Coordinator of the FP7 Factories of the Future MSEE (Manufacturing SErvice Ecosystem) Integrated Project, promoting service innovation in virtual factories and enterprises through enterprise modeling and enterprise interoperability. In the field of Technology Enhanced Learning, Sergio will soon coordinate the TELL ME (Technology Enhanced Learning Livinglab for Manufacturing Environments) Integrated Project, aiming at developing new participative and creative methods and tools for re-skilling and up-skilling blue collar workers at the manufacturing workplaces.

Building a New Eco-System to Transform a Smarter Logistics Industry with Smarter Logistics Cloud

Lei Qin

Cloud Labs, Smarter Commerce Lab. Based Service, IBM CGC, China
qinlei@cn.ibm.com

Abstract. China is well known as a "World Factory", where logistics is one of the key service industries. The market of logistics in China is huge. The logistics cost is over 18% of Chinese GDP, and it is rapidly growing at 14% increasing rate yearly. However, the logistics industry in China is inefficient and fragmentary. The rate of total logistics cost of entire GDP is even twice times bigger than developed countries. IBM is now working with the Chinese Government and local business partners to deliver a "Smarter Logistics Cloud" by applying IBM technologies such as Smarter Commerce, Cloud, Business Optimization, Business Analytics, Mobile technologies etc. Ningbo is one of the largest ports in China. We will implement in market innovation and start the transformation of service industry from Ningbo, roll it out it China, and eventually spread out to other emerging countries.

Keywords: smarter logistics, cloud computing, industry transformation, Ningbo logistics.

Brief Biography

Lei (Larry) Qin joined the IBM Software Group in 1997. During the period 1997 to 2004, Mr. Qin served the IBM Software Group as IT engineer and senior IT expert respectively, and in these capacities he had a leading role in projects concerning Lotus groupware, Internet security, and enterprise content management in various areas of design and implementation of a series of success stories including Industrial and Commercial Bank of China, people's Bank of China, Bank of China, Beijing Mobile, and China Life Insurance.

From 2004 to 2007, Mr. Qin served as Technical Sales Manager of the IBM Software Group being responsible for the Tivoli line of products in China, technical sales, and support and promotion work. In the beginning of 2008, Mr. Qin became software architect and technical director of IBM's Software Group, leading the software division team for a number of industrial customers including government, business, manufacturing, distribution, transportation, retail, software architecture design, and software and industry solutions. In 2009, Mr. Qin also served as vice president of the IBM China Development Center.

The original version of this chapter was revised: The copyright line was incorrect. This has been corrected. The Erratum to this chapter is available at DOI: 10.1007/978-3-642-33068-1_20

M. van Sinderen et al. (Eds.): IWEI 2012, LNBIP 122, pp. 3–4, 2012.
© IFIP International Federation for Information Processing 2012

From the end of 2009, Mr. Qin served as general manager of the Greater China Group (GCG) cloud computing laboratory and high-performance solutions within the IBM China Development Center.

Since 2012, Mr. Qin is also e-commerce director of laboratory services of the IBM China Development Center GCG, and serves as the Ningbo smart logistics cloud project director.

Innovation Management Needs
an Interoperable Requirements Management

Katja Landgraf[1] and Roland Jochem[2]

[1] Slitisa Inc., Schwarzer Stock 8, 36110 Schlitz, Germany
landgraf@slitisa.de
[2] Berlin Institute of Technology,
Institute of Machine Tools and Factory Management,
Chair Quality Management,
Pascalstr. 8-9, 10587 Berlin, Germany
roland.jochem@tu-berlin.de

Abstract. In a world of fast changing environments for business, the need for innovation is one of the most stable items. On the other hand, innovation is influenced by more and more factors, like increasing products and service complexity ore growing numbers of partners, involved into a single product innovation. This paper introduces interoperability problems related to simultaneous business and product development.

Purpose – This paper introduces the L-model^{Agile}, an advancement of the V-model. Due to interoperability is essential during the product development process, overall aim of the L-model^{Agile} is to improve the quality and rate of innovation within complex systems during the early stages of a stable and simultaneously agile innovation process.

Design/methodology/approach – The basis of the L-model^{Agile} consists of the interoperability between the innovation process and the requirements management & engineering process (RM&E process) as well as the agile method Scrum. To link these processes, a best practice model inclusive a capability model and a performance measurement system has been developed.

Findings – An increase of innovation quality and innovation speed at complex systems during the early stage of a reliable and simultaneous agile innovation process.

Originality/value – The paper focuses on the innovation process during the product development and how to improve its quality.

Keywords: Interoperability, innovation management, requirements management & engineering process.

1 Introduction

Innovations and their transformation into the product development process must be made comprehensible and assessable, in order to be able to minimize the associated risks. The planning of preventive quality measures to avoid unnecessary iterations and

The original version of this chapter was revised: The copyright line was incorrect. This has been corrected. The Erratum to this chapter is available at DOI: 10.1007/978-3-642-33068-1_20

M. van Sinderen et al. (Eds.): IWEI 2012, LNBIP 122, pp. 5–19, 2012.
© IFIP International Federation for Information Processing 2012

interface problems during the innovation and product development process are tasks, which shorten development times dramatically. There is no lack of innovative ideas, but their application and marketing in the form of innovative products, services and procedures. Thus for example each fourth patent of a patenting enterprise is not brought on the market in Germany - the German economy sits thereby on not realized assets of at least 8 billion Euros in terms of innovative products, services and procedures [8]. The consequences of a suboptimal innovation process can be dramatically: Who did not carry out innovations, is often to be found on the list of those ranges, which are dropped out of the market [4].

By modeling of business and product development processes the goal is pursued to increase clarity and comprehensibleness in the product development. Process admission, visualization and partially also simulation are state of the art. Today the problem is seen in the missing systematic connection between the business and the product development process, the associated models exists to a large extent independently and changes in one model are only comprehensible manually in another model. That leads to the fact that such models are not "living" and find no acceptance in the operational departments. Context and/or view-referred exchange of information and models are missing.

A substantial deficit of present processes is still the missing systematic continuity in communication between the specialized divisions and to the suppliers. System specifications during the collaborative product development process must be described more precisely, semantically clearly and above all computer-interpretable, in order to eliminate for example misunderstandings and to test the development results against the requirements.

2   Innovation Management

The innovation is the result of a process or even the process itself, all phases by the idea preparation over the idea conversion up to the idea utilization, or differently said to the introduction on the market and economic use. Innovation, and the scientific analysis of this area, is no new topic of the economy. Already in 1931 the Austrian political economist Alois Schumpeter has innovated an "Enforcement of new combinations", with which enterprises leave from pecuniary reward them, "reeled out courses of the static economy" [13]. The enforcement of new combinations Schumpeter refers to the production of a novel product or a new production method, the development of a new sales market or the reorganisation of an enterprise.

This traditional understanding of innovation has changed particularly in the last years. Besides the radical-revolutionary changes, as they are connected with the application of new active principles or a complete reorganization of processes and structures, also incremental evolutionary innovations have increasingly obtained attention, as for example the continuous improvement of single product or process parameter [10].

Innovation management is understood as systematic planning, conversion and control of ideas in organizations. The management of innovations is part of the enterprise strategy and can refer to products, services, manufacturing processes, organisational structures or management processes. While product innovations usually aim at to satisfy the needs of customers better, process innovations are usually aligned to improvement of effectiveness and efficiency of procedures.

The continuously decreasing developmental periods, the increasing number of technologies and their system connections, the numerous global process interfaces during and besides the product engineering process, the extension of customer markets, increased expense pressure and much more – all this leads to a more and more complex innovation process which needs to be stably controlled [3, 6] and at the same time flexible and agile enough to fit changing circumstances (of customers, of markets, of laws, etc.).

The manufacturers along the value chain have to develop and produce more and more efficient and innovative products of higher quality, providing a large number of individual variants. [14] To develop innovative product in short clock cycles, interoperability between standards in quality and processes inside and outside the company is essential. Thereby it is a general rule to keep the balance between the required stability and needed process agility, operations and methods. The stability is primarily gained by the definition of standards in quality and processes. But what is the required level of standardization at a creative innovation process?

If the complex standards are completely realized and lived out within the process, the coefficients "time" and "expenses" get out of hand. Due to this, innovations might reach the market too late, possibly accompanied by significant expenses.

The target has to be the definition of a reliable standard in quality and processes and to simultaneously be flexible or agile enough to fit rapidly changing circumstances.

3   Basic Concept of the L-model^{Agile}

The L-model^{Agile} is concerned in detail with these early stages of the innovation process of complex systems at the vehicle industry with the target of securing and improving the innovation quality using the agile Scrum methods. The application of Scrum at the early stages of the innovation process shall enable a focused communication of the required inputs and outputs between all participants with the right quality, the respective expenses and at the scheduled time. Besides the application of Scrum for planning and controlling the innovation process, the requirements management & engineering (RM&E) plays another key role for the communication of quality requirements within the innovation process. By the interoperability of RM&E at the early stages of the innovation process a structured approach for identification, documentation and administration of relevant market, competition and customer requirements is given. This ensures the communication between all relevant quality requirements.

The L-model^{Agile} consists of four parts. The first one is the so called innovation requirements process (IR process^{Agile}). It includes a methods catalogue, process templates and a role model. For its execution are two essential documents provided, which enables a prototypical realization.

Second part of the L-model^{Agile} is a catalogue of indication numbers which was developed to control and improve the process. The third part, the so called innovation requirements maturity model rates the execution of the L-model^{Agile} and suggests actions for a continuous improvement.

Afterwards, as part four, the whole information is summarized into a web-based approach guideline.

The Structure and the four parts of the model are explained below.

The intention of the L-model^{Agile} is to build on existing and established research concepts. The V-model is already established at the whole vehicle industry, it was seen as a starting point for the L-model^{Agile}.

The V-model is applied at almost every company of the vehicle industry. The name occurs from the v-shaped structure of the project elements. The "V-shape" expresses the equivalent verification and validation step at each conception step. The needed requirements on the developed system of the later user for instance are specified at a product requirement document or a requirements specification. The approach during the development is supported by concepts and proposals. [7, 11]

Another basis for the L-model's structure besides the V-model is the interoperability of the RM&E and the innovation management with Scrum to a so called innovation requirements process^{Agil} (IR process^{Agil}).

The created IR process^{Agil} illustrated that the V-model and in concrete the first element of the V-model, the "requirements identification and specification", was not sufficient for the required context at a systematic analysis and valuation of ideas, resp. future innovations. Therefore the approach of the L-model^{Agile} is to expand the V-model by the context, resp. the stages of the idea development and thereby the fragmentation and specification of an idea.

The expansion consists of three elements:

- Element 1: Potential determination and first framework conditions
- Element 2: Idea determination, including first requirements
- Element 3: Idea release for execution

To keep the "symmetry" at the L-model, the elements of the V-model have been turned by 45° and expanded by the elements of idea fragmentation and specification.

The components of the V-model including the extensions build the structure of the L-model^{Agile} (Figure 1).

The elements of the structure of the L-model^{Agile} work as gates within the IR prozess^{Agile}, illustrated by a traffic light. The elements of the left stem are, as at the V-model, validated with the requirements of the right stem. The first three elements are proven by identified lessons learned information from the whole supply chain and thereby the innovation process is continuously improved.

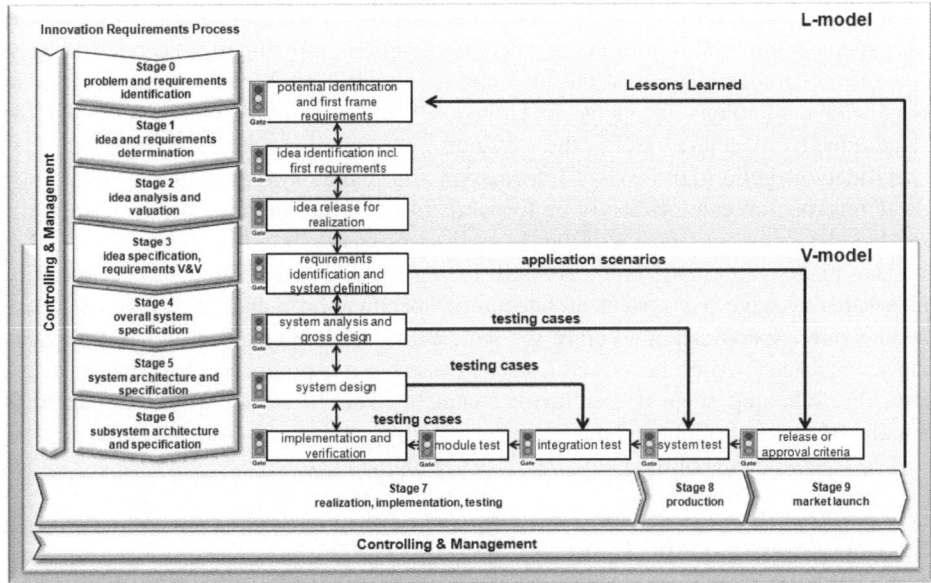

Fig. 1. Structure of the L-model[Agil]

As shown in Figure1, the IR process starts with the systematic generation of an idea – stage 0, the "problem and requirements identification".

The stakeholder identification and the competitive intelligence at this stage should in concrete identify the heterogeneous customer wishes and the requirements of the market and the competition which are later integrated to stage 1, the "idea and requirements identification". The gate between stage 0 and 1 is considered as a quality check for the collected information. The quality control ensures a qualitatively high level of information of each requirement, resp. information. This prevents misunderstandings by the systematic generation and collection of information and requirements.

Within the IR process[Agile] an idea can be generated systematically from the market (at stage 0) or "unsystematically"(without market research directly at stage 1), e.g. by employees in shape of lessons learned. Thereby an early requirements analysis and modeling (by UML/SysML/Swimlane) at stage 1, the "idea and requirements identification", improves the quality of analysis and valuation of ideas already at the beginning and supports the decision makers at the valuation process. In turn this minimizes the miscalculations and improves the innovation quality. Using the model-based and systematic analysis and valuation helps to make out risks early. A gross valuation of the idea finishes stage 1.

At stage 2, the "idea analysis and valuation", the analysis and valuation of an idea gets refined with support of the RM&E. By doing so, risks can be rated successively and measures can be initialized early. The development expenses and time can be minimized by early detection of risks and an exact, model-based specification. Afterwards the decision maker at the stage 2 gate decides about release and realization of the idea, another improvement loop or the abandonment.

When the decision is made to release the idea for realization, stage 3 begins - the idea specification and requirements v&v (verification and validation). Focus of stage 3 is the exact specification of the idea and the quality check of the requirements. In parallel a marketing concept is developed. By the support of the RM&E and the requirements structure from the systems engineering, the model-based idea specifications get a high level of information and reduce miscalculations. In addition these information can efficiently be forwarded to adjacent process interfaces, e.g. the product development (stage 4 of the "overall specification").

The respective subsystems as well as their architecture are further specified afterwards at stage 5 ("system architecture / specification") and stage 6 ("subsystem architecture / specification") before the realization, the implementation and the testing happen at stage 7. After the system tests are passed, series production happens at stage 8 with the following stage 9, the "market launch". The 10 stages are accompanied in parallel by the controlling and management.

The four elements of the L-model^{Agile} are explained below.

4   Elements of the L-model^{Agil}

As already introductorily mentioned, the four main elements of the L-model^{Agil} are, besides the IR process^{Agil} (element 1), a key figures catalogue for process controlling (element 2), a maturity level model for model realization valuation (element 3) and a web-based approach guideline which shows the whole information, including an implementation concept (element 4). These four elements are now introduced below. This paper focuses in concrete on the early stages of the innovation process, the so called idea development stages at the IR process^{Agil}.

4.1   The Innovation Requirements Process at the L-model^{Agile} (Methods & Elements)

An innovation process has to continuously fit new framework conditions. Due to this time pressure, a substantial application of the processes isn't always possible. Additionally, especially at this stages of creativity, communication inside and outside the company are an important factor of success. Therefore the innovation process has to be agile. The agile approach within the L-model^{Agile} is explained below.

Agile methods are based upon the four basic rules of the "agile manifest": [1]

"Individuals and interactions over processes and tools
Working software over comprehensive documentation
Customer collaboration over contract negotiation
Responding to change over following a plan"

An agile approach is especially defined by the great variance of methods, their appropriate choice, continuous valuation and their change of necessary. Agile means to choose the appropriate method out of an obviously endless amount of possibilities and to use & abuse it. [11] Scrum was chosen for the integration of an agile method into the model.

Scrum shows rules for the planning and controlling of projects. A Scrum project consists of several iterations (sprints) which are supported by team conferences (sprint meetings). Responsibilities, deadlines and results are clearly defined by sprints. Thanks to scrum, the IR process[Agile] consists of a clearly structured approach and due to this it is easily and systematically realizable. The sprints are determined by the stages of tie IR process. A sprint lasts approx. 30 days, but it's duration is company-dependent and is therefore defined as a "time box" at the L-model[Agile] (see Figure. 2). [12]

Before each spring information is taken from a pool, the so called product backlog, and afterwards processed by the scrum team. Depending on the stage, this can be a pool of requirements, potentoials, frame conditions or ideas. [15]

Before a sprint can start, the sprint result or output is exactly defined. During the sprint, the scrum master cares for the scrum team not to be interrupted or disturbed in developing the sprint output. The team acts selforganizingly and comes together in sprint meeting during the sprint which happen daily or in larger periods. Questions on the commission side, the product owner, can be cleared and problems can be discussed by the scrum master moderated meetings. The product owner in this case represents the technical commission side. [12]

The defined sprint results are presented to the product owner (ort in case to the customer) at the sprint review to obtain a recent feedback. Every sprint review is defined by the gates of the L-model[Agile]. At the review the decision is made whether the predefined sprint output has been reached or not. If not, either the specific sprint has to be repeated or the product backlog has to be updated. The following sprint restrospective meeting contains the continuous improvement and lessons learned at the process. Supported by the innovation maturity level, potentials can be identified and realized at this point to rise in efficiency and effectiveness. [12]

The approach of the agile methods at the IR process[Agile] is introduced below by reference of the stages 0-3.

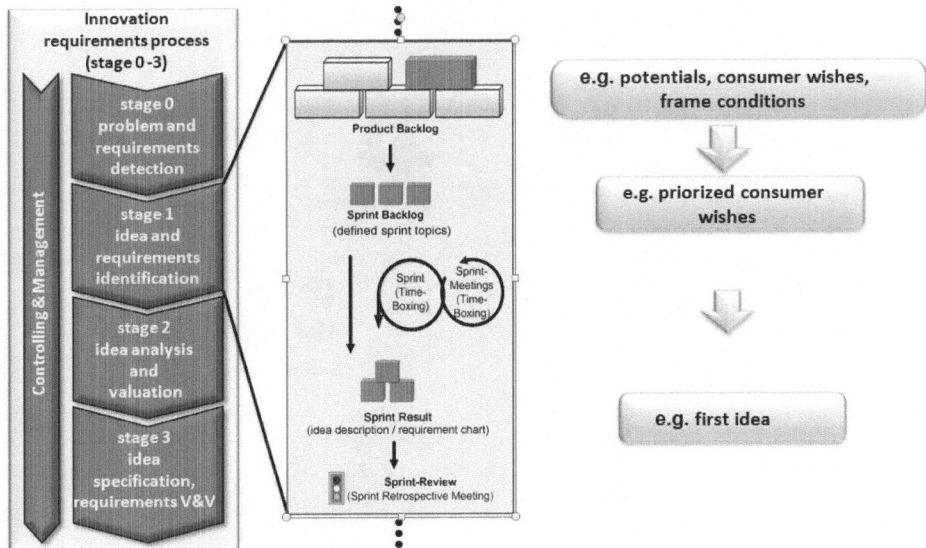

Fig. 2. Scrum at the L-model[Agile]

Deadlines, responsibilities and the result to be developed can be clearly defined and realized for each stage by scum. Due to this, decisions can quickly be made and aren't placed on hold if the scum rules are attended.

4.2   The Process Templates

At the L-model^{Agile}, the model merely serves as reference book which constists of four additional process templates besides the IR process^{Agile}, which show the IR process without the scrum support and seperately illustrates the innovation and RM&E process. The fifth process template consists of the innovation requirements process especially for the generation and implementation of innovations in process, socials and organization, because the IR process moreover focuses on the product innovations.

4.3   The Methods Catalogue

The provided methods catalogue consists of valuation, quality and risk management methods, determination techniques and modeling models which support the process for an improvement of innovation quality at the vehicle construction. The exact and process-oriented assignment of methods enables a context- and company-dependent choice of the methods per process. The methods catalogue provides overall 106 methods and model diagrams (e.g. UML/SysML diagrams or a feasibility and economy) which are available to the involved persons.

The Role Model

The IR process^{Agile} consists of six roles at the stages 0-3 (see Figure 3).

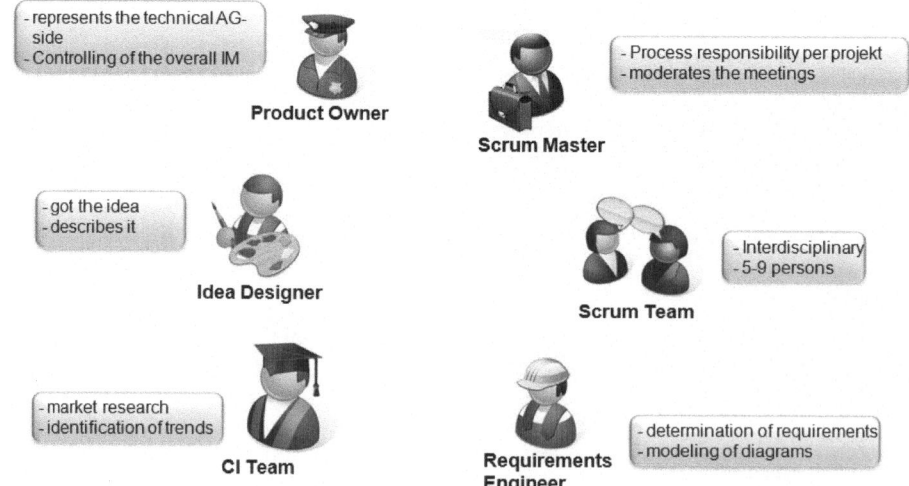

Fig. 3. Role model of the L-model^{Agile}

Due to the role description of the L-model, personal tasks, the requirements on a role occupant, the competences and duties are exactly defined. All roles of the model permanently have to stay in contact to each other to be able to efficiently and effectively analyze and rate an idea.

As communication media and checklist, the involved persons are supported in the process by two central documents, the idea description and the requirements chart. Each role has access to these documents to write down their knowledge, resp. their results. With this systematic and transparent collection of information and requirements, the flood of documents and the search for the location of a specific information for an idea shall be minimized.

The Central Documents

There are two key documents at the L-model^{Agil}, the idea description and the requirements chart, which ensure communication between quality criteria.

The idea description displays all relevant information about an idea. Here, all required information of each stage and process, including the responsibilities, are illustrated in the form of a checklist. In parallel, the required input and output are necessary as well as the applicable methods are shown for each process in a table.

The second key document at the IR process^{Agil} is the requirements chart. All existing requirements, framework conditions, and others belonging to the idea are collected here and assigned to a system structure. The existing requirements, including the attributes, the system elements of the system requirements and, if possible, up to the component requirements are honed down thereby.

By means of the idea description and the requirements chart, the ideas are continuously refined and specified from stage to stage. Due to this, the collected information can be delivered to the product development process afterwards in a transparent and systematic way.

The connection between the idea description and the requirements chart ensures a continuous information flow and by association a communication between quality criteria within the IR process at stages 0 to 3. Figure 4 illustrates through an example the flow of methods and information. In this case exemplary with the methods QFD and FMEA.

The Figure 4 illustrates that at stage 0 the detection of first customer requirements into a requirements chart and thereby a direct assignment into the process structure can be done. A Transformation of customer requirements into system requirements as well as the integration of lessons learned at previous projects happens at stage 1, the determination of ideas and requirements. For example, the requirement/features, the requirement title as well as possible stakeholders and the originator of the requirement are rudimentarily specified at this point.

Basing on this information, requirements can now be technically prioritized by the QFD at stage 2 (analysis and valuation of ideas), as well as malfunctions and prevention actions can be generated for the product development with the aid of FMEA.

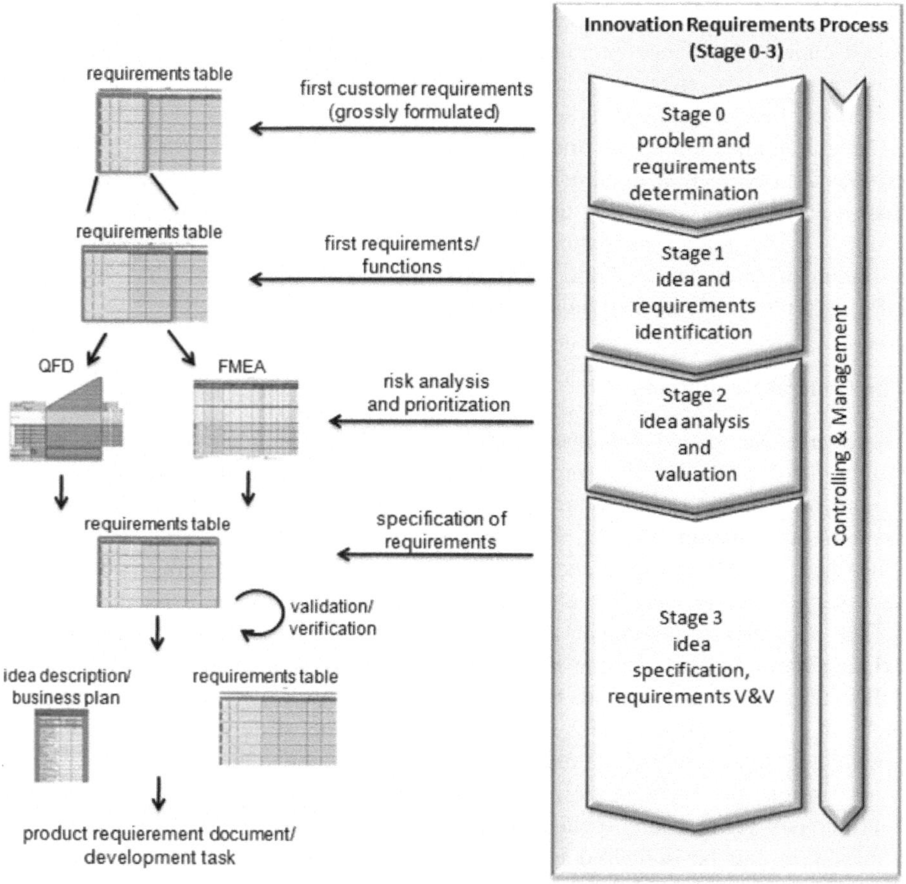

Fig. 4. Connection between requirements and methods from the IR process[Agil] – here exemplary with the methods QFD and FMEA

Stage 3 completes the requirements chart by filling out the relevant attributes of each idea. Among the specification of stage 3 is the verification and validation of the requirements. Only if verification and validation are passed successfully, the idea description and the requirements chart can be forwarded to the product development, resp. stage 4 of the IR process[Agile]. In this case, the verification and validation ensure a high standard in quality of the relevant information of an idea and a high level of communication between quality requirements.

The introduced methods and elements are the first part of the L-model[Agile]. The following chapter shows the three other elements of the L-model[Agile].

4.4   The Key Figure Catalogue at the L-model[Agile]

Elementary for the consequent controlling of the process is the definition and detection of key figures. The L-model[Agile] got a key figure catalogue, consisting overall 80 key figures and metrics, e.g. the number of ideas or the productivity at the IR process[Agil].

Thereby the key figure categories are organized in four organization fields. The organization fields are in a complex correspondence with each other. [15] They are deducted basing on specific (corresponding to the process field) and generic targets (process overlapping) and their critical success factors and (time) drivers.

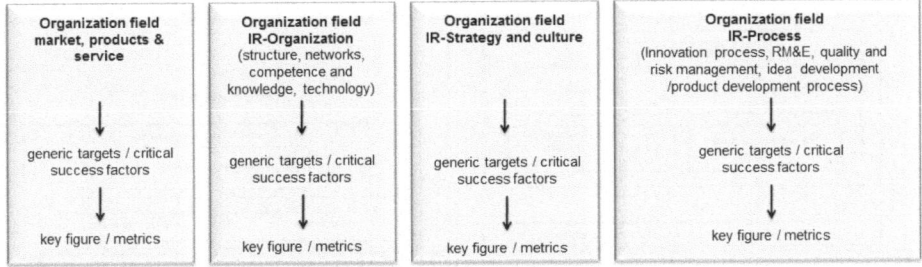

Fig. 5. Organization fields of the key figure system

Among the process controlling, the valuation of the process realization is appreciable for the continuous improvement. A specific maturity model, the so called innovation requirements maturity level model, which is explained below, has been developed for the IR process at stages 0 to 3.

4.5 The Maturity Model of the L-model[Agile]

The application of the innovation requirements maturity model refers to the stages 0 to 3 of the IR process at the vehicle construction. Thereby it does not only consider the realization of the early stages of the innovation process at complex systems, it also considers the implementation of RM&E at these stages up to the product development process.

The IRM refers on the four organization fields of the key figure development. At the IRM one can choose of two valuation schemes. Thereby a distinction is made between the determination of the maturity level and the determination of the ability level.

- **Valuation procedure 1:** This procedure identifies the maturity level of the innovation requirement. Thereby the abilities of the organization [9] referring to the thematic of the L-model[Agile] based on the four organization fields are rated.
- **Valuation procedure 2:** Procedure 2 is used to identify the ability level of a process field. [9] The valuation of the IR ability bases on the "IR process" organization field. Within this organization field, the process field innovation management, RM&E, risk management, quality management and idea-development/product-development process interface are rated.

Depending on the chosen valuation procedure, follows an actual-theoretical comparison on basis of interviews, respectively metrics, identification of the maturity level, respectively the ability level, and the identification of recommendations and improvements to obtain the next level. The following Figure 6 once again shows the two valuation procedures and their points of maturity level identification, respectively ability level identification.

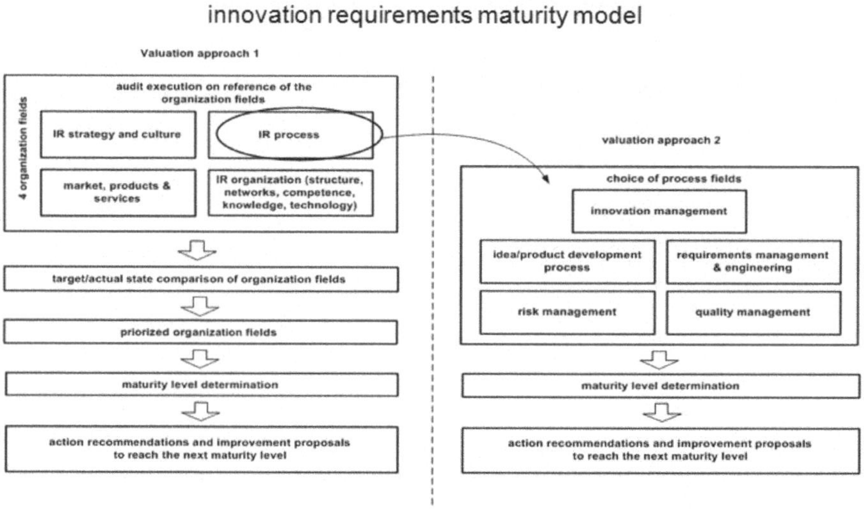

Fig. 6. Valuation approaches at the innovation requirements maturity model

Basing on a valuation scale, the characteristics of organization fields can be measured and then be used for action advices to reach the next level. The results of these valuations can be categorized in 5 maturity levels.

Besides the already shown parts of the L-model[Agile], comes up a fourth part now, the web-based approach guideline.

4.6   Web-Based Approach Guideline of the L-model[Agile]

The approach guideline is meant to support the vehicle construction companies at the introduction and realization of the L-model[Agile]. The process-oriented approach guideline can be used to look up in which order the processes at the L-model, respectively the IR process, are run through, which methods can be applied and which information is required for a specific result. After the adoption on the respective company, the approach guideline is primary suitable as a job instruction and a reference book, or secondarily as an addition to schoolings on the model. Due to the html format, the user can obtain information on each process, data or the roles at the model by the data structure of directly process-oriented. The Figure 7 illustrates that html format.

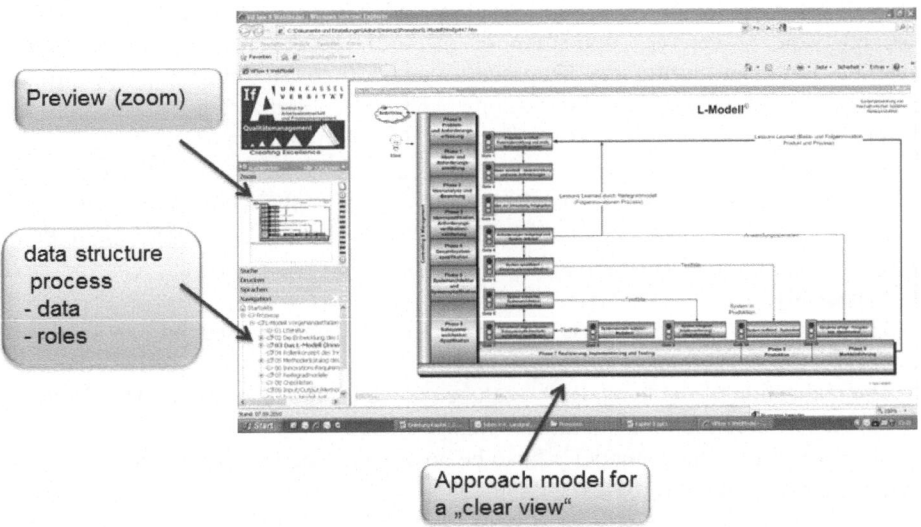

Fig. 7. Web-based approach guideline

The web-based approach guideline is the fourth part at the L-modelAgil. The main parts of the L-model[Agil] are once again represented in summary below.

5 Summary of the L-model[Agile]

Until now the knowledge in innovation and engineering processes, for example why the approach to a solution was dropped or followed up at the concept phase, usually just remains at the constructers and the developers. A whole view about the product and the experiences made during the development is limited to the parties concerned to the project.

How far the knowledge is going to be shared and used for new developments just depends on the communication and informal networks of the employees within the company. Because of this, the goal is to optimize the innovation realization process to raise the innovation-tempo and quality by model based consistent systems engineering at the product development process. Thereby innovations have got to describe formal and systematic. The degree of performance (maturity) along the product development process has to become measurable. Therewith it is possible to achieve an essential part to the input of innovation quality and to the decrease of costs (for example by discontinuation of additionally prototypes by using documented experiences at the model) (see [2, 5]).

The L-model[Agil] provides an approach for increasing the innovation quality and communication at the early stages of vehicle construction. The L-model[Agile] exhibits a standardized process (IR process[Agile]) with methods, procedures and checklists, which enables the formal and systematic description and valuation of ideas and due to this, it simplifies the communication between quality criteria. Ideas can systematically be created, referring to the innovation strategy and the ideas identified at the market research. The preventive application of methods reduces needless iterations and interface problems during the IR process (stages 0 to 3) right up to the product creation process interface. Innovations and their realization at the product development process are reconstructable and valuable in order to reduce risks.

Thereby the description and valuation of ideas is done by two key documents, the idea description and the requirements chart. By doing so, the whole information of an idea is described by to documents or at least by multiple documents referring to them. Due to this, the information collected at the innovation process can be used systematically.

The realization of the process can be controlled using the second part of the L-model^{Agile}, the key figures.

The realization of the L-model^{Agile} can be valued by the maturity model afterwards to generate a guideline for a continuous improvement.

The four parts of the L-model^{Agile} can be provided to the vehicle industry by a web-based approach guideline.

The L-model^{Agile} is a reference book and offers an agile but although stable approach in quality communication to quickly obtain first successes in increasing quality and rate of innovation with minimal bureaucracy and maximum discretionary.

References

[1] Agile Alliance, Manifesto for Agile Software Development (2001),
    http://agilemanifesto.org (last update 2001) (last check October 11, 2010)
[2] Ahlemann, F., Schroeder, C., Teuteberg, F.: Kompetenz- und Reifegradmodelle für das Projektmanagement - Grundlagen, Vergleich und Einsatz, ISPRI-Arbeitsbericht Nr. 01/2005 (2005)
[3] Becker, H.: Phänomen Toyota, Erfolgsfaktor Ethik. Springer, Heidelberg (2006)
[4] Bericht zur technologischen Leistungsfähigkeit Deutschlands, BMBF (2005)
[5] Carnegie Mellon University Software Engineering Institute (SEI): CMMI-DEV, V1.2
[6] Doppler, K., Lauterburg, C.: Change Management, den Unternehmenswandel gestalten. Campus Verlag, Frankfurt (2002)
[7] Ebert, C.: Systematisches Requirements-Engineering und Management. Anforderungen ermitteln, spezifizieren, analysieren und verwalten. 2., aktualisierte und erw. Aufl. dpunkt-Verlag, Heidelberg (2008)
[8] Institut der deutschen Wirtschaft Köln (IW): Das Innovationsverhalten der technikaffinen Branchen. (Gutachten) Studie im Auftrag des Vereins Deutscher Ingenieure, VDI (2006)
[9] Liggesmeyer P. : Software-Qualität – Testen, Analysieren und Verifizieren von Software; 2. Auflage. Spektrum Akademischer Verlag, Heideberg (2009)
[10] Pleschak, F., Sabisch, H.: Innovationsmanagement, Stuttgart, S.6 (1996)
[11] Rupp, C.: Die Sophisten: Requirements-Engineering und -Management. Professionelle, iterative Anforderungsanalyse für die Praxis. 4., aktualisierte und erw. Aufl. Carl Hanser Verlag, München (2007)
[12] Rupp, C., Hruschka, P., Starke, G.: Agility kompakt; Spektrum. Akademischer Verlag, Heidelberg (2009)

[13] Schumpeter, J.A.: Theorie der wirtschaftlichen Entwicklung. In: Vahs, D., Burmester, R.:
     Innovationsmanagement, S. 3, Stuttgart (1999)
[14] Siemens, A.G.: Transformation des Innovationsprozesses in der Kraftfahrzeugindustrie.
     Siemens Product Lifecycle Management (2008)
[15] Spath, D., Wagner, K., Aslanidis, S., Bannert, M., Rogowski, T., Paukert, M., Ardilio, A.:
     Die Innovationsfähigkeit des Unternehmens gezielt steigern. In: Bullinger, J.H. (Hg.)
     Fokus Innovation. Kräfte bündeln – Prozesse Beschleunigen, pp. 41–109. Carl Hanser
     Verlag, München (2006)

A Goal Decomposition Approach
for Automatic Mashup Development

Lin Bai, Dan Ye, and Jun Wei

Technology Center of Software Engineering,
Institute of Software, Chinese Academy of Sciences,
Beijing, China
{bailin,yedan,wj}@otcaix.iscas.ac.cn

Abstract. Automatic mashup aims to discover desired mashlets according to user goals automatically and combine them into an entirely new application. However, the user goals are usually high-level and coarse-grained while the mashlets are low-level and fine-grained. How to fill in the gap becomes a challenge when addressing automatic mashup development. This paper proposes a novel goal decomposition and refinement approach to handle this problem. We defined a goal model based on which we proposed a history heuristic based algorithm to build a Mashup Goal Ontology repository to enable the auto-decomposition of user goals. Then mashlets which are matching with the refined user goals can be found out and mashed up. We evaluate our approach through experimental results which demonstrate acceptable performance of the decomposition.

Keywords: goal decomposition, Mashup Goal Ontology, mashup, mashlet.

1   Introduction

Mashup is an emerging application development paradigm and has gained much attention in recent years. Wikipedia explains mashup as a web page or application that uses and combines data, presentation or functionality from two or more sources to create new services [1]. For its easy and fast integration of online resources, mashup becomes another attractive technology for enterprises who are following the SOA (Service Oriented Architecture) paradigm.

Just like service discovery in SOA, mashlet discovery is also an indispensable part in mashup. Mashlet is a general term of online resources, including data, functions and presentations, which are ready to be combined and reused to coin new applications. The difference lies in that the executors of service discovery are professionals who are familiar with service description language (e.g. WSDL), service communication protocol (e.g. SOAP), etc, while the executors of mashlet discovery are usually end users without any knowledge or experience in development. This brings great challenges to mashlet discovery. For example, when we are going to transport good from one chain store to another, we can merge the following information together: the exact addresses of the two stores, the possible routes

The original version of this chapter was revised: The copyright line was incorrect. This has been corrected. The Erratum to this chapter is available at DOI: 10.1007/978-3-642-33068-1_20

M. van Sinderen et al. (Eds.): IWEI 2012, LNBIP 122, pp. 20–33, 2012.
© IFIP International Federation for Information Processing 2012

between them, and the distance of each route. In fact, there may be more than one mashlet that provides the same or similar services with different quality, performance, or user preference. Novice users usually do not know their differences and thus confused to select the one which is appropriate for their current situations most. Further, novice user may lose some important services sometimes. For example, to plan a shorter and faster route, traffic is another necessary aspect (except for distance) to be concerned, which is prone to be omitted by novice users.

To release the users from the hard and error-prone mashlet searching, automatic mashup platform aims to discover mashlets automatically according to user goals. However, the fact is that user goals are generally high-level and coarse-grained, like "transport good as fast as possible", while the mashlets which are registered in the repository to be combined are usually low-level and fine-grained with explicit functional descriptions, like "get distance", "get directions", "get traffic volume", etc. How to find out the concrete mashlets for the general user goals becomes a challenge when addressing automatic mashup development. This paper proposed a novel goal decomposition and refinement approach to fill in the gap between them. We defined a goal model based on which we proposed a history heuristic based algorithm to build a goal-ontology repository to enable the auto-decomposition of user goals. Then mashlets which are matched with the refined user goals can be found out and mashed up. Experimental results demonstrate that our approach is effective for user-goal decomposition and thus gives helpful guidance to novice users on developing their own mashup applications.

The remainder of the paper is organized as follows: We will summarize and analyze some existing solutions to the decomposition and refinement of user goals in current automatic goal-driven mashup development in section 2. Then, section 3 presents a novel history heuristic based algorithm leveraging collective intelligence of historic users to guide the decomposition of current user goals. In section 4, we evaluate our approach by a group of experiments, and section 5 concludes this paper with some discussions and future works.

2 Related Work

Goal-driven development is the main strategy adopted by current automatic mashup platform. To resolve the mismatch between the general user goals and the concrete mashlets, two kinds of approaches can be summarized from current research work.

Eric Bouillet et al [3-7] eliminate above mismatch by restricting users to specify their goals with registered mashlet descriptions, which are expressed in tags. Since registered mashlet may be numerous (considering ProgrammableWeb.com [21] as an example, there have already been 6602 mashups and 5757 APIs registered by 26/4/2012), finding out the exact mashlet description tags as user goals are tedious and toilsome. To facilitate end users to specify their goals, Eric Bouillet et al, on the one hand, categorize tags into facets which mean a category of tags with some common features. Therefore, a hierarchical goal structure is built and end users can refine their goals step by step in a navigation manner. On the other hand, the authors propose a goal refinement strategy, prompting users with possible goals which are generated by a customized AI planner, to guide users to refine their current goals. However, as the authors claim that this approach is proposed to be applied in flow-based information processing systems. The flow planning based goal refinement mechanism is limited for other mashup scenarios, such as event-triggered mashup which contains no evident data flows or logic flows but glues mashlets together through a set of discrete events in a "wiring[18]" manner (Compared with the "wiring" manner, there is a "piping[18]" manner which means mashlets are linked with a explicit data flow or logic flow). Furthermore, the navigation from high-level goals to lower level goals lacks of necessary guidance and depends totally on users' own subjective experience. In this paper, we also adopt a hierarchical goal structure, which we call goal-ontology, to guide users to decompose and refine their initial goals. The difference is we defined rich semantic association (including "is-a", "has-a", etc.) between the father goal and the child goal rather than just subordinate relationship like in [3-7]. Referencing to the goal-ontology as a shared vocabulary on goal concepts, users are more knowledgeable and instructed when choosing sub-goals and therefore feel better experience.

Different from above user-involved goal decomposition, Jian Cao et al [25] integrate the concept of goal-ontology into customized web service models. By defining the relationship among goal concepts (i.e. specialization and decomposition), the general user goals can be easily decomposed into more concrete and fine-grained sub-goals. However, this paper doesn't mention how to create such a goal-ontology and this is the key issue in the ontology-driven goal decomposition problem. Hua Xiao et al present an ontology based automatic goal decomposition approach in [10-13]. The high-level user goals are extended automatically into a set of sub-goals according to a collection of ontologies which can be achieved by dedicated ontology search engines. For the reason that no human interaction is involved, the results of goal decomposition are totally dependent on the quality of pre-chosen ontologies. However, the ontologies searched by ontology search engines are usually too general to guide mashup development. Considering the example discussed in section 1, the initial goal "fast transport" can be extended, for example according to AKT Reference Ontology [14], into sub-goals like "things act on", "receipt agent", "loc@start", "loc@end", "means of transport", which make a radical departure from our expectation by providing redundant sub-goals like "things act on" and missing necessary sub-goals like "get directions", "get traffic volume", etc. Evren Sirin et al also adopt ontology-based approach to deal with automatic goal decomposition in [15]. The difference is that the ontology, which is represented as "domain" in HTN planning problem, is translated from existing OWL-S process definition and therefore more instructive on development than that searched from network by search engine. However, the process-dependent (i.e. "piping") ontologies are not applicable to process-independent (i.e. "wiring") mashup, such as event-triggered mashup mentioned before. Different from above works, in this paper, we will present a historic heuristic based algorithm to mine knowledge and experience from those already developed mashup applications (including both "piping" manner and "wiring" manner) and build up a goal-ontology dedicated to mashup development. Referenced to the goal-ontology, sub-goals, which have higher popularities for example, can then be recommended to the user with a higher probability to be choosen.

3   An Ontology-Driven Approach to Goal Decomposition

Ontology is a formal representation of knowledge as a set of concepts within a domain, and the relationships between those concepts [17]. It is widely used as a shared vocabulary in semantic web, artificial intelligence, etc. In this paper, we utilize it as the knowledge to direct end users to decompose and refine their goals by recommending possible sub-goals and other correlated goals. For example, if a user indicates "fast transport" as his initial goal, "get directions", "get traffic volume" may be recommended as its sub-goals and "cars rent service" as a possible complement, which is usually accompanied by the transport-related concept.

Ontology-based modeling and reasoning enables automatic and intelligent software development. But at present, the approved united and consistent ontology specific for mashup development is still missing. Manually creation of such a normative ontology is not only time-consuming and expensive, but also error-prone. In this paper, we propose to leverage collective intelligence that web 2.0 encapsulates and advocates, and present a history heuristic based approach to create goal-ontology for mashup development by reversely analyzing existing mashup applications.

Mashup Goal Ontology, in this paper, means the formal representation of knowledge which is used to guide the decomposition and refinement of user goals in mashup development. It can be viewed as a hierarchical goal tree, along which the high level goal can be decomposed into sets of sub-goals. Based on our observation that the architecture of mashup application also presents a hierarchical structure for the reason of nested composition of mashlet, and moreover the concepts of Mashup Goal Ontology (i.e. user goals) can be viewed as functional descriptions of the components of mashup architecture, we define the Mashup Goal Ontology model by referring to the architecture of mashup application. The goal decomposition process is essentially the design procedure of mashup architecture, and the sub-goals are actually the requirements for mashup constructs, namely mashlets.

3.1   Mashup Goal-Ontology Model

In this section, we analyze the architecture of mashup application, based on which we define the Mashup Goal Ontology model for mashup development.

Mashup Architecture. In [18,19], the authors present an enterprise mashup stack like "resource-page-component-mashup" from the point of view of programming. However, as the authors state, the "page" designers should be "characterized by basic programming skills in order to bind the resources to user interfaces". This is far beyond the capability of novice end users. In this paper, we will look at the mashup architecture from a requirement perspective which may be more acceptable for end users.

As shown in Fig. 1, a mashup application is a collection of mashlets which are loosely coupled through event mechanism. Further, we distinguish two categories of mashlets, infoMashlet and actMashlet, based on their different purpose and logical structures. infoMashlet is a kind of mashlet used to display a group of data. The result data to be displayed and its presentation (i.e. Graphical User Interface) are the most concerned factors for users. Usually, the result data are calculated by a flow of data processing operations on multiple data sources, and the procedure how the data is processed is not cared about by users. Thus, from the requirement respect, infoMashlet is comprised of data items to be displayed and their presentation in our mashup architecture. Correspondingly, actMashlet is a kind of mashlet used to execute a series of interactive actions, such as "making an internet phone call" involves a sequence of actions of "calling" and "hanging up". Each interactive action, such as the "calling" in an internet phone call procedure, is actually implemented by a series of services, e.g. "connecting with the call server", "routing", "creating speech channels", etc. From the users' respect, it is transparent how these services are bound together and how they are implemented in the background. What the users care about is what functions the composed services can provide, i.e. the operations covered by an actMashlet.

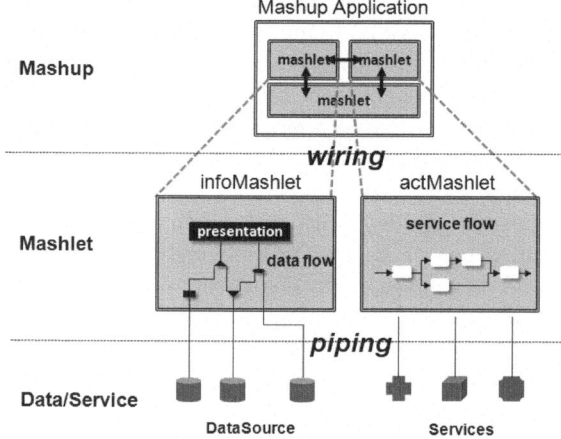

Fig. 1. Architecture of Mashup Application

Mashup Goal Ontology Model. Referenced to above mashup architecture, we define mashup goal-ontology model as a tree structure shown in Fig. 2.

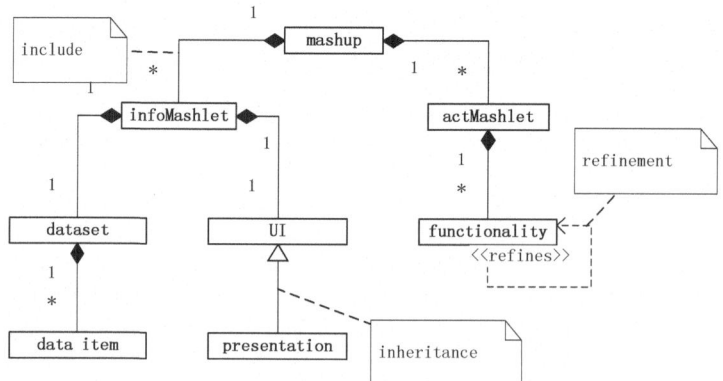

Fig. 2. Mashup Goal Ontology Model

The concepts of Mashup Goal Ontology are derived from the components of mashup architecture. The hierarchical relationship between the super-concept and the sub-concept means "containing" or "involving". For example, a mashup application may contain 1 to n mashlets which are complementary to each other, while an actMashlet, providing certain functions, may involve 1 to n implementations which are mutually exclusive. Further, we characterize three types of relationships among sub-concepts. For the complementary relationship, we mark it as OR, meaning each sub-concept is optional to be a content of the super-concept and the super-concept is called OR-Concept in this paper. For the coordinative relationship, marked as AND, meaning each sub-concept is indispensable to its super-concept which is called And-Concept. For the mutually exclusive relationship, marked as XOR, meaning the candidate sub-concepts are functionally equivalent or similar and can be replaced with each other. We call their super-concept as an XOR-Concept.

To specify the contribution of each sub-concept to his parent, we label each sub-concept with a weighted value, W, indicating its importance and popularity. We assume that one sub-concept contribute more to his parent if it has been appeared in more existing applications. We will discuss it in detail in the following section. To be an exception, the sub-concepts of infoMashlet, "dataset" and "UI", have no weighted value attached for the reason that dataset and UI are the two static constructs of infoMashlet. They will not be instantiated in the model instantiation procedure.

User Goal Definition. User goal can be viewed as an instance of Mashup Goal Ontology model. Based on the model, we define user goal as a set of mashelts, being infoMashlet or actMashlet.

Goal{Mashlet$_i$| i=1...k, Mashelt=infoMashlet|actMashelt}

We define infoMashlet as a tuple of Dataset and UI where Dataset means a set of date items and UI means a set of presentations. *"OR"*, *"XOR"*, *"AND"* are the three types of relationships between data items and presentations which we have discussed above.

infoMashlet <Dataset, UI>
Dataset{dataitem$_i$ | i=1...n, dataitem = dataitem OR dataitem | dataitem XOR dataitem | dataitem AND dataitem}
UI{presentation$_i$ | i=1...m, presentation=presentation XOR presentation}

We define actMashlet as a set of functionalities. Besides *"XOR"* and *"AND"*, relationship of "refinement", marked as "->", is also defined, which means the sub functionality is more specific than its father. For example, "get Traffic Volume" -> "get Traffic Volume of Beijing".

actMashlet{functionality$_i$|i=1...t, functionality=functionality -> functionality | functionality XOR functionality | functionality AND functionality}

An instance of user goal can be described as:

"Fast Transport"{
  MapView < "labels of source&destination" AND "street names" AND "live traffic", "maps mode" XOR "satellite mode">,
  PlanView { "planning" -> ("time-shortest planning" XOR "distance-shortest planning") }
}

3.2   A History Heuristic Based Approach to Mashup Goal Ontology Creation

Mashup Goal Ontology is the shared knowledge which can be used to guide end users to create their own situational mashup applications. In this section, we present a history heuristic based approach to create Mashup Goal Ontology. We think that the mashup application which has already been implemented and published contains some knowledge that can be reused when addressing the same kind of problems. We analyze each mashup application and parse its core elements out according to the Mashup Goal Ontology model we defined in the last section. That is we translate each mashup application into a Mashup Goal Ontology instance.

For the reason that the Mashup Goal Ontology instances derived from mashup applications may overlap in semantics, we take a semantic merging algorithm on those instances in an iterative manner to form a Mashup Goal Ontology repository for automatic mashup development.

Ontology Merging

Algorithm: Ontology_Merging

Input: <H<>, N>,   //H<>: existing set of ontology instances,   N: new ontology instance to be merged
Output: H'<>,   //H'<>: set of ontology instances after merging
1   for each H in H<>
2   if (Similarity(MashupH, MashupN)>= threshold)   // MashupH and MashupN are similar, then merge them
3   for each infoMashletN
4   for each infoMashletH
5   if (Similarity(infoMashletH, infoMashletN) >= threshold)
6   infoMashletH.presentations=infoMashletH.presentations ∪ $_{semantic}$ infoMashletN.presentation
7   infoMashletH.data = infoMashletH.data ∪ $_{semantic}$ infoMashletN.data
8   if no similar infoMashletH exist, infoMashletsH=infoMashletsH ∪ infoMashletN
9   for each actMashletN
10   for each actMashletH
11   if (SynSet(actMashletH, actMashletN)) // actMashletH and actMashletN are synonymous
12   actMashletH.weight++
13   if (Hypernym(actMashletH, actMashletN)) // actMashletH is more generic than actMashletN
14   actMashletH.functions=actMashletH.functions ∪ $_{semantic}$ actMashletN
15   if (Hyponym(actMashletH, actMashletN)) // actMashletH is more specific than actMashletN
16   continue
17   if (Coordinate(actMashletH, actMashletN)) // actMashletH and actMashletN are coordinate
18   actMashletH' = actMashletH
19   actMashletH = GetHypernym(actMashletH, actMashletN)
20   if (actMashletH'.functions = = null)
21   actMashletH.functions=actMashletH' ∪ actMashletN
22   else
23   actMashletH.functions=actMashletH'.functions ∪ $_{semantic}$ actMashletN
24   if no similar actMashletH exist, actMashletsH=actMashletsH ∪ actMashletN
25   H'<> = H<>
26   else   H'<> = append(H<>, N) // append N into H<>

The inputs of the algorithm are two ontology instances to merge. $H<>$ means the existing set of instances, while N means the current instance to be merged. The output is the new merged instance set, marked as $H'<>$. In the body of the algorithm, we take each ontology instance, H, in $H<>$ to compare with N. First, we calculate the semantic similarity between the root nodes of H and N. If it falls in an acceptable threshold, it means that the goals of mashup H and N are similar and can be merged together to form a more complex ontology instance. Otherwise, it means H and N are two unrelated instances and we just put N into $H<>$ as a new set element without any merging operations.

When merging the two ontology instances H and N, we first compare their infoMashlet nodes. For the infoMashlets which have high semantic similarities, we merge them by taking a $U_{semantic}$ operation on their data and presentation nodes respectively. For the remained infoMashlets of N which do not have high semantic similarity with any infoMashlets in H, we just put them into the infoMashlet set of H. Likewise, we compare actMashlet nodes of H and N (marked as actMashletH and actMashletN respectively). We characterize four relationships between actMashletH and actMashletN:

- **Synonym**: if they are synonymous, we just need to plus one to the weight of actMashletH node, meaning the contribution of this actMashlet node of H is increased by one.
- **Hypernym**: if they are hypernymic, meaning actMashetH is more generic than actMashletN, we join actMashletN into actMashletH as one of its sub-nodes.
- **Hyponym**: if they are hyponymic (i.e. actMashletH shares an "is-a" relationship with actMashletN), we just discard actMashletN for it is too generic to make contributions to refine the actMashlet node of H.
- **Coordinator**: if they are coordinate, we shall first calculate the mutual hypernym of both actMashletH and actcMashletN as the new actMashlet node of H, and then join actMashletH and actMashletN together as the sub-nodes of the new node.

To calculate the similarity between OR-Concepts and AND-Concepts, we define:

$$\text{Similarity(word1, word2)} = \begin{cases} \alpha/(\alpha+d), & d<\text{threshold} \\ 0, & \text{otherwise} \end{cases} \qquad (1)$$
$$d = \text{Distance(word1, word2)} .$$

Distance(word1, word2) is the distance between word1 and word2 in the WordNet [26] architecture. α is an adjustable parameter which we take 1 in this paper.

For the XOR-Concepts, we leverage the open APIs provided by WordNet to determine the semantic relation between ontology concepts, including synonym, hypernym, hyponym and coordinator.

When merging subnodes of two concepts, we define a $U_{semantic}$ operation which includes three sub-operations: 1) union set A and set B to form set C, 2) remove synonyms in set C and meanwhile 3) modify the weight of remaining elements of set C. For example, if $c1 \in C$, $c2 \in C$, $c1$ is synonym of $c2$, after $U_{semantic}$ operation, only $c1$(or $c2$) is remained in set C with its weight plus one, while $c2$(or $c1$) is removed.

3.3   Recommendation-Based Goal Decomposition

Referenced to Mashup Goal Ontology, an initial user goal may be decomposed into a set of sub-goals. To facilitate users to pick out their most interested sub-goals, a recommendation mechanism is used to rank those sub-goals according to their contributions to their parent and push the top-k [22,23] sub-goals to the users.

Specifically, except for above contribution metric, the ranking metric may also involve user preference which can be achieved by either pre-defining or mining through the history of user operations or feedbacks. In the current implementation, we just take the frequency of sub-goal in the existing mashup applications as the ranking metric. Fig. 3 shows the whole procedure of goal decomposition.

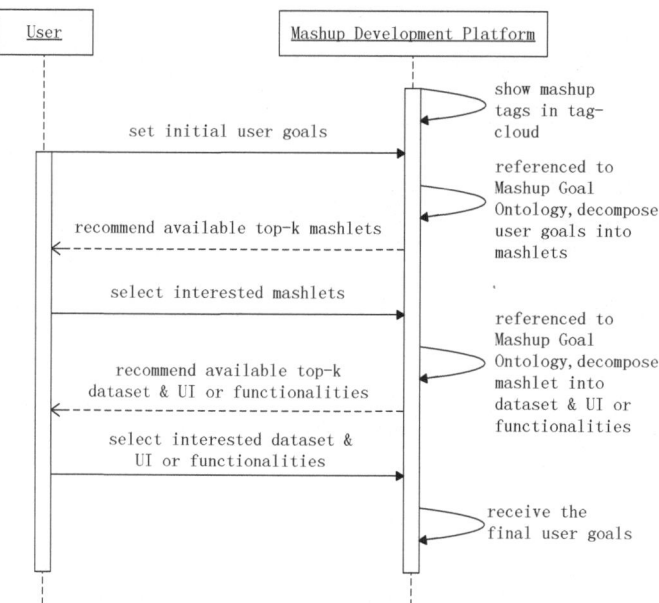

Fig. 3. Procedure of Goal Decomposition

4   Evaluation

We designed and carried out a set of experiments to evaluate the effectiveness of our Mashup Goal Ontology for decomposing and refining user goals in mashup development.

For the evaluation metric, we adopt precision and recall which are widely used to measure user satisfaction in searching or recommendation field.

$$\text{Precision: } P = (A \cap B)/A \qquad\qquad (2)$$
$$\text{Recall: } R = (A \cap B)/B \ .$$

In (2), A is the set of sub-goals that are decomposed according to the Mashup Goal Ontology, B is the set of sub-goals that the user really required or interested in, $A \cap B$ represents the "hit" sub-goals which are correctly decomposed into. Precision is the ratio of "hit" sub-goals to the total decomposed sub-goals according to the Mashup Goal Ontology. Recall is the ratio of "hit" sub-goals to the total required sub-goals.

We download 6000 mashups and 2500 APIs from ProgrammableWeb.com and divide the mashups into two groups: one is used to construct the Mashup Goal Ontology repository, the other is used to evaluate the performance (i.e. precision and recall) of our Mashup Goal Ontology for decomposing and refining user goals.

Step_1: Construct Mashup Goal Ontology Repository

Select randomly 5000 mashups and parse out 5000 Mashup Goal Ontology instances. After performing Ontology_Merging algorithm on those ontology instances, we then get a united Mashup Goal Ontology repository, marked as Mashup_Goal_Ontology_5000.

Step_2: Evaluate Mashup Goal Ontology on the Remained Mashups

Select randomly 100 mashups in the remained 1000 mashups as the benchmark for evaluating the precision and recall of our decomposition approach, based on the belief that the mashup which has been developed and published represents the real goal of the developer. We parse the benchmark mashup and take its functional description as the user's initial goal. Then we apply our decomposition approach on those initial goals and get a set of sub-goals, i.e. set A in (1). Further, we translate the benchmark mashup into a Mashup Goal Ontology instance and take it as the desired user goals, i.e. set B in (1). Specifically, to improve the efficiency of the experiment, we will simulate user interactions by clustering algorithm. For the OR-Concept, we cluster its sub-goals in groups by their weights and pick up the group with the highest weight as the sub-goal set that the user may select. For the XOR-Concept, we just need to choose the sub-goal that has the highest weight.

We repeat above steps for twenty times and calculate the mean of precision and recall respectively. The results are shown in Fig. 4-7.

In Fig. 4, Y-axis represents the ratio of precision and recall. X-axis represents the level of decomposition in which 1 means the 1st-level decomposition (i.e. initial user goals decompose into mashlets) and 2 means the 2nd-level decomposition (i.e. mashlets decompose into dataset & UI or functionalities). From the results, we see that after applying our approach, we can get a mean precision (and recall) beyond seventy percent, which means our approach plays a positive effect in guiding the decomposition of user goals. Specifically, we note that the precision and recall of the 2nd-level decomposition are both lower than that of the 1st-level. It can be explained that we simulate user interactions by clustering algorithm in the experiment and the error of 1st-level decomposition is propagated into 2nd-level decomposition.

We then change the mashup numbers in step_1 to be 3000, 1000 (the corresponding goal-ontologies are marked as Mashup_Goal_Ontology_3000 and Mashup_Goal_Ontology_1000) and repeat above experiment. We have the following results in Fig. 5 and Fig. 6.

Fig. 7 shows the comparative results with different Mashup Goal Ontology repository. We can see that the precision and recall both reduced with the size of Mashup Goal Ontology repository decreased. The reason is obvious that decreasing Mashup Goal Ontology instances means weakening the knowledge that is used to guide the goal decomposition. This may lead to some goals failed to be decomposed or miss some important sub-goals because of the limited knowledge.

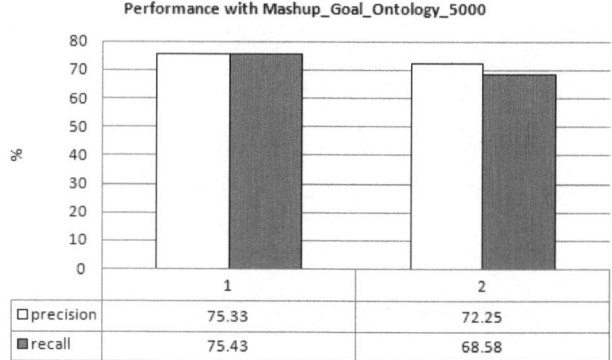

Fig. 4. Precision and Recall of Decomposition with Mashup_Goal_Ontology_5000

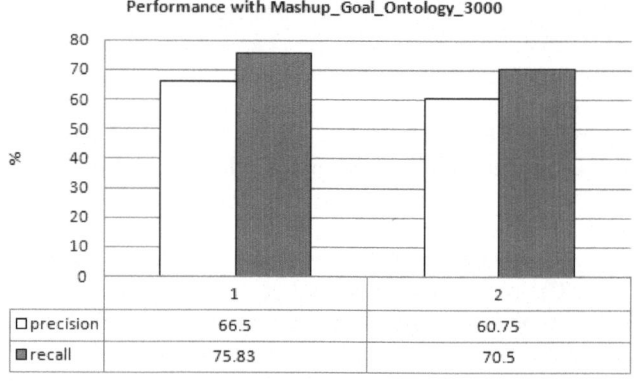

Fig. 5. Precision and Recall of Decomposition with Mashup_Goal_Ontology_3000

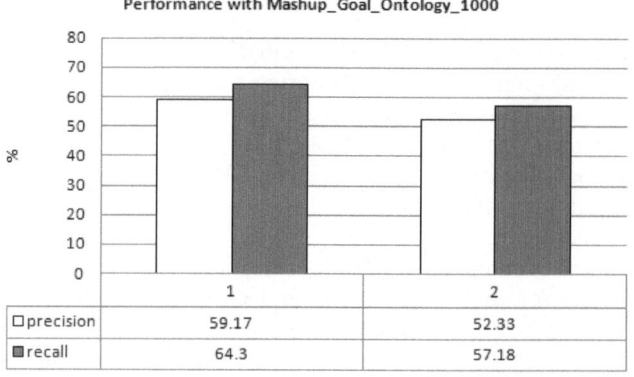

Fig. 6. Precision and Recall of Decomposition with Mashup_Goal_Ontology_1000

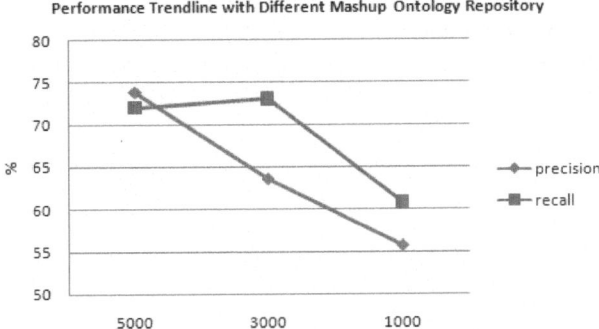

Fig. 7. Tendency of Precision and Recall with Different Mashup Goal Ontology Repository

5   Conclusion and Future Work

It is a great challenge on how to map general user goals into low-level and concrete mashlets in automatic mashup development. In this paper, we explored a goal decomposition and refinement approach aiming at enhancing the automation of mashup development. We defined a Mashup Goal Ontology model based on which Mashup Goal Ontology instances can be derived. Further, we proposed an ontology merging algorithm to create a union Mashup Goal Ontology repository for automatic decomposition of user goals. Meanwhile, leveraging recommendation methodology, we involve user interactions in the whole decomposition process to adjust the results of auto-decomposition and ensure the decomposition goes in the way that users expect.

Mashup development is a new pattern of End-User Programming. Considering the capability of end users in development, we explore mashup applications from the user requirement perspective and in a coarse-grained manner, e.g. data item, UI and operational functionality that have something to do with user interactions. While for the low-level and non-user-interactive services, e.g. the data operations like filtering, merging, et al., it is outside the discussion of this paper. Composition of these fine-grained mashup resources can be achieved, for example, by intelligent planning approach proposed in [3,8,9].

This paper presents a history heuristic based approach to create Mashup Goal Ontology repository. The quality of the ontology is dependent on the quantity and quality of the existing mashups and mashlets which have been developed and registered in the network, for example, whether the mashup specification is well-defined or whether the mashlet is accessible. Matured mashup community, like ProgrammableWeb.com, plays a fundamental role in our approach.

In this paper, we mainly considered perceptible user goals. In the future, we will take implicit user goals into consideration, which may not be perceived by the user himself but could have a great effect on his current goals, e.g. the user's geographical location, preference, or knowledge background, etc. How to model and measure these kinds of goals is our next work.

Acknowledgments. This work is supported by the National Basic Research Program of China (973 Program) under Grand No. 2009CB320704, the National Natural Science Foundation of China under Grant No. 61170074 and the National Science and Technology Major Project of the Ministry of Science and Technology of China under Grand No. 2010zx01045-001-006-1.

References

1. Wikipedia, http://en.wikipedia.org/wiki/Mashup_(web_application_hybrid) (accessed by March 21, 2012)
2. Bouguettaya, A., et al.: End-to-End Service Support for Mashups. IEEE Transactions on Services Computing 3(3), 250–263 (2010)
3. Bouillet, E., et al.: A tag-based approach for the design and composition of information processing applications. In: Proceedings of the 23rd ACM SIGPLAN Conference on Object-Oriented Programming Systems Languages and Applications. ACM, Nashville (2008)
4. Bouillet, E., et al.: A Folksonomy-Based Model of Web Services for Discovery and Automatic Composition. In: IEEE International Conference on Services Computing, SCC 2008 (2008)
5. Bouillet, E., et al.: A Faceted Requirements-Driven Approach to Service Design and Composition. In: IEEE International Conference on Web Services, ICWS 2008 (2008)
6. Ranganathan, A., Riabov, A., Udrea, O.: Mashup-based information retrieval for domain experts. In: Proceeding of the 18th ACM Conference on Information and Knowledge Management. ACM, Hong Kong (2009)
7. Riabov, A.V., et al.: Wishful search: interactive composition of data mashups. In: Proceeding of the 17th International Conference on World Wide Web. ACM, Beijing (2008)
8. Riabov, A., Liu, Z.: Scalable Planning for Distributed Stream Processing Systems. In: Proceedings of the Sixteenth International Conference on Automated Planning and Scheduling, ICAPS 2006, Cumbria, UK, June 6-10. AAAI (2006)
9. Riabov, A., Liu, Z.: Planning for stream processing systems. In: Proceedings of the 20th National Conference on Artificial Intelligence, vol. 3. AAAI Press, Pittsburgh (2005)
10. Xiao, H., Zou, Y., Tang, R., Ng, J., Nigul, L.: A Framework for Automatically Supporting End-Users in Service Composition. In: Chignell, M., Cordy, J., Ng, J., Yesha, Y. (eds.) The Smart Internet. LNCS, vol. 6400, pp. 115–136. Springer, Heidelberg (2010)
11. Xiao, H., et al.: An Approach for Context-Aware Service Discovery and Recommendation. In: Proceedings of the 2010 IEEE International Conference on Web Services. IEEE Computer Society (2010)
12. Hua, X., et al.: An automatic approach for ontology-driven service composition. In: Proceedings of the 2009 IEEE International Conference on Service-Oriented Computing and Applications (2009)
13. Xiao, H., et al.: Personalized Service Discovery and Composition. In: Pre-proceedings of SITCON: The CAS / NSERC Strategic Workshop in Smart Internet Technologies, Canada (2009)
14. Advanced Knowledge Technologies, http://www.aktors.org/ontology/ (accessed by December 23, 2010)

15. Sirin, E., et al.: HTN planning for Web Service composition using SHOP2. Web Semantics: Science, Services and Agents on the World Wide Web 1(4), 377–396 (2004)
16. Wu, D., Parsia, B., Sirin, E., Hendler, J., Nau, D.S.: Automating DAML-S Web Services Composition Using SHOP2. In: Fensel, D., Sycara, K., Mylopoulos, J. (eds.) ISWC 2003. LNCS, vol. 2870, pp. 195–210. Springer, Heidelberg (2003)
17. Wikipedia,
    http://en.wikipedia.org/wiki/Ontology_(information_science)
    (accessed by April 10, 2012)
18. Hoyer, V., Janner, T., Delchev, I., Fuchsloch, A., López, J., Ortega, S., Fernández, R., Möller, K.H., Rivera, I., Reyes, M., Fradinho, M.: The FAST Platform: An Open and Semantically-Enriched Platform for Designing Multi-channel and Enterprise-Class Gadgets. In: Baresi, L., Chi, C.-H., Suzuki, J. (eds.) ICSOC-ServiceWave 2009. LNCS, vol. 5900, pp. 316–330. Springer, Heidelberg (2009)
19. Hoyer, V., et al.: Enterprise Mashups: Design Principles towards the Long Tail of User Needs. In: IEEE International Conference on Services Computing (2008)
20. Rodriguez, M.A., Egenhofer, M.J.: Determining semantic similarity among entity classes from different ontologies. IEEE Transactions on Knowledge and Data Engineering 15(2), 442–456 (2003)
21. http://www.programmableweb.com/
22. Akbarinia, R., Pacitti, E., Valduriez, P.: Best position algorithms for top-k queries. In: Proceedings of the 33rd International Conference on Very Large Data Bases. VLDB Endowment, Vienna (2007)
23. Wang, J., et al.: TFP: an efficient algorithm for mining top-k frequent closed itemsets. IEEE Transactions on Knowledge and Data Engineering 17(5), 652–663 (2005)
24. Wu, J., et al.: Web Service Discovery Based on Ontology and Similarity of Words. Chinese Journal of Computers 28(4), 595–602 (2005)
25. Cao, J., et al.: A Goal Driven and Process Reuse Based Web Service Customization Model. Chinese Journal of Computers 28(4), 721–730 (2005)
26. WordNet, http://wordnet.princeton.edu/wordnet/

Benefits of Enterprise Integration: Review, Classification, and Suggestions for Future Research

Ariyan Fazlollahi[1], Ulrik Franke[1,2], and Johan Ullberg[1]

[1] Industrial Information and Control Systems, KTH Royal Institute of Technology,
Osquldas v. 12, SE-10044 Stockholm, Sweden
ariyan@kth.se, {ulrikf,johanu}@ics.kth.se
[2] Swedish Defence Research Agency, SE-164 90 Stockholm, Sweden

Abstract. This article reports the findings of a literature review concerning the potential benefits of Enterprise Integration (EI) for organizations. The review reveals the current state of the scientific literature concerning the potential benefits of EI, classified using a conceptual model of the enterprise. We believe that the results provide a consolidated and comprehensive picture of such potential benefits, useful as a baseline for future research. Additionally, the review is expected to assist practitioners in establishing business cases for EI by means of scientifically grounded reasoning about how EI benefits can contribute to the achievement of certain business goals. Additionally, results could be employed to develop methods or models capable of measuring such benefits in financial terms.

Keywords: Enterprise Integration, Enterprise Systems, Benefits, Classification, Literature Review.

1   Introduction

Large multinational enterprises operating in global markets, continuous development of computing technologies, and the extended, dispersed and continuously interconnected enterprise information systems, has caused a fundamental transformation of the economy [1]. Moreover, the migration of organizations toward greater complexity with global presence, sever economic pressures, the need for enhanced innovation and more participative and learning-oriented management practices call for change in organizational life regarding the technology-organizational relationship [2]. Considering such forces, studies in organizational sciences generally agree on the evolution of organizational forms towards decentralized and more flexible approaches and structures [2].

In order to evolve, survive and thrive in these competitive markets, enterprises must find a way to cope with rapid changes in both internal and external environments. As a strategy to be able to rapidly respond to a changing environment, business functions can be integrated in order to efficiently utilize information technology, and share data with third-party actors in the marketplace [3].

The original version of this chapter was revised: The copyright line was incorrect. This has been corrected. The Erratum to this chapter is available at DOI: 10.1007/978-3-642-33068-1_20

M. van Sinderen et al. (Eds.): IWEI 2012, LNBIP 122, pp. 34–45, 2012.

It is believed that the cost advantages of enterprise integration systems are significant [3]. The authors in [4] have estimated the benefits of improved information exchanges using electronic data interchange (EDI) between Chrysler and its suppliers to an annual amount of 220 million US$. In another study in the health care industry, Walker et al. [5] assessed the net value of a fully implemented electronic health care information exchange and interoperability as $77.8 billion per year. However, it should be considered that enterprise integration is expensive and time-consuming [3]. Gartner [6] estimates the total revenue of application integration infrastructure as $5 billion per year in 2011.

The scientific literature has touched upon the topic of benefits and effects of enterprise integration on organizations from different viewpoints. However, there has been no effort to date to comprehensively evaluate these benefits. This paper outlines how enterprise integration can be useful to organizations, and provides guidelines for how future research might be conducted. In short, the purpose of this paper is to review the current state of research on the benefits of Enterprise Integration, thus providing a useful baseline for future research. This paper presents the literature review from a master thesis project [7] with the goal of developing a method capable of measuring the benefits of EI in quantitative terms.

2 Defining Enterprise Integration

A variety of terms are presented in the literature to denote the integration area. Examples of such terms are enterprise integration (EI) [8, 9], application integration (AI) [10], systems integration [11], and enterprise application integration (EAI) [3].

Vernadat [9] contrasts Enterprise Integration (EI) with systems interoperability, designating EI by a "strong organizational dimension" while considering interoperability more of a technical nature. From a pure technical perspective, EI is considered to denote connecting computer systems and IT applications to support business process operations [9]. On the other hand, from an organizational perspective, EI facilitates information, control, and material flows across organization by connecting all the necessary functions and functional entities to improve communication, cooperation, and coordination within the enterprise [9].

Adopting application integration (AI) term as the umbrella term for integration, the authors in [10] introduce three main subcategories, namely (1) intra-organizational AI, (2) inter-organizational AI, and (3) hybrid AI. They thus differentiate the integration of internal applications from cross-enterprise business processes and systems. The term hybrid is used to denote that in some cases, these applications function as intra-organizational AI and in others as inter-organizational applications.

Markus [11] defines systems integration as establishment of "tighter linkages between different computer-based information systems and databases". By this definition, the author views systems integration as a requirement to achieve business integration. In this context, enterprise application integration (EAI) is defined as an systems integration strategy to achieve data and process integration [11].

Lee et al. [3] uses enterprise integration and systems integration synonymously as "the capability to integrate a variety of different system functionalities". Similar to [11], Lee et al. [3] considers EAI as an approach to systems integration.

In this article enterprise integration (EI) is adopted to refer to the entire integration area. Most importantly, this definition of EI encompasses various perspectives and levels of integration, namely systems integration (interconnection of devices via computer networks), application integration (integration of software applications and database systems), and business integration (co-ordination of functions that manage, control and monitor business processes) [8]. Moreover, the term itself possess the required comprehensiveness to be considered as the umbrella term incorporating other related terms mentioned for integration.

3   Benefits of Enterprise Integration

The authors in [12] propose a framework as a decision-making tool regarding the adoption of EI. The proposed framework considers four integration layers, namely the connectivity layer, transportation layer, translation layer, and the process automation layer. In the connectivity layer, integration elements like data and objects are extracted from source systems and are transferred to the integration infrastructure by the transportation layer. Transported elements are translated and reformatted for target systems using the translation layer. The process automation layer is responsible for routing the translated elements to target systems.

Based on the classification of ERP benefits proposed by [13], Themistocleous [14] classifies the benefits of EI in five different types; organizational (e.g. more organized business processes), managerial (e.g. ROI), strategic (e.g. increase collaboration among partners), technical (e.g. achieve data, object and process integration), and operational (e.g. reduce cost). However, it could be argued that such scheme imposes a subjective classification rather than an objective one, i.e. the decision to classify one benefit in a category depends on the researcher rather than the characteristics of the benefit itself. In this sense, these types could overlap, which makes it is difficult in practice to make a distinction between them.

Enterprise Integration Council suggests flexibility and agility, defined as the ability to rapidly respond to new business opportunities, as the ultimate goals of EI [3]. Moreover, it proposes cycle time reductions, cost reductions, and cost containment as benefits of enterprise integration systems [3]. In acclaiming such benefits, Chari and Seshadri state that "adopting standards-based integration solutions is the most promising way to reduce the long-term costs of integration and facilitate a flexible infrastructure" [15].

Themistocleous and Irani [16] view the benefits of EI as reduced integration time, more flexible and maintainable solutions, and the easing of migration to new technologies due to conformance of EI systems to common standards [16]. They argue that these benefits ultimately result in reduction of overall integration costs due to the reduction of both integration time and maintenance costs.

Ruh et al. [17] face the challenge of determining the effects of EI from the organizational perspective. The authors claim that an integrated infrastructure allows companies to improve their performance, increase their productivity and increase the quality of services offered to their customers. Similarly, Themistocleous and Irani assert that EI strengthens supply chains [16]. Manouvrier and Menard [1] also stress improvements in quality of service as the most significant benefit of integration systems.

From another point of view, Shin [18] claims that EI is generally effective for large firms, with size above some critical point. They stress that in order to rationalize the initial fixed cost of EI systems, companies shall have conditions such as a mass of complicated information systems.

In addition to increasing reactivity, adaptability and the ability to manage external exchanges optimally, Manouvrier and Menard [1] suggest accelerating time-to-market as another effect of EI.

Tackling the problem of determining the effects of EI, Themistocleous and Irani in [19] and [20] propose that Information systems that benefit from integration with others can arguably be viewed as no longer having a definitive start and end. The authors claim that such systems are evolving entities that grow and develop over time, in tune with the business environment.

Analyzing the benefits of enterprise integration on the data level, the authors in [21] suggest business benefits such as improved productivity, improved data accuracy, greater agility and flexibility, and system replacement/organizational mergers.

3.1   A Classification of Benefits

In order to present the identified benefits of EI for an enterprise, a classification scheme is employed. This scheme is intended to unite different perspectives of enterprise integration benefits that can be found in the literature. The classification scheme is based on the conceptual model proposed for enterprise integration in [22]. The authors in [22] proposed a model in which an enterprise is seen as a layered framework of related activities sharing common goals, which as a whole, describe an organization. Each of these layers can be seen independently as a view of the enterprise. These layers are network, information, application, work processes and organization. The integration goal at the network layer is to provide connectivity, defined as the linkages between systems, applications, and modules. Thus the integration issue addressed at this layer is the physical heterogeneity of the hardware and their operating systems in a physical network. In our model, however the notion of the network layer is excluded (cf. figure 1). Such exclusion could be justified considering that the network layer is deemed to be too fundamental to give rise to benefits.

The information layer is the view incorporating data sharing issues, as it involves enabling organizational sub-units to understand and use data from other subunits. The application layer describes the systems used by the organization. The integration goal at this layer is application interoperability which is defined as "the ability of one software application to access/use data generated by another software system" [22].

Tasks and the manner and order in which they are conducted in order to produce an output are the core of the work processes layer. In the last layer, organization layer is where the different strategies including business strategy, organizational design strategy and information systems strategy must all be aligned with one another.

The described scheme provides an abstraction mechanism in order to unite various perspectives of enterprise integration benefits in different literature. Moreover, it offers the possibility to picture the relation between various benefits related to the different layers.

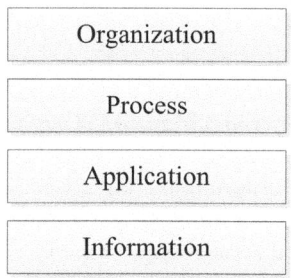

Fig. 1. Classification scheme; based on [22]

Table 1. Classified benefits of enterperise integration

Organization	– customer relationship improvements – enterprise flexibility improvements – facilitating organizational mergers – costs reduction – revenue growth – supply chain improvements
Process	– Business-to-Business (B2B) processes improvement – decision making processes improvements – processes flexibility/agility improvements – processes performance improvements
Application	– applications switching costs decrease – data analysis capabilities improvements – systems interoperability improvements – systems modifiability improvements – total cost of ownership (TCO) decrease – systems reusability improvements
Information	– data entry/processing automation and data quality improvements – enhanced data accessibility and reusability – superior data standardization

The presented scheme differs essentially from both models proposed in [12] and [14]. By classifying the workflow of a typical integration scenario, the model proposed in [12] provides a layered view over EI activities (how it is performed) rather than the benefits of EI (what is achieved). The scheme proposed in this paper, however, aims to describe an organization as a layered framework of related independent activities which share common goals. The classification presented in [14] provides a classification model for the benefits of EI. On the other hand, the model limits its perspective to the point of view of an organization's senior management.

With the aim of providing a comprehensive view over the benefits of EI, each of the layers in the presented scheme (cf. figure 1) can independently be seen as a view of the enterprise. In this way, the proposed scheme covers all the layers of an enterprise. This can also be justified by the similarity of the proposed layers to the enterprise layers in the enterprise architecture (EA) literature. For instance, the three layers presented in Archimate [23] could be associated with the proposed scheme:

– Archimate's technology layer could be associated with scheme's information layer;
– application layers of both could be related to each other;
– business layer of Archimate could be linked with the process and organization layers of the proposed scheme.

3.2   Information Layer

Benefits identified from the literature related to the information layer are data entry/processing automation and data quality improvements [14, 21], enhanced data accessibility and reusability [3, 9, 14, 17, 21], and superior data standardization [3, 14].

Data Entry/Processing Automation and Data Quality. The authors in [21] discuss that enterprise integration minimizes data entry points, automates data entry, business rules execution against data, and data transformation. They argue that such automation minimizes the opportunity for human error, which in turn results in improvements in data accuracy. Moreover, according to [14], EI results in data with increased reliability, which is defined as a data quality dimension indicating whether the data can be relied on to convey the right information [24]. To indicate the significance of data quality improvements by enterprise integration, the authors in [14] discuss that such improvements supports the decision-making process, which in turn, improves performance and management of the organization.

Data Accessibility and Reusability. Providing support for more efficient data sharing and more reusable data is mentioned as one of the results of employing enterprise integration in organizations [14]. However, more emphasis has been placed on enhanced data accessibility, which is discussed to be achieved through information exchanges [17, 21]. More specifically, it is argued that enterprise integration improves data accessibility by facilitating greater degree of communication [3] by connecting all the necessary functions and heterogeneous functional entities [9].

Data Standardization. Considering automated data entry and execution of business rules against the data as a feature of enterprise integration, Lee et al. [3] argues that this would lead to improved data standardization. The authors in [14] posit that an implication of enterprise integration is reduced data redundancy, resulting in less data and application, and less maintenance effort.

3.3   Application Layer

The application layer contains the following benefits: applications switching costs decrease [3, 10], data analysis capabilities improvements [14], systems interoperability improvements [3, 9, 14, 25], systems modifiability improvements [1, 10, 14, 21, 25], total cost of ownership (TCO) decrease [10, 14, 26, 27], and systems reusability improvements [14, 27].

Applications Switching Costs. The authors in [10] and [3] argue that by enabling organizations to conform to common standards, enterprise integration facilitates easier and quicker migration to new technologies and reduces switching costs of systems.

Systems Interoperability. The literature relates improvements in systems interoperability achieved by enterprise integration to the standardization of interfaces [3, 14], which allows greater degree of cooperation between different applications [3, 9]. Brunnermeier et al. [25] discuss that enterprise integration reduces problems caused by imperfect interoperability.

Systems Modifiability. Providing a common integrated infrastructure, enterprise integration minimizes the changes to application code [10, 14], and leads to more flexible, manageable and maintainable solutions [10, 14, 21] with higher scalability [14, 21]. Moreover, mediation and transformation functionalities of enterprise integration and provided asynchronous communication results in higher degrees of loose coupling between applications [1], which yields in increased information systems flexibility and reactivity [1]. Additionally, enterprise integration makes it possible to position business rules outside the code for applications, thus rendering maintenance and adaptability of systems much simpler and faster. Furthermore, the authors in [25] discuss that the improvements in systems interoperability reduce related mitigation and reworking activities and corresponding time and resources, which could be discussed that increase systems modifiability.

Total Cost of Ownership (TCO). As discussed, lower applications switching costs and enhanced systems interoperability decrease the lifecycle cost of the information systems within the organization. Additionally, improved systems modifiability results in reduced purchasing, maintaining and training efforts [25]. In overall, enterprise integration reduces the total cost of ownership for information systems in the organization, including cost of managing, running and maintaining the IT infrastructure, and the time required to conclude systems integration [10, 14]. On the other hand, increased flexibility and software reuse extends the information systems lifecycle, which could significantly reduce the total cost of ownership for information systems within the organization [26, 27].

Systems Reusability. The authors in [27] state that the new integrated information system resulting from integrating multiple information systems offers software reuse through the adaptability provided by integration. In the results of multiple case studies, Themistocleous [14] also supports this finding.

3.4   Process Layer

This layer includes Business-to-Business (B2B) processes improvement [1, 12, 14, 17], decision making processes improvements [14, 17], processes flexibility/agility improvements [3, 14, 21, 25], and processes performance improvements [3, 9, 14, 16, 17, 21, 25].

Business-to-Business (B2B) Processes. The integrated IT-infrastructure enables sharing information between the partners of a supply chain [14, 17], which increases collaboration among trading partners [12], and strengthens supply chains [17]. Moreover, internal and external supply chains are integrated, resulting in improvements in supply chain planning. From the perspective of organization's customers, this would yield in improvements in the quality of services offered to customers [1].

Decision Making Processes. Enterprise integration mediates the flow of information from stovepipe applications to the common warehouse and supports the conversion of data from various applications' formats to a common format. This facilitates the construction of a data warehouse which could provide integrated information for decision support of the organization. [17]

Processes Flexibility/Agility. As a consequence of enterprise integration, process scalability is increased [14], delays in activities of value chain could be decreased [25], organization could quickly respond to changes in its environment by providing new products, services and information [3], quickly modifying its business methods [3], or bringing new business lines [21].

Processes Performance. The authors in [9] argue that by connecting all the necessary functions and heterogeneous functional entities (e.g. information systems, devices, applications, and people), enterprise integration facilitates information, control, and material flows across organization boundaries, aids data and information exchanges (i.e. interoperation between applications), which in turn improves timely orchestration of process steps within the enterprise. Moreover, business processes are optimized in terms of productivity by reducing manual tasks [12, 14], eliminating unnecessary or redundant tasks by letting systems share data across the enterprise [14, 21], providing employees with better access to the information they need to do their jobs [17], and reducing time and resource required for reworking tasks [25]. Additionally, if processes are reengineered during implementation of enterprise integration, business processes would become more organized, which would lead to increases in business processes understanding and control, resulting in increased performance [14].

3.5 Organization Layer

The layer with highest abstraction level encompasses the following benefits: customer relationship improvements [14, 17], enterprise flexibility improvements [1, 3, 9, 14, 17, 21], facilitating organizational mergers [21], costs reduction [14], revenue growth [1, 14, 25], and supply chain improvements [14, 17, 28].

Customer Relationship. In an integrated IT infrastructure, all information relevant to a customer would be available in an integrated form, which provides a 360-degree view of customer relationships, resulting in improved services quality for customers and increased services/products value to customers [14, 17]. Such increased value could build customer loyalty, which in turn could generate profit for the organization [29–31].

Enterprise Flexibility. Connecting all the necessary functions and heterogeneous functional entities allows for a greater degree of communication, coordination, and cooperation in human factors as well as information technologies. This enables organizations to continuously monitor market demand, quickly respond by providing new products, services, information, and application, and quickly introduce new technologies and modify business methods [3, 9, 21]. Moreover, not only does EI reduce the time-to-market [1, 14, 17], but also due to cross-department standardization to all domains of the enterprise, the resulting increased reactivity can manifest itself by a reduction in loss of revenues or an increase of quality of service [1].

Organizational Mergers. In case of organizational mergers or acquisitions, when new business units enter the mix, enterprise integration facilitates incorporating new systems into the enterprise architecture [21].

Costs Reduction. Reengineering processes, during implementation of enterprise integration, results in more organized business processes and increases business processes understanding and control. This leads to business processes improvement, resulting in increased organizational performance.

Revenue Growth. Imperfect interoperability could lead to delays in key activities in value chain. Such delays yield to reduction in market share and the associated revenues. Another consequence could be delays in revenue [1, 14, 25].

Supply Chain. By integrating internal and external supply chains, enterprise integration improves planning in supply chain management [14], and therefore improves supply chains [17, 28].

4   Discussion

This research sought to reveal the current state of the scientific literature concerning the potential benefits of EI. Our research results provide a consolidated view of the scientifically established picture of such potential benefits.

The literature suggests benefits of EI, related to various aspects of an enterprise. However, the results of many studies are limited to specific cases due to the research methodologies adopted. Some studies also suffer from limited understandability and reusability, since they lack a classification scheme or proper taxonomy. Moreover, disperse backgrounds of the studies conducted regarding EI benefits causes an ambiguity with regard to the context where the perceived benefits are applicable. To address such voids, the presented research provides an account of the available research findings of EI benefits, classified using a conceptual model of the enterprise.

The results have several implications for both researchers and practitioners. First of all, the provided information on potential EI benefits and their applicability (enterprise layer) enhances the understanding of EI. Moreover, the list and classification of EI benefits provided can function as a source for defining relevant objectives for EI projects, which is useful in business cases. Additionally, the results could be used to define EI effectiveness metrics. Within a more ambitious research agenda, the classified benefits could be employed to develop methods or models capable of measuring such benefits in financial terms.

Certain benefits have been found to semantically overlap or to group more than one notion, while some might appear vague or of high-level abstraction. This reflects the different intentions of the original studies' authors. However, the affected benefits were incorporated without any modifications to avoid potential semantic inconsistencies.

In addition to the context within which certain benefits appear as results of EI, future studies are recommended to understand and report the causal mechanisms behind these benefits. Identifying the relations between different benefits of EI with the specific mechanisms that generate them provides insight on how the benefits were actually brought about. Such causal relationships could offer additional and critical understanding regarding the benefits of EI, not least for decision-makers running actual integration projects.

Although the study aimed to be highly inclusive regarding the studies available on the subject of benefits of EI, it might not have covered the entire span of available literature. To increase the comprehensiveness, additional studies could be conducted to consider additional studies in other languages than English (which was the focus of the search in this study), as well as the gray literature (e.g. organizational statistics, internal reports).

Moreover, based on the results of this research, one future study could be to perform more rigorously designed EI research on benefits of EI. This would lead to more reproducible results, a crucial need for the area.

References

1. Manouvrier, B., Ménard, L.: Application Integration: EAI, B2B, BPM and SOA. Wiley-IEEE Press (2008)
2. Fulk, J., DeSanctis, G.: Electronic communication and changing organizational forms. Organization Science 6, 337–349 (1995)

3. Lee, J., Siau, K., Hong, S.: Enterprise integration with ERP and EAI. Commun. ACM. 46, 54–60 (2003)
4. Mukhopadhyay, T., Kekre, S., Kalathur, S.: Business Value of Information Technology: A Study of Electronic Data Interchange. MIS Quarterly 19, 137–156 (1995)
5. Walker, J., Pan, E., Johnston, D., Adler-Milstein, J., Bates, D.W., Middleton, B.: The value of health care information exchange and interoperability. Health Affairs, W5:10–W5:18 (2005)
6. Lheureux, B.J., Skybakmoen, T., Thompson, J., Malinverno, P., Biscotti, F., Wilson, D.R., Schulte, W.R., Beyer, M.A., Knipp, E., Pezzini, M.: Taxonomy, Definitions and the Vendor Landscape for Application Integration Solutions (2011)
7. Fazlollahi, A.: Benefits of Enterprise Integration Systems (Master thesis). KTH, Industrial Information and Control Systems, Stockholm (2012)
8. Chen, D., Doumeingts, G., Vernadat, F.: Architectures for enterprise integration and interoperability: Past, present and future. Computers in Industry 59, 647–659 (2008)
9. Vernadat, F.B.: Enterprise Integration and Interoperability. In: Nof, S.Y. (ed.) Springer Handbook of Automation, pp. 1529–1538. Springer, Heidelberg (2009)
10. Themistocleous, M., Irani, Z.: Novel taxonomy for application integration. Benchmarking: An International Journal 9, 154–165 (2002)
11. Markus, M.L.: Paradigm shifts-E-business and business/systems integration. Communications of the Association for Information Systems 4 (2000)
12. Themistocleous, M., Irani, Z.: Towards a novel framework for the assessment of enterprise application integration packages. In: Proceedings of the 36th Annual Hawaii International Conference on System Sciences. IEEE (2003)
13. Shang, S., Seddon, P.B.: A comprehensive framework for classifying the benefits of ERP systems. In: AMCIS 2000 Proceedings, p. 39 (2000)
14. Themistocleous, M.: Justifying the decisions for EAI implementations: a validated proposition of influential factors. Journal of Enterprise Information Management 17, 85–104 (2004)
15. Chari, K., Seshadri, S.: Demystifying integration. Communications of the ACM 47, 58–63 (2004)
16. Themistocleous, M., Irani, Z.: Benchmarking the benefits and barriers of application integration. Benchmarking: An International Journal 8, 317–331 (2001)
17. Ruh, W.A., Brown, W.J., Maginnis, F.X.: Enterprise application integration: a Wiley tech brief. John Wiley & Sons, Inc., New York (2001)
18. Shin, I.: Adoption of Enterprise Application Software and Firm Performance. Small Business Economics 26, 241–256 (2006)
19. Puschmann, T., Alt, R.: Enterprise application integration-the case of the Robert Bosch Group. IEEE Comput. Soc. (2001)
20. Themistocleous, M., Irani, Z., Psannis, K., Vrehopoulos, A.: Application Integration of Information Technology: Classification of Benefits and Barriers. Information Systems,156–164 (2001)
21. Gleghorn, R.: Enterprise application integration: a manager's perspective. IT Professional, 17–23 (2005)
22. Giachetti, R., Hernandez, P., Nunez, A., Truex, D.: A research framework for operationalizing measures of enterprise integration. Knowledge Sharing in the Integrated Enterprise, 237–247 (2005)
23. The Open Group: ArchiMate® 2.0 Specification. The Open Group, Berkshire, UK (2012)
24. Wand, Y., Wang, R.Y.: Anchoring data quality dimensions in ontological foundations. Communications of the ACM 39, 86–95 (1996)

25. Brunnermeier, S.B., Martin, S.A.: Interoperability costs in the US automotive supply chain. Supply Chain Management: An International Journal 7, 71–82 (2002)
26. Themistocleous, M., Irani, Z., Kuljis, J., Love, P.E.D.: Extending the information system lifecycle through enterprise application integration: a case study experience. In: Proceedings of the 37th Annual Hawaii International Conference on System Sciences, p. 8 (2004)
27. Irani, Z., Themistocleous, M., Love, P.E.D.: The impact of enterprise application integration on information system lifecycles. Information & Management 41, 177–187 (2003)
28. Mentzer, J.T., DeWitt, W., Keebler, J.S., Min, S., Nix, N.W., Smith, C.D., Zacharia, Z.G.: Defining supply chain management. Journal of Business Logistics 22, 1–26 (2001)
29. Hallowell, R.: The relationships of customer satisfaction, customer loyalty, and profitability: an empirical study. International Journal of Service Industry Management 7, 27–42 (1996)
30. Edvardsson, B., Johnson, M., Gustafsson, A., Strandvik, T.: The effects of satisfaction and loyalty on profits and growth: Products versus services. Total Quality Management & Business Excellence 11, 917–927 (2000)
31. Heskett, J.L., Jones, T.O., Loveman, G.W., Earl Sasser Jr., W., Schlesinger, L.A.: Putting the service-profit chain to work. Harvard Business Review 72, 164–174 (1994)

A Resource Virtualization Mechanism
for Cloud Manufacturing Systems

Ning Liu and Xiaoping Li

School of Computer Science and Engineering, Southeast University,
Nanjing 211189, P.R. China
{ningliu,xpli}@seu.edu.cn

Abstract. Virtualization is critical for resource sharing and dynamic allocation in cloud manufacturing, a new service-oriented networked collaborative manufacturing model. In this paper, an effective method is proposed for manufacturing resources & capabilities virtualization, which contains manufacturing resources modeling and manufacturing cloud services encapsulation. A manufacturing resource virtual description model is built, which includes both nonfunctional and functional features of manufacturing resources. The model provides a comprehensive manufacturing resource view and information for various manufacturing applications. The OWL-S is adapted to an upper level ontology model, according to which manufacturing resources & capabilities are encapsulated into manufacturing cloud service. The proposed method is applied to the virtualization process of an aerospace company. Effectiveness and efficiency are illustrated for the manufacturing cloud services discovery and management.

Keywords: virtualization, manufacturing cloud service, cloud manufacturing, resource integration.

1   Introduction

Cloud manufacturing, as the manufacturing version of cloud computing, offers a new manufacturing model for collaborative manufacturing. Virtualization is the prerequisite for achieving cloud manufacturing, because it determines the robustness of a cloud manufacturing system [1]. By virtualized and encapsulated as cloud services, manufacturing resources & capabilities can be shared over the manufacturing cloud platform. It is very important to investigate an effective virtualization method for capturing information of manufacturing resources & capabilities, enhancing the performance of resource sharing and discovery, reducing the holding cost of inventory, and improving the ROI (Return on Investment) of manufacturing resources.

Compared with the virtualization in cloud computing, the cloud manufacturing virtualization is more challenging due to the following considerations. (1)Besides computing resources, manufacturing resources (such as equipment, materials, human)

The original version of this chapter was revised: The copyright line was incorrect. This has been corrected. The Erratum to this chapter is available at DOI: 10.1007/978-3-642-33068-1_20

M. van Sinderen et al. (Eds.): IWEI 2012, LNBIP 122, pp. 46–59, 2012.

with complex features also need to be virtualized in an isomorphic manner. It is hard to establish a comprehensive information model for representing manufacturing resources & capabilities. (2)Cloud manufacturing represents a dynamic organizational structure. In contrast to static mapping between physical resources and logical resources, cloud manufacturing needs a flexible mapping strategy to avoid resource failure caused by uncertain factors. (3)Resources selection in cloud manufacturing largely depends on the granularity of manufacturing demands. For example, the collaboration among enterprises focuses on resources with large granularity, such as transport capacity, warehouse capacity. On the contrary, the collaboration among stations focuses on resources with fine granularity, such as machining tool, warehouse location. Therefore, it is insufficient to describe simple manufacturing capabilities of a manufacturing resource. It is desired to describe manufacturing capabilities of multiple cooperative manufacturing resources. (4)The current standards (XML/SOAP /WSDL/UDDI/OWL) related to web services and semantic web cannot be applied to manufacturing resources directly, because the meaning and usage of manufacturing services are different from traditional web services. A lot of critical information on manufacturing domain cannot be represented by existing service description methods.

Based on the above analysis, this paper explored manufacturing resource & capability virtualization from Enterprise Interoperability and Collaboration(COIN) perspective. By describing manufacturing capabilities with multi-granularity, the proposed method provides sufficient information for manufacturing demands coming from different collaboration levels. By extending OWL-S, manufacturing resources and capabilities can be encapsulated as manufacturing cloud services, which contribute to resource sharing and dynamic allocation. The paper is organized as follows. Section 2 presents a comprehensive review on manufacturing resources modeling and service encapsulation. Then a cloud manufacturing virtualization framework is described in Section 3. Based on the proposed framework, an effective method for manufacturing resource & capability virtualization is introduced in Section 4. Section 5 gives a case study to illustrate the advantages of the proposed method. Finally, conclusions are given in Section 6.

2 Related Work

Cloud manufacturing focuses on the flexibility and scalability of cooperation among heterogeneous manufacturing resources. Manufacturing resource modeling and manufacturing service description are the critical issues for cloud manufacturing virtualization.

2.1 Manufacturing Resources Modeling

Standards as STEP and enhancements of STEP were recognized to play an important role in manufacturing resources modeling [2]. However, the standards only focused on products while overlooked the manufacturing equipment. Vichare et al [3] proposed a unified manufacturing resource model(UMRM), which is based on modeling kinematic chains of machines and is more concentrated on geometric aspects of the system. Compared with an assembly system composed of multiple individual devices, UMRM is not adequate to describe the capability of the system. Shen et al [4] provided an agent-based service-oriented integration architecture for collaborative intelligent manufacturing. A unique property of the proposed approach is that the scheduling process of an order is orchestrated on the Internet through the negotiation among agent-based web services.

In the process of product development, manufacturing capabilities determine whether manufacturing resources can reach requirements of product design. Therefore, the representation of various manufacturing capabilities is necessary in virtualization. Liang et al [5] defined resource element as the similar and exclusive capabilities of manufacturing resources, and discussed resource element modeling approach in detail. The proposed method can represent the multi-functional resource closely, reduce the complexity of manufacturing system and improve the agility and flexibility of manufacturing systems. Zhang et al [6] presented a multi-perspective modeling approach to systematically manage distributed manufacturing knowledge on the semantic web. By integrating the industrial, software engineering techniques into ontology-based knowledge engineering process, the proposed approach facilitates the implementation of computer supported cooperative work in distributed manufacturing for semantic web application. These methods can be introduced to model cloud manufacturing resources.

2.2   Manufacturing Service Description

Web service technologies are widely used in service-oriented computing. Services description, discovery and integration are based on a series of standards(XML, SOAP, WSDL, UDDI). To improve the resource sharing in a manufacturing grid environment, Shi et al [7] encapsulated resource information by employing XML schema and defined all accessing operations to resources by using WSDL. However, the proposed method is lack of expressing semantic description about manufacturing services.

Ontology and semantic web technology describe web services in a computer-interpretable form, which enables the intelligent interoperation of web services. OWL-S is an ontology-based approach providing a standard for semantic web services. However, OWL-S only addresses the communication capabilities of the services. IOPR-based approaches fall short of logical relationships for the underlying inputs and outputs. Based on an environment ontology, Wang et al [8] built capability specifications of web services. Algorithms for constructing the domain ontology and the matchmaking between the web service capability specifications are presented. The proposed approach can support automated web service discovery. Jang et al [9] defined manufacturing service capability profiles by using OWL and presented a reasoning procedure for matching queries to service description based description logic. The proposed method contributes to intelligent manufacturing service discovery. Ameri et al [10] described manufacturing services formally by manufacturing service description language(MSDL), which has two major parts. The core is composed of basic classes for manufacturing service description.

The extension includes a collection of taxonomies, subclasses, and instances built by dispersed users from different communities based on their specific needs. Due to lack of semantic description standard for manufacturing services, the above mentioned methods require human involvement to some extent when services interactions are engaged. As a result, the scalability of manufacturing services is limited and the expected economic value of manufacturing services is reduced.

3   Cloud Manufacturing Virtualization Framework

Fig.1 illustrates a cloud manufacturing virtualization framework, which consists three layers, manufacturing resource layer, virtual description layer, and service encapsulation layer.

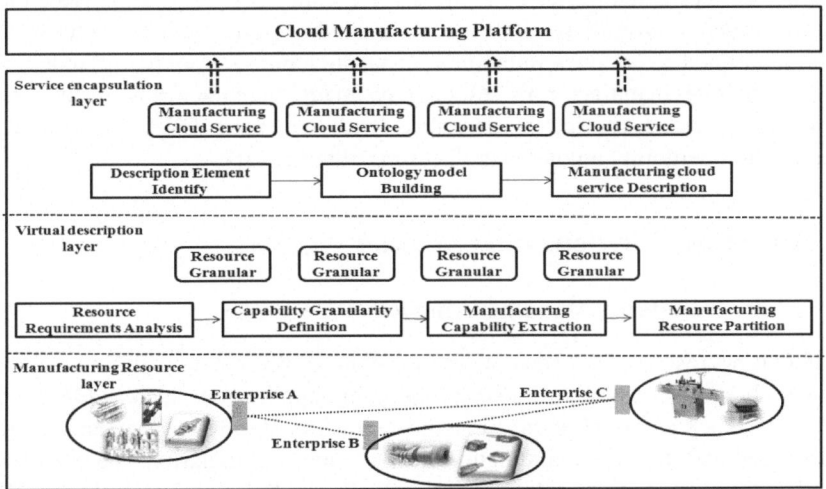

Fig. 1. Cloud manufacturing virtualization framework

In manufacturing resource layer, distributed manufacturing resources can be intelligently sensed and connected into cloud manufacturing systems by using advanced information and communication technologies [11] such as RFID, sensors, GPS. Manufacturing resources refer to various elements to support manufacturing activities throughout product lifecycles. They are the cornerstone of the cloud manufacturing and can be divided into financial resource, technical resource, equipment resource, human resource, software resource, logistics resource, and warehouse resource.

Virtual description layer aims to provide a comprehensive information view for various applications. Manufacturing resource information takes two forms, physical resource information and manufacturing capability information. Physical resource information describes static manufacturing facilities with actual existence. Manufacturing capability information represents an assembly of various operations provided by physical resources. It can be considered as the behavior of the physical resource undertaking a particular manufacturing activity with certain constraints. Manufacturing resources can be divided into different results according to manufacturing capabilities with different granularity. Then manufacturing resources with the same or similar capabilities can be aggregated into one granular. An appropriate manufacturing resource model includes both nonfunctional and functional features of manufacturing resources based on a full consideration for both the resource provider and the resource requestor.

Based on ontology modeling approach, manufacturing resources and capabilities are encapsulated as manufacturing cloud services in service encapsulation layer. By this way, manufacturing resources are managed and operated in a service-oriented and flexible way. Furthermore, they can be discovered, selected, and composited in a cost-effective manner through the manufacturing cloud platform. Manufacturing cloud service providers are motivated by the profits to be made by charging consumers for accessing services. Manufacturing cloud service consumers request services ranging from all stages of overall product lifecycle. In this paper, a manufacturing cloud service is defined as an encapsulation of a manufacturing resource granular, which may contain one manufacturing resource or many manufacturing resources. The manufacturing cloud service is described with extended OWL-S to implement semantic interoperability among manufacturing enterprises.

4   Proposed Virtualization Method

4.1   Multi-granularity Manufacturing Resource Model

Manufacturing resource information is the digital representation for manufacturing resources. It is the base for various manufacturing applications such as CAD, CAPP, CAM, CAE, ERP etc. In cloud manufacturing, manufacturing resource information is characterized with multi-domain, multi-level, and multi-granularity. The granularity is defined as the measure extent that characterizes the scale or level of problems. Within the field of granular computing, information granularity usually refers to "structural granularity", which signifies the structural abstraction of information items [12]. A structural abstraction can be based on a relatively large information item, such as a document, or its constituent parts. For example, chapters, sections, pages, paragraphs are the different structural abstractions of a book. Similarly, in the process of performing large-scale collaborative manufacturing, complex manufacturing problems are usually recursively decomposed according to the product structure. The matching between complex manufacturing problems and manufacturing resources involves heterogenic system levels (line, cell, station, device), as shown in Fig.2.

Manufacturing capabilities of a physical resource have the characteristics of multiple granularities because a physical resource displays different manufacturing capabilities in different activities and different collaborative demand levels. Within an enterprise, manufacturing resource information with fine granularity is more effective. It is convenient to manage manufacturing resources in a global way. While outside the enterprise, manufacturing resource information with coarse granularity is more popular. It is conductive to release manufacturing resources in an understandable way.

Therefore, product structure is the basis for measuring manufacturing resources and manufacturing demands. Flexible and effective matching of manufacturing resources against manufacturing demands requires formalized and structured description of the manufacturing capabilities and constraints with multi-granularity.

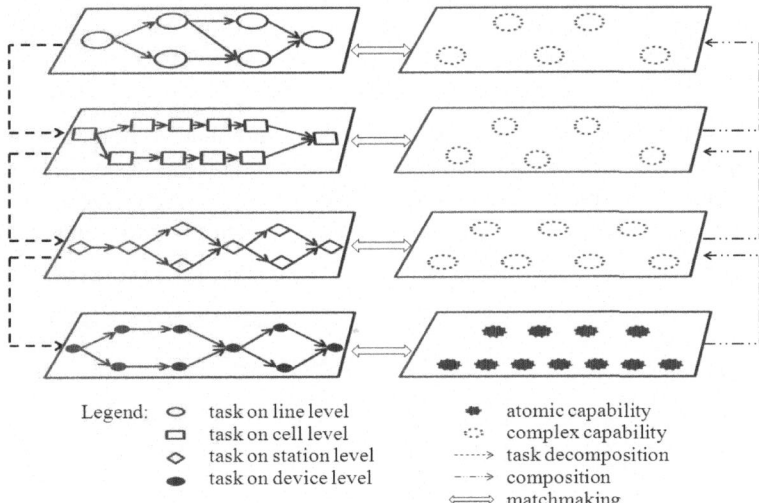

Legend: ○ task on line level   ✹ atomic capability
         ▢ task on cell level   ⊙ complex capability
         ◇ task on station level   ┈┈┈▶ task decomposition
         ⬤ task on device level   ╌ ╌▶ composition
                                         ⟺ matchmaking

Fig. 2. Multi-granularity matching between manufacturing task and manufacturing capabilities

Definition 1. Let MR be the collection of manufacturing resources, which are connected in cloud manufacturing systems. Let g be a equivalence relation over MR. If $g : MR \rightarrow 2^{|MR|}$, then $MR = \bigcup_{i=1}^{n} B_i$ and $\{B_j\}$ is a division of MR. B_j is called a manufacturing resource granular. $Gr(\{B_i\}) = |\{B_i\}|/|MR|$ is the refinement degree of $\{B_j\}$.

Manufacturing resources can be divided into different results according to different manufacturing capability demands. Through a proper abstraction of manufacturing capability, a manufacturing task can easily find the eligible manufacturing resources among all the available ones. When $Gr(\{B_i\}) = 1$, $\{B_j\}$ is the finest division of MR. Manufacturing capabilities according to the finest division are called atomic capability. In the same way, manufacturing capabilities are called complex capability, which are according to the division with $Gr(\{B_i\}) < 1$.

Definition 2. A manufacturing resource is represented as a triple, MResource::= (MR_Id, NFeature, FFeature).

(1) MR_Id is the identification of the manufacturing resource. It can be represented by the Uniform Resource Identifier of the manufacturing resource.
(2) NFeature represents the nonfunctional features of the manufacturing resource, which can be used to efficiently evaluate the resource organization, storage, management, and utilization. Furthermore, it can be divided into static information and dynamic

information. NFeature::=(StaticInfo, DynamicInfo). Static information is relatively stable in manufacturing resource lifecycles, such as resource type, resource structure, resource provider etc. Dynamic information changes over time, such as resource state, resource inventory, resource planning etc.

(3) FFeature presents functional features of the manufacturing resource, which are equivalence to the inherent manufacturing capabilities of the manufacturing resource. The detail information of each functional feature is consisted of three parts. FFeature::={(B_j , CapaInfo, CstrInfo)}. B_j is the manufacturing resource granular which is dependent on the manufacturing demands. CapaInfo represents the operations included in the corresponding manufacturing capability. CstrInfo is the specific constraint information of the manufacturing capability. Fig.3 illustrates an example of the manufacturing resource with multi-granularity capabilities.

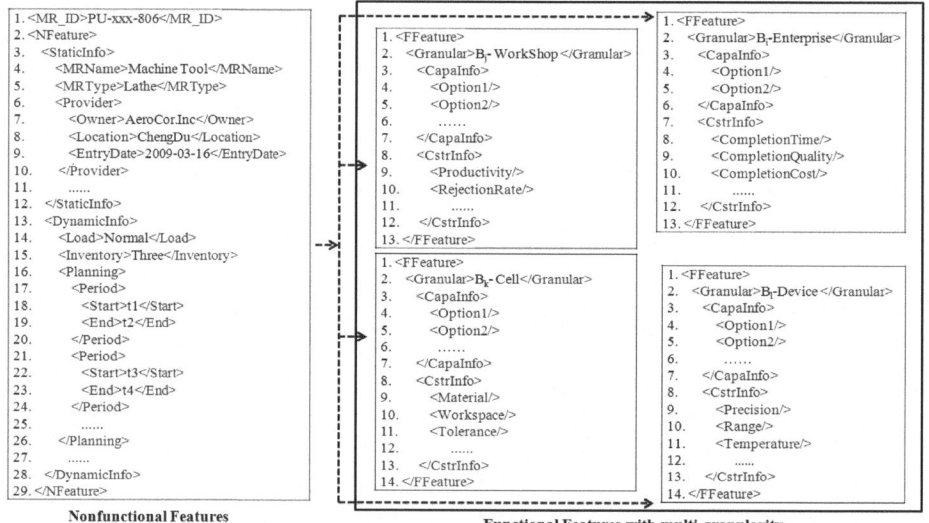

Nonfunctional Features   **Functional Features with multi-granularity**

Fig. 3. An excerpt of a manufacturing resource description

The described manufacturing resource are included in four different manufacturing resource granular, which are on enterprise level, workshop level, cell level, and device level respectively. For example, the manufacturing capability in the manufacturing resource granular on device level can be described from process type, geometrical characteristic, speed etc. Accordingly, constraints for the manufacturing capability are related to parameters such as processing precision, part range, processing temperature etc. Each resource can be viewed as the combination of nonfunctional features and functional features. Based on object-oriented methodology, each resource inherits all attributes from its superclass and can have its own new attributes on demand. By the flexibility and openness of the proposed description model, the templates of each special kind of manufacturing resources can be customized.

4.2   Manufacturing Cloud Service Encapsulation Using Extended OWL-S

OWL-S is a web ontology language for web services which supports the dynamic services discovery, invocation, composition and mediation. A complete description of web service capabilities can be deployed through three modules, service profile, service model, and service grounding. However, OWL-S is insufficient for manufacturing cloud services because manufacturing cloud services are different from traditional web services. A web service is applied to the software development. It transforms information entities. While a manufacturing cloud service is associated with manufacturing equipment. It transforms the raw materials into physical objects with specific geometry. The capabilities of a web service are associated with input, output, precondition, effect. While manufacturing capabilities contain a variety of complex information, such as processing object, available product etc. Furthermore, information of manufacturing capabilities must be as precise and rich as possible. For example, a web service requestor only concerns about the QoS indicators. The invocation and composition of manufacturing cloud services are more complex. It is related to many factors, such as service location, service state. Therefore, in addition to the QoS indicators are needed to expose to the requestor, performance indicators of manufacturing cloud services are also needed to be described.

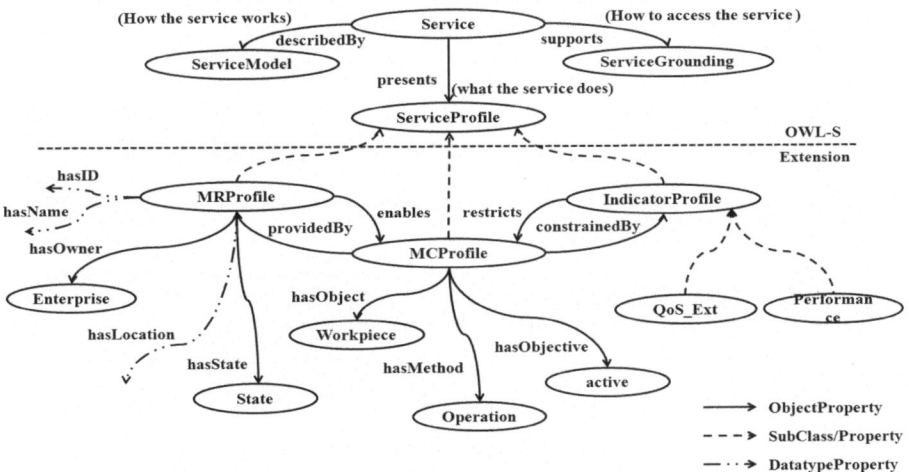

Fig. 4. Ontology model by extending OWL-S

An effective virtualization method requires formalized and structured representations of manufacturing resources. The information of manufacturing capabilities and their constraints plays an important role in manufacturing service discovery and matchmaking. This paper extends OWL-S by defining three classes in order to represent the indispensable information of manufacturing cloud services. As shown in Fig.4, the extended ontology model concerns the issues and elements related to collaborative manufacturing, such as available raw materials or castings, available equipment, available products, resource state, and various performance indicators relevant to manufacturing capabilities. MRProfile, MCProfile, and IndicatorProfile are the subclasses of ServiceProfile. MRProfile represents the nonfunctional information of the entities that enables manufacturing capabilities. MCProfile describes the functionalities of the manufacturing resource. It gives a detailed description of how the manufacturing cloud service operates. Manufacturing capabilities can be divided into atomic capability and complex capability. Complex capabilities are combinations of atomic capabilities, usually formed by a combination of devices, such as a machine tool, fixture, and a worker. IndicatorProfile presents constraint information from both providers and requestors perspectives.

```
1. <owl:Class rdf:ID="MCServiceProfile">
2.  <owl:equivalencClass>
3.   <owl:Class>
4.    <owl:intersectionOf rdf:parseType="Collection">
5.     <rdfs:label>Manufacturing Cloud Service Profile</rdfs:label>
6.     <rdfs:subClassOf rdf:resource="&service;#ServiceProfile"/>
7.     <rdfs:subClassOf>
8.      <owl:Restriction>
9.       <owl:onProperty rdf:resource="#supportedBy"/>
10.      <owl:allValuesFrom rdf:resource="#MRProfile"/>
14.     </owl:Restriction>
15.     <owl:Restriction>
16.      <owl:onProperty rdf:resource="#owns"/>
17.      <owl:allValuesFrom rdf:resource="#MCProfile"/>
18.     </owl:Restriction>
15.     <owl:Restriction>
16.      <owl:onProperty rdf:resource="#merit"/>
17.      <owl:allValuesFrom rdf:resource="#IndicatorProfile"/>
18.     </owl:Restriction>
19.     </rdfs:subClassOf>
20.    </owl:intersectionOf>
21.   </owl:Class>
22.  </owl:equivalencClass>
23. </owl:Class>
```
(a)The ontology description of manufacturing cloud service

```
1. <owl:Class rdf:ID="MCProfile">
2.  <owl:equivalencClass>
3.   <owl:Class>
4.    <owl:intersectionOf rdf:parseType="Collection">
5.     <rdfs:label>Manufacturing Capability Profile</rdfs:label>
6.     <rdfs:subClassOf rdf:resource="&service;#ServiceProfile"/>
7.     <rdfs:subClassOf>
8.      <owl:Restriction>
9.       <owl:onProperty rdf:resource="#providedBy"/>
10.      <owl:allValuesFrom rdf:resource="#MRProfile"/>
11.      <owl:minCardinality rdf:datatype="&xds;#nonNegativeInteger">
12.      1
13.      </owl:minCardinality>
14.     </owl:Restriction>
15.     <owl:Restriction>
16.      <owl:onProperty rdf:resource="#constraintedBy"/>
17.      <owl:allValuesFrom rdf:resource="#IndicatorProfile"/>
18.      <owl:maxCardinality rdf:datatype="&xds;#nonNegativeInteger">
19.      1
20.      </owl:maxCardinality>
21.     </owl:Restriction>
22.     </rdfs:subClassOf>
23.    </owl:intersectionOf>
24.   </owl:Class>
25.  </owl:equivalencClass>
26. </owl:Class>
```
(b)The ontology description of manufacturing capability

```
1. <owl:Class rdf:ID="MRProfile">
2.  <owl:equivalencClass>
3.   <owl:Class>
4.    <owl:intersectionOf rdf:parseType="Collection">
5.     <rdfs:label>Manufacturing Resource Profile</rdfs:label>
6.     <rdfs:subClassOf rdf:resource="&service;#ServiceProfile"/>
7.     <rdfs:subClassOf>
8.      <owl:Restriction>
9.       <owl:onProperty rdf:resource="#enables"/>
10.      <owl:allValuesFrom rdf:resource="#MCProfile"/>
11.      <owl:minCardinality rdf:datatype="&xds;#nonNegativeInteger">
12.      1
13.      </owl:minCardinality>
14.     </owl:Restriction>
15.     </rdfs:subClassOf>
16.    </owl:intersectionOf>
17.   </owl:Class>
18.  </owl:equivalencClass>
19. </owl:Class>
```
(c)The ontology description of manufacturing resource

```
1. <owl:Class rdf:ID="IndicatorProfile">
2.  <owl:equivalencClass>
3.   <owl:Class>
4.    <owl:intersectionOf rdf:parseType="Collection">
5.     <rdfs:label>Manufacturing Cloud Service Indicator Profile</rdfs:label>
6.     <rdfs:subClassOf rdf:resource="&service;#ServiceProfile"/>
7.     <rdfs:subClassOf>
8.      <owl:Restriction>
9.       <owl:onProperty rdf:resource="#restricts"/>
10.      <owl:allValuesFrom rdf:resource="#MCProfile"/>
11.     </owl:Restriction>
12.     </rdfs:subClassOf>
13.    </owl:intersectionOf>
14.   </owl:Class>
15.  </owl:equivalencClass>
16. </owl:Class>
```
(d)The ontology description of indicator

Fig. 5. The OWL schema for core concepts in ontology model

The description of the core concepts are given in Fig.5 by OWL. Manufacturing resources and manufacturing capabilities are the general objects consisting of manufacturing cloud services. Manufacturing resources enable various manufacturing capabilities while manufacturing capabilities are provided by different manufacturing resources. They have multiple to multiple mapping relationship. In this paper, both manufacturing resources and manufacturing capabilities cannot exist independently. A manufacturing resource enables at least one manufacturing capability. In the same way, a manufacturing capability is provided by at least one manufacturing resource. The indicator information enhances the possibility and accuracy of manufacturing cloud service discovery. The three extended classes form the core concepts of ontology model for manufacturing cloud services. Concepts of relevant product and resource elements needed for matchmaking are also formalized defined.

5   Case Study

5.1   Background

The proposed method is demonstrated by a manufacturing resource in a big aerospace company of China, which owns its core competence with coordinating partners include designers, suppliers, and testers in various fields. Various manufacturing resources are distributed among partners. Because of the importer virtualization for resources, existing collaborative manufacturing operational forms could not be directly used to cloud manufacturing environments. We implemented the proposed virtualization method and applied it to the aerospace company to promote its manufacturing resources and capabilities sharing in cloud manufacturing.

5.2   The Description of Manufacturing Cloud Services

To illustrate the significance of the proposed method, this paper gives the description of a manufacturing cloud service which has an atomic manufacturing capability of "joining" on device level, as depicted in Fig.6. The manufacturing capability is provided by a joining machine. The document on the left side is described based on OWL-S and the document on the right side is described based on the proposed method. The code lines are numbered to facilitate discussion. Obviously they are not a part of the service description.

In the description of manufacturing cloud service based on OWL-S, the information of both joining machine and joining capability are included in the same profile, such as Lines 10-25 in the figure 6(a). This means that the manufacturing resource and its manufacturing capability are tightly coupled with each other. That is not conductive to deal with the matchmaking between manufacturing resources and manufacturing tasks on different collaboration levels. When the manufacturing resource unexpectedly exits cloud manufacturing systems, or it suddenly stops running for some reasons, the manufacturing cloud service cannot be invoked normally. From another perspective, the information is not sufficient to represent complex manufacturing capabilities from both structure and constraints aspects. Manufacturing requestors cannot find their interest information in the document. As a result, the resource utilization of the cloud manufacturing systems is reduced.

(a)The description of manufacturing cloud service based OWL-S

(b)The description of manufacturing cloud service based proposed method

Fig. 6. The comparison of manufacturing cloud service description

In the description of manufacturing cloud service based on the proposed method, the information of manufacturing resource, manufacturing capability and performance indicators are described separately. In figure 6(b), Lines 1-6 specify the basis of XML coding and the namespaces declaration of the ontologies exploited by the description of the manufacturing cloud service. Lines 7-11 introduce a description of the manufacturing cloud service, identified as JOINING_MANUFACTURING_ CLOUD _SERVICE, showing the relationship between manufacturing cloud service and the core concepts in the extended ontology model. Lines 12-26 focus on the manufacturing resource description. The manufacturing resource profile, named JOINING_MACHINE_PROFILE provides the resource name, the serial number, a textual description, the provider, the location, the state, the maintenance times, the failure rate and the associated capability. Lines 27-37 focus on the manufacturing capability description. The manufacturing capability profile, named JOINING_ CAPABILITY_PROFILE provides the capability name, the capability provider, the performance indicator, the capability level, the precondition, the processing object, the method, and the objective. Lines 38-43 present indicator profile description. The indicator profile named JOINING_INDICATOR_PROFILE provides the productivity, the rejection rate. The information is the performance indicators when the manufacturing resource provides the manufacturing capability. In other words, the capability is provided by the manufacturing resource named JOINING_MACHINE_ PROFILE and takes material "aluminum" as processing object and returns the plane body. As precondition, the capability checks the validity of the material, whereas as result, it completes the product with specific performance. By this way, manufacturing capabilities are artificially decoupled with manufacturing resources to support agile and flexible resource discovery and sharing.

5.3   Discussion

The proposed method and OWL-S present several similarities and differences. Like the OWL-S, the proposed method describes manufacturing cloud services from semantic perspective. Both of them aim to contribute to service discovery, matching, and composition automatically. However, unlike OWL-S, which represents web service capabilities in the service profile, the proposed method describes manufacturing cloud services based on three profiles. The description of multi-granularity manufacturing capabilities and related performance indicators are more suitable to the requirements of the requestors. By this way, an effective and efficiency matching approach can be developed. Manufacturing resources can be easily discovered by demands coming from different collaborative levels in two steps. Firstly, based on manufacturing capabilities, the product requirement can rapidly select a set of manufacturing resource candidates. Then based on the performance indicators, the best service among the candidate services can be determined.

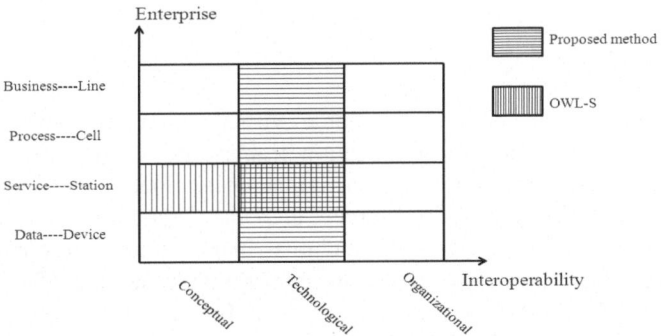

Fig. 7. The comparison from enterprise interoperability perspective

From enterprise interoperability point of view, Chen et al. [13] proposed an enterprise interoperability framework with two basic dimensions, as shown in Fig.7. Enterprise dimension represents enterprise levels(business, process, service, data), which has the similar meaning of collaborative levels in cloud manufacturing. Interoperability dimension represents interoperability barriers (conceptual, technological, organizational). The intersection of a level category (row) and a barrier category(column) constitutes an interoperability sub-domain. The proposed method contributes to remove technological barrier on various levels of enterprise dimension, while OWL-S addresses the conceptual and technological barriers on service level. Knowledge aspect is not explored in depth by the proposed method. In order to manage distributed manufacturing resources, a semantic manufacturing resource meta-model can be designed based on the core concepts proposed in this paper.

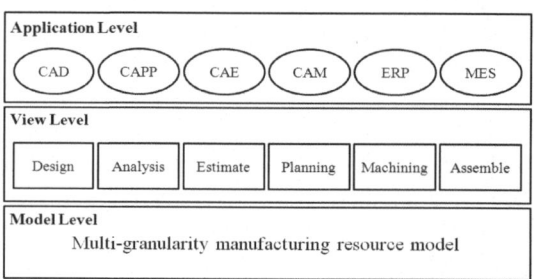

Fig. 8. The significance from collaborative point view

From enterprise collaboration point of view, the proposed method provides a feasible solution to enhance the competitive advantages of the collaborative networks. As shown in Fig.8, the multi-granularity manufacturing resource model includes comprehensive information on the phases of product development. Information views can be derived from the model to support various manufacturing applications. Manufacturing enterprises can achieve their business objectives in a time, quality and cost effective manner.

6   Conclusions

This paper presents an effective resource virtualization mechanism for cloud manufacturing. A three layers virtualization framework is proposed to transform distributed manufacturing resources into manufacturing cloud services. By analyzing the features of manufacturing resources and the granularity requirements of manufacturing capabilities, a multi-granularity manufacturing resource model is described. Manufacturing capabilities are encapsulated as manufacturing cloud services by extending OWL-S with three classes. Instead of building a centralized manufacturing resources repository, the multi-granularity manufacturing resource model manages manufacturing resources based on manufacturing capabilities. During the process of collaborative manufacturing, manufacturing resources are changeable while manufacturing capabilities are relatively sustained. Therefore, the proposed mechanism is flexible and scaleable because manufacturing cloud services are decoupled with manufacturing resources. In addition, manufacturing resources can be located and obtained according to multi-granularity manufacturing capabilities and related constraints. That contributes to support dynamic and automatic services discovery and composition.

Acknowledgment. This work was supported by National Natural Science Foundation of China under Grant 61070160.

References

1. Xu, X.: From cloud computing to cloud manufacturing. Robotics and Computer-Integrated Manufacturing 28, 75–86 (2012)
2. Laguionie, R., Rauch, M., Hascoet, J.Y., Suh, S.H.: An extended manufacturing integrated system for feature-based manufacturing with STEP-NC. International Journal of Computer Integrated Manufacturing 24, 785–799 (2011)
3. Vichare, P., Nassehi, A., Kumar, S., Newman, S.T.: A unified manufacturing resource model for representing CNC machining systems. Robotics and Computer-Integrated Manufacturing 25, 99–1007 (2009)
4. Shen, W.M., Hao, Q., Wang, S.Y., Li, Y.S., Ghenniwa, H.: An agent-based service-oriented integration architecture for collaborative intelligent manufacturing. Robotics and Computer-Integrated Manufacturing 23, 315–325 (2007)
5. Liang, F., Fung, R.Y.K., Jiang, Z.: Modeling approach and behavior analysis of manufacturing resources in virtual cellular manufacturing systems using resource element concept. International Journal of Computer Integrated Manufacturing 24, 1168–1182 (2011)
6. Zhang, W.Y., Cai, W., Qiu, J., Yin, J.W.: Managing distributed manufacturing knowledge through multi-perspective modeling for semantic web applications. International Journal of Production Research 22, 1144–1153 (2009)
7. Shi, S.Y., Mo, R., Yang, H.C., Chang, Z.Y., Chen, Z.F.: An implement of modeling resource in a manufacturing grid for resource sharing. International Journal of Computer Integrated Manufacturing 20, 169–177 (2007)
8. Wang, P.W., Jin, Z., Liu, L., Cai, G.Q.: Building towards capability specifications of web services based on an environment ontology. IEEE Transactions on Knowledge and Data Engineering 20, 547–561 (2008)
9. Jang, J., Jeong, B., Kulvatunyou, B., Chang, J., Cho, H.: Discovering and integrating distributed manufacturing services with semantic manufacturing capability profiles. International Journal of Computer Integrated Manufacturing 21, 631–646 (2008)
10. Ameri, F., Dutta, D.: A matchmaking methodology for supply chain deployment in distributed manufacturing environments. Journal of Computing and Information Science in Engineering 8, 001002:1–001002:9 (2008)
11. Atzori, L., Iera, A., Morabito, G.: The internet of things: a survey. Computer Networks 54, 2787–2805 (2010)
12. Yan, X., Lau, R.Y.K., Song, D., Li, X., Ma, J.: Toward a semantic granularity model for domain-specific information retrieval. ACM Transactions of Information Systems 29, Article 15 (2011)
13. Chen, D., Doumeingts, G., Vernadat, F.: Architectures for enterprise integration and interoperability: past, present, and furture. Computers in Industry 59, 647–659 (2008)

Manufacturing Software Interoperability Services Which ISO 16100 Brings about

Michiko Matsuda

Kanagawa Institute of Technology,
1030 Shimo-ogino, Atsugi-shi, Kanagawa, Japan
(ISO/TC 184/SC 5/WG 4 convenor)
matsuda@ic.kanagawa-it.ac.jp

Abstract. ISO 16100 series provides a standardized methodology for the interoperability of manufacturing software using capability profiling. The method for describing software capability as Capability Profile and the way for exchanging software capability as information through Capability Profile are provided by ISO 16100. By using these two fruits from ISO 16100, two new interoperability services are proposed. One is a new manufacturing application developing method using the manufacturing software capability catalogue as cloud service. The other is a new manufacturing system configuration method by plug-and-play of manufacturing software. Finally, further enhancement of interoperability services are discussed.

Keywords: manufacturing software interoperability, capability profiling, capability template, MSU(Manufacturing Software Unit), software integration.

1   Introduction

The ISO 16100 series which is titled 'Manufacturing Software Capability Profiling for Interoperability,' consists of six parts. Part 1 is titled 'Framework [1].' Part 2 is 'Profiling methodology [2].' Part 3 is 'Interface services, protocols and capability templates [3].' Part 4 is 'Conformance test methods, criteria, and report [4].' Part 5 is 'Methodology for profile matching using multiple capability classes [5].' The last: Part 6 is 'Interface services and protocols for matching profiles based on multiple capability class structures [6].' All parts of ISO 16100 have been published by spring of 2010. Now, all parts are ready for use. The ISO 16100 series enables manufacturing software integration by providing the followings: 1) standard interface specifications that allow information exchange among software in industrial automation systems developed by different vendors, 2) software capability profiling using a standardized method to enable users to select software that meet their functional requirements, and 3) a conformance test method that ensures the integrity of the software integration. The ISO 16100 methodology is also applicable and usable for developing general software applications and for describing capabilities of application software.

The original version of this chapter was revised: The copyright line was incorrect. This has been corrected. The Erratum to this chapter is available at DOI: 10.1007/978-3-642-33068-1_20

M. van Sinderen et al. (Eds.): IWEI 2012, LNBIP 122, pp. 60–70, 2012.

In this paper, two new directions and usages of ISO 16100 are proposed. One is a new manufacturing software developing methodology corresponding to globalization and the trend of the open system architecture, by using ISO 16100 as tools to find and use skillfully software units which are provided by various vendors and to reuse existing software units. The other is a new manufacturing system configuration methodology by using ISO 16100 as information exchange tools which have abilities for describing software capabilities and interface services. Finally, enhancements and extensions of the ISO 16100 methodology are discussed to proceed in the proposed directions.

2   Manufacturing Software Capability Profiling in ISO 16100

As a premise of a proposal, the methodology for manufacturing software capability profiling and elements for capability profiling in ISO 16100 are introduced [7].

2.1   Capability Profiling of Manufacturing Software Units

Capabilities of a manufacturing application are represented as an activity tree structure that is both nested and hierarchical. The activity tree is structured based on its associated manufacturing domain. To distinguish a particular activity in an activity tree, an activity has an unambiguous and unique name, along with semantic information expressed. The Capability Class Structure (CCS) is formed from the activities in the activity tree. As shown in Fig. 1, a CCS corresponds to the activity tree and a Capability Class is unique when the activity can be pointed to in the activity tree. An activity tree and a CCS have a one to one mapping. This means the activity tree is modeled as a CCS. The capability of a Manufacturing Software Unit (MSU) is expressed in terms of Capability Classes. At each level, the MSU is modeled as a set of Capability Classes organized in a similar structure. At the bottom level, the MSU is modeled as one Capability Class. These classes denote the combination of the manufacturing functions, resource, and information handled by the MSU according to the requirements of the manufacturing process.

A MSU that enables or supports an activity with an associated Capability Class is concisely described in a Capability Template. A Capability Template is unique when a Capability Class can be pointed to. In other words, one Capability Class has one corresponding Capability Template as shown in Fig. 1. This means that a Capability Template is a concrete class for a Capability Profile. MSU's Capability Profiles are obtained by filling adequate Capability Templates.

If a MSU vendor wants to widely distribute his developed MSU, the vendor makes several Capability Profiles for one MSU corresponding to each CCS. A MSU vendor registers a Capability Profile of a MSU so that it is widely available to many potential users of the MSU. When a manufacturing system configurator or manufacturing application developer wants to search proper MSUs, they create the Capability Profile by filling the Capability Template with the required capabilities and seek a matching of the required Capability Profile and MSU's Capability Profiles.

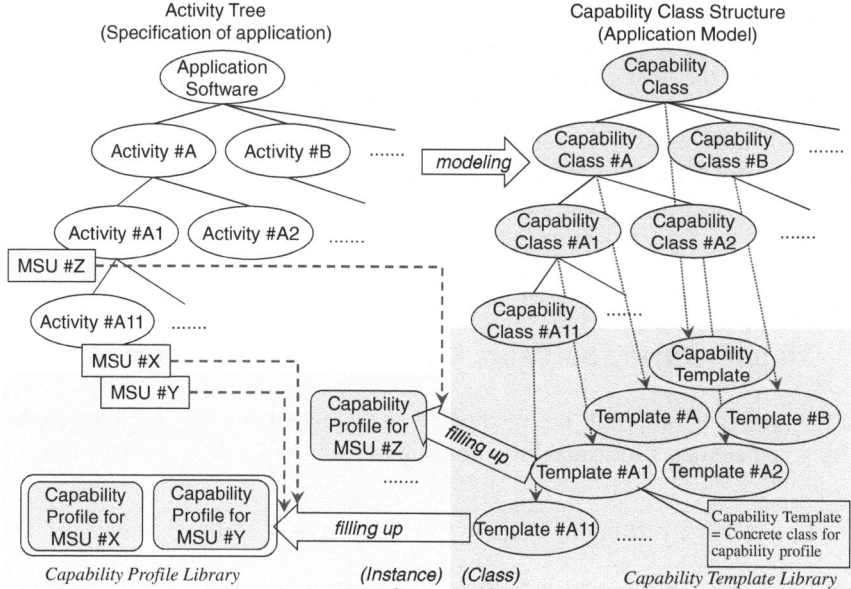

Fig. 1. Capability templates and capability profiles

2.2   Elements for Capability Profiling

A manufacturing application in a specific domain is enabled by manufacturing processes, manufacturing information and manufacturing resources as shown in Fig. 2. A manufacturing process is composed on a set of manufacturing activities. A manufacturing process may have a nested or hierarchical structure of manufacturing activities. The sequence and schedule of functions performed is determined by the sequence and schedule of the activities that comprise a particular process. The MSUs deployed to perform the functions are considered to execute according to the required sequence and schedule of their associated functions. A MSU consists of one or more manufacturing software components, performing a definite function or role within a manufacturing activity while supporting a common information exchange mechanism with other MSUs. In this framework, MSU's capabilities are profiled using CCS and a Capability Template as mentioned in Sec. 2.1.

The relationships of important elements for capability profiling such as Capability Template and Capability Profile, and elements in the above mentioned framework are shown in Fig. 2. Furthermore, two new elements are introduced for capability profiling. One is the MDM: Manufacturing Domain Model. The other is the MDD: Manufacturing Domain Data. The MDM is a particular view of a manufacturing domain, consisting of MDDs and relationships among them, corresponding to the domain's applications. A set of MDDs works like a terminology set in the applicable domain.

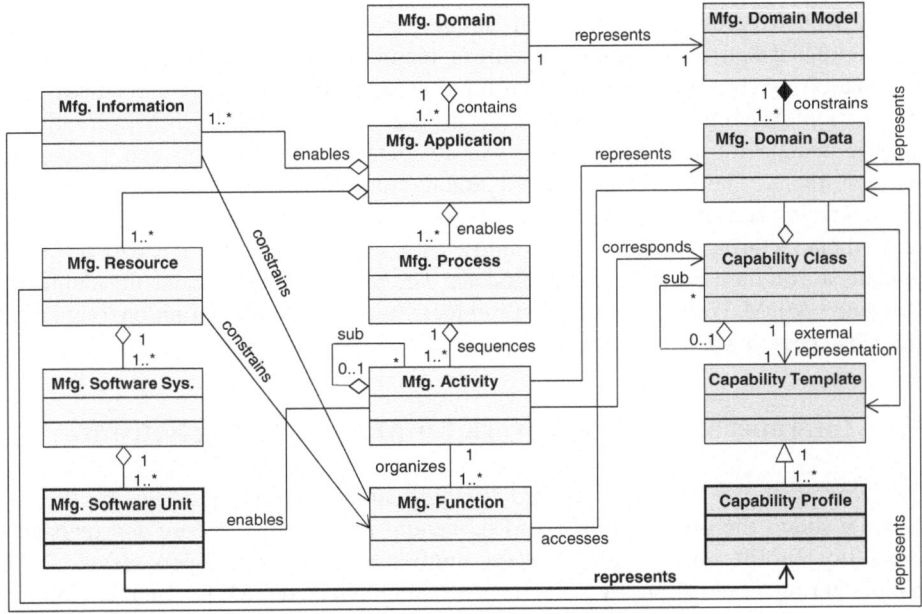

Fig. 2. Elements for capability profiling

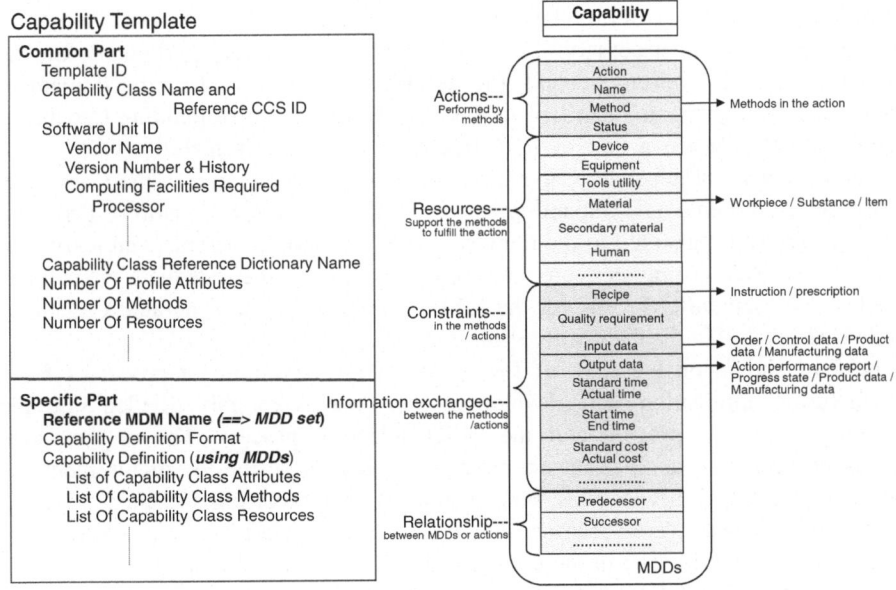

Fig. 3. Manufacturing domain data and a capability template

An MDD represents information about various aspects of a manufacturing application such as manufacturing resources, manufacturing processes, manufacturing information exchanged, and relationships among the resources, processes and information exchanged as shown in the right part of Fig. 3 [8]. Each MDD within a specific manufacturing domain consists of attributes, operation types and a mapping between them. The MDD exchanged among manufacturing functions or among manufacturing activities is descriptively named such that each MDD is unique in the target manufacturing domain. A Capability Template shown in the left part of Fig. 3 contains a Common Part and a Specific Part. The Specific Part contains the elements: Reference MDM Name, list of MDD objects, and capability definition (e.g. time ordered access to MDD objects).

3   Interoperability Framework for Manufacturing Software

The Interoperability framework in ISO 16100 is summarized in Fig. 4 [7]. On the left the flow shows the procedure that a MSU vendor performs to prepare and register a Capability Profile of a MSU. System configurators or developers develop the manufacturing application by searching existing adequate MSUs and combining them. The flow on the right shows the procedure that system configurators or developers perform to develop a new manufacturing application.

The flow shown on the left of Fig. 4 shows the whole process for Capability Profile registration. When a Capability Profile is first registered, the adequate Capability Template selection is necessary. First, a suitable manufacturing domain for the registering MSU is chosen. Second, the applicable activity tree in the domain is adopted and the activity is identified in the tree. Third, the corresponding Capability Class is adopted. When a new activity tree is created, new Capability Classes are generated. Fourth, an adequate Capability Template corresponding to the Capability Class is set up. When a new Capability Class is generated, a new Capability Template is also created and registered to the library. If one MSU could use different activities, several Capability Templates are selected. By filling the adequate Capability Template, the Capability Profile for the MSU is generated. The generated Capability Profile is registered in the Capability Profile library.

The flow shown on the right of Fig. 4 shows the development processes for a manufacturing application. The development process is roughly divided into the requirement analysis process and the MSU selection process. The requirements analysis process is to analyze the requirements and to describe the requirements as required by the Capability Profiles. First, a suitable manufacturing domain is selected. Second, requirements are decomposed into several primitive requirements by reference to the activity tree in the domain and activities are then appointed from the primitive requirements. Third, the Capability Class is adopted. Forth, the adequate Capability Template corresponding to the Capability Class is set up. The Capability Template is filled with specific requirements in order to generate a required Capability Profile. Next is the MSU selection and verification process. A MSU selection process starts with a required Capability Profile for a given activity.

A desired set of MSUs has a corresponding set of Capability Profiles that match the capabilities required for a given activity. For each required Capability Profile, a search for matching Capability Profiles that represent available MSUs is performed. When a match exists, the MSU is added to a list of candidates. When a match does not exist, a new MSU is developed to meet the required Capability Profile, the required Capability Profile is decomposed into a combination of several Capability Profiles, or requirements are reconsidered against existing profiles. The selected MSUs are verified against the manufacturing application requirements according to interoperability criteria. Manufacturing system configurators or developers develop the manufacturing application by combining MSUs in the candidate list.

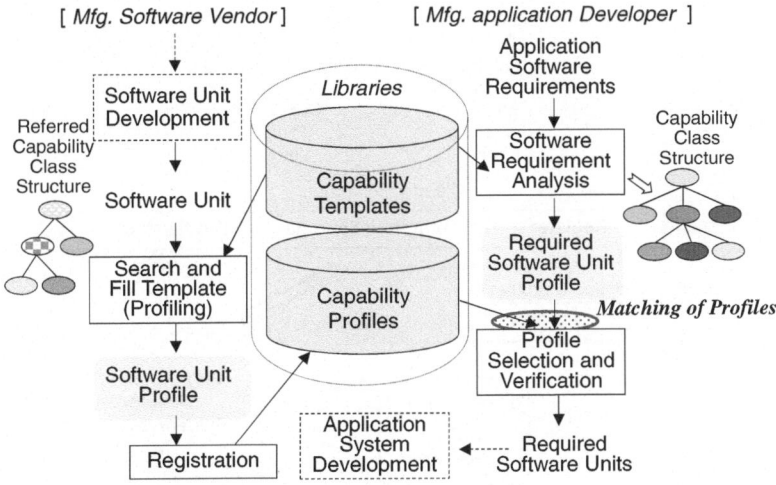

Fig. 4. Basic services using capability profiles

4   Extended Services Provided by Using Capability Profiling

Using the capability profiling methodology provided by ISO 16100, new extended interoperability services are proposed.

4.1   Development of the Manufacturing Application by Integration of Manufacturing Software Units

ISO 16100 provides a standardized method to describe capabilities of manufacturing software in terms of the MSU Capability Profile. To use this, the manufacturing software capability catalogue can be organized. The manufacturing software capability catalogue is constructed by the Capability Template libraries and the Capability Profile libraries. The Capability Templates are registered with the identifier of the MDM. Probably, each vendor or vender group has their own MDM. The Capability Templates are categorized by MDM. Each library corresponds to a

MDM. Each Capability Profile has an identifier of the Capability Template used. As a result, Capability Profiles are also categorized by MDM. MSUs themselves are in the corresponding vender's database. When the manufacturing software capability catalogue is open, the system configurator or developer use the catalogue to find and select an adequate MSUs, and develop the manufacturing application by integrating MSUs which are downloaded from each vendor's database.

Fig. 5 shows the case where the manufacturing software capability catalogue is in the cloud environment. The function for registration of the Capability Template and Capability Profile, the function for selection of an adequate Capability Template to describe requirements, and the function for matching the required Capability Profile with MSU's Capability Profiles are also provided as cloud services.

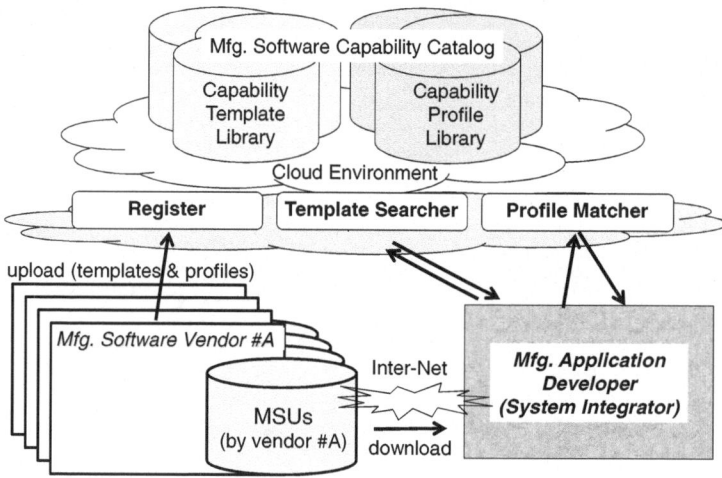

Fig. 5. Development of the manufacturing application using the cloud environment

4.2   Extended Information Exchange

ISO 16100 also provides the way to exchange MSU's capability as information through a Capability Profile. This enhances interoperability services. On the dynamic configuration of manufacturing application, adequate MSU can be invoked when its capability is required through matching of Capability Profiles. The system configurator has required Capability Profiles, and organizes the manufacturing application by plug-and-play of MSUs which have the Capability Profile matched with the required profile. The MSU itself could become the configurator. In this case, the application is autonomously organized by direct communication among MSUs and plug-and-play of MSUs. The Capability Profile Library for searching adequate MSUs is connected through the Capability Profile Interface (CPI). An MSU can have its own Capability Profile inside itself. In this case, the MSU itself has an interoperability function. Fig. 6 shows a configuration of the manufacturing application using plug-and-play of MSUs

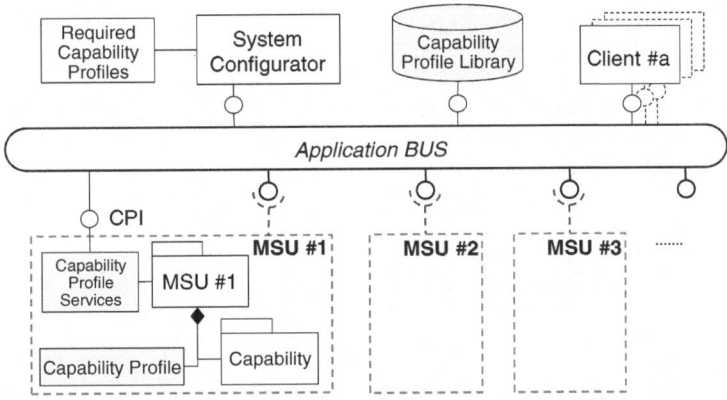

Fig. 6. Configuration of the manufacturing application by plug-and-play of MSUs

5   Extension of Methodology for Manufacturing Software Capability Profiling

Extensions of the capability profiling methodology provided by ISO 16100 are required for implementation of proposed interoperability services. Some of required extensions are introduced.

5.1   Integration of Local Manufacturing Domains

For the matching procedure of two Capability Profiles, the MDDs has an important role. When considering the enhancement of interoperability services as mentioned in Chapter 4, integration of local MDD sets are required. One solution is proposed below.

In every MDM, one unique set of MDDs is available. In a Capability Template in terms of the Capability Class, the capabilities of required and existing MSUs are described using MDDs. An adequate Capability Template is selected corresponding to the activity which an MSU enables or supports. If there are several MSUs which enable the same activity, each profile is generated using the same Capability Template. A company and/or a company group usually has their own MDM and set of MDDs. If a manufacturing software vendor wants to widely distribute his developed MSU, the vendor makes several profiles for one MSU corresponding to each MDM. When naturally considering a manufacturing domain, the manufacturing domain corresponds to a manufacturing phase such as machining, assembly and diagnosis. Fig. 7 shows the above mentioned consideration.

When extending the manufacturing domain to this manufacturing phase, the MSU's interoperability is also extended. To extend the manufacturing domain concept, sets of MDDs for each company group should be integrated to make one MDM corresponding to a manufacturing phase. As one of solution, a MDD dictionary is introduced.

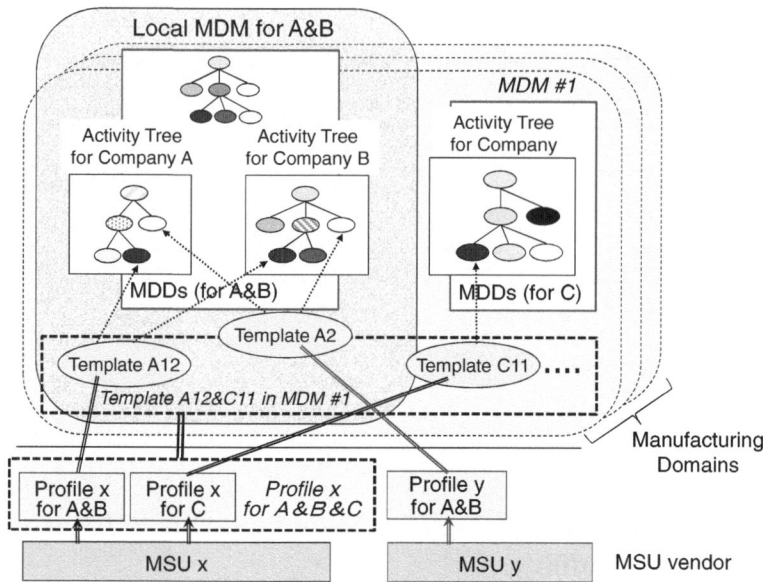

Fig. 7. Extension of MDM concept and integration of MDDs

5.2   MDD Dictionary as an Domain Integration Tool

Items in the MDD Dictionary can be MDD classes, attributes, values of attributes, units of measure, qualifiers of measure, currency, data types, representations such as definitions, terms, abbreviations, images and languages, and other things that need to be referenced to within the Capability Profiles and Capability Templates. Here the ISO 22745 methodology [9] is applicable to construct the MDD Dictionary as shown in Fig. 8. In order to be compatible with ISO 22745, the Identification Schema in eOTD shown at the bottom left of Fig. 8, is used. ISO 22745 specifies a system of descriptive technology for representing, handling and exchanging master data. The registration authority identifier (RAI), data identifier (DI) and version identifier (VI) constitute the global unique identifier. Items in the MDD Dictionary can be created in two ways. The first one is that items are standardized by authorities as the data sources. The second one is that items are informatively copied from other local dictionaries which would be the sources of these items. Here, other local dictionaries include sets of MDDs in some MDMs and some other standards. Each item in the MDD Dictionary has one or more definitions, one or more terms or abbreviations and corresponding sources. For each such source, the link would be added to the item record in the MDD Dictionary. The MDD Dictionary serves as a 'Bridge' among different local dictionaries [8].

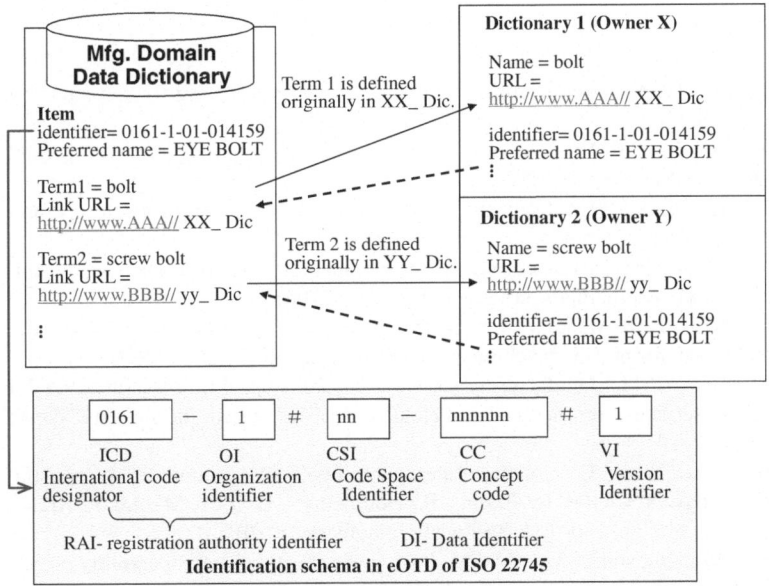

Fig. 8. The Domain Data Dictionary as a "Bridge" among different local manufacturing domains [8]

6   Conclusions

New manufacturing application development methods using the manufacturing software capability catalogue as a cloud service and a new manufacturing system configuration method using plug-and-play of manufacturing software are newly proposed. To enhance such interoperability services, extensions and intensions of ISO 16100 are required. For example, there are work items such as standardization of the construction method for MDM and MDDs, standardization of interface service including CPI, standardization for a manufacturing software capability catalogue such as contents and format, and standardization of service access to a Capability Profile and Capability Template. Now, the new project: ISO 16300 series is planed for these extensions. Furthermore, the implementation of ISO 16100 methodology would be expected to provide useful experience and help to define future directions.

Acknowledgments. The author thanks ISO/TC 184/SC 5/ WG 4 members and MESX joint WG in MSTC members for fruitful discussions and their useful effort to complete international standards. The author is also grateful to Dr. U. Graefe, the previous convenor of ISO/TC 184/SC 5/ WG 4 for his helpful assistance with the writing of this paper in English.

References

1. ISO 16100-1:2009 Manufacturing software capability profiling for interoperability Part 1: Framework (2009)
2. ISO 16100-2:2003 Manufacturing software capability profiling for interoperability Part 2: Profiling methodology (2003)
3. ISO 16100-3:2005 Manufacturing software capability profiling for interoperability Part 3: Interface services, protocols and capability templates (2005)
4. ISO 16100-4:2006 Manufacturing software capability profiling for interoperability Part 4: Conformance test methods, criteria and reports (2006)
5. ISO 16100-5:2009 Manufacturing software capability profiling for interoperability Part 5: Methodology for profile matching using multiple capability class (2009)
6. ISO 16100-6:2011 Manufacturing software capability profiling for interoperability Part 6: Interface services, protocols for matching profiles based on multiple capability class structure (2010)
7. Matsuda, M., Wang, Q.: Software Interoperability Tools: Standardized Capability-Profiling Methodology ISO16100. In: Bernus, P., Doumeingts, G., Fox, M. (eds.) EAI2N 2010. IFIP AICT, vol. 326, pp. 140–151. Springer, Heidelberg (2010)
8. Wang, Q., Matsuda, M.: Manufacturing application interoperability using software capability catalogue. In: Enterprise Interoperability V: Shaping Enterprise Interoperability in the Future Internet, IFIP WG5.8, pp. 141–152. Springer (2012)
9. Radack, G.: ISO 22745: The Standard for Master Data November 28 (2009), http://findarticles.com/p/articles/mi_qa3766/is_200710/ai_n27997247/

A Confidentiality-Guarantee Mechanism for SaaS

Guozhen Ren, Qingzhong Li, Yuliang Shi, and Lizhen Cui

School of Computer Science and Technology
Shandong University
Jinan, China
{rgz,lqz,liangyus,clz}@sdu.edu.cn

Abstract. In SaaS Applications, the data of tenants are stored in the untrusted service provider side, this case increases the risk of data leakage, and becomes the brief reason to prevent people and enterprise from taking SaaS mode for their applications. Correspondingly, confidentiality-guarantee has become the key factor of its large scale promotion. In this paper we propose a general secure mechanism that allows the sensitive data of tenants to be stored in encrypted mode, which guarantees data confidentiality on the assumption that application server is trusted, and then put forward the analysis of its security and performance.

Keywords: SaaS, data confidentiality, trusted application server.

1 Introduction

In software as a service (SaaS) applications, high efficiency of deployment, upgrading, and maintenance are the motivation of its development. But in this case, the data of tenants are stored in the service provider side, which increases the risk of data leakage. No tenants wish to lose data confidentiality in any case, therefore, data confidentiality-guarantee is very important for tenant deciding to adopt SaaS.

In the related research works, the secure problems of SaaS are usually divided into secure access control, data integrity protection, data privacy protection and data confidentiality protection[4]. Some research results focused on secure access control and data integrity had been put forward, and most of them were based on corresponding mechanisms in DAS and Web fields. But in SaaS applications, business logic calculation is executed in the service provider side and multiple tenants share data storage, which is essentially different from traditional applications, such that the traditional data confidentiality control mechanism cannot be directly applied to SaaS confidentiality-guarantee mechanism.

In this paper, we put forward a confidentiality-guarantee mechanism for typical SaaS framework under the trusted application computing environment. In this mechanism, we refer to the remote attestation method for trusted computing environment [2], and give the key agreements protocols which can transfer the data encryption key to the application server in security, and so the server can transparently encrypt/decrypt the data of tenants through the confidential engine in processing. And this can make the data of tenants to be stored in encrypted mode in database. This mechanism is secure supposing application system is trusted.

The original version of this chapter was revised: The copyright line was incorrect. This has been corrected. The Erratum to this chapter is available at DOI: 10.1007/978-3-642-33068-1_20

M. van Sinderen et al. (Eds.): IWEI 2012, LNBIP 122, pp. 71–80, 2012.
© IFIP International Federation for Information Processing 2012

In fact, the data leakage events occurred in the data storage is the most of the actual data leakage occurrence. In our mechanism, sensitive data defined by tenants stored in the physical storage are all encrypted, thus to prevent this kind of leakage events completely. So our research work has practical significance. Specifically, this paper makes the following contributions:

1) We propose a confidentiality-guarantee framework supposing the application server is trusted, and point out its practical significance.
2) Design of a confidential-guarantee mechanism under the typical SaaS framework, and this mechanism secures data transparently to application developer.

The rest of this paper is organized as follows. Section 2 introduces the related works. Section 3 analyzes the confidential problem in general SaaS model, and gives the hypothesis and the practical application of the scene of our research. Section 4 address a security framework in SaaS. Section 5 gives the corresponding security protocols and data encryption mechanism of the framework. Section 6 analyzes the security and performance of the mechanism. Experimental results are reported in Section 7. The paper concludes in Section 8 with the summary and future works.

2   Related Work

At present, the research works for data confidentiality-guarantee mechanism for SaaS is in its infancy. In the related area, research works focused on secure access control and integrity of data in SaaS, secure Data As Services (DAS), new encryption algorithms for database and trusted computing etc.

The research works of confidentiality in DAS can be divided into two cases which depend on the data be stored in document or database. For the former, there are key word query mechanism in literature based on document encryption storage [8,9,12,13]. In these mechanisms, documents are switched to cipher before stored to untrusted service center, mechanisms offer key word search when customers use these documents, the inquired content will be decrypted and used after being transferred to client side, which realizes confidentiality protection of document content. And, the literature [1] puts forward a multiple key words query mechanism over documents encrypted, in condition of the main document encryption, it storages multiple keywords based on message hidden methods, and gives a multiple key word query mechanism which supports and/or query operation of query builder. Literature [1] also give a complete solution about database mode on base of literature[6,7,9,10]. Based on order preserving encryption algorithm and fully homomorphic encryption, the mechanism supports basic compare operator and arithmetic operator and SPJ (select-project-join) operations for SQL query, and gives the query optimization mechanism.

With the development of SaaS application, Secure problems quickly become a hot spot in the study of the industry, literature [4,14] classify secure problems systematically. Now there are dual authentication and RBAC mapping for tenants to answer for problems in secure access control and authorized management[19]. With redundant tuples and digital signature technology, problems are partly solved in data integrity protection. But for data privacy and data confidentiality, Only SSL, AS2, S-FTP are put forward, these mechanisms can only solve data leakage problems in transmission, but can't solve leakage problems in the database level and application service level when sensitive data of tenants are stored in the untrusted service provider side. Literature [14] puts forward that data confidentiality as a challenge in SaaS.

Research works about trusted platform are abundant, and the remote attestation mechanism under the TCG framework gets closed attention, integrity measure framework IMA [15] and remote attestation mechanism based on the attribute certificate proposed by IBM research institute are typical in all of the works, in this direction, article [2] analyzes the problems of dynamic characteristic, concurrency and consistency for multiple remote attestation instance(Multi-RAI) in trusted computing environment, and propose a complete dynamic update attestation mechanism for Multi-RAI in trusted computing environment. This also provides a good reference for solving secure problems in SaaS.

In addition, in order to improve efficiency of data query over the encrypted messages, there are some research works about new practical encryption algorithm such as order preserving encryption. Literature [17,18] give practical methods and make high efficient query over the integral and string data types, which provides very good help for SaaS confidentiality study.

3 Confidential Problem Analysis for SaaS

Participators here can be Tenant, SP and Attacker in general.

1) Tenant: Data owner in SaaS, hopes its sensitive information not to be snooped during information storage, transmission, and computational process.
2) SP: Service provider in SaaS, provide data storage and application service.
3) Attacker: Any offensive person or group except data owner, including other Tenant.

Considering data processing procedure in SaaS, the attacks can be classified in 3 cases.

1) Data storage attack: Data stored in SP maybe stolen by attackers who attack the system to get privileges of authority, or obtained by the data administrator who take advantage of the privileges of authority.
2) Data processing attack: Business logic is caculated in the SP application servers. It could be obtained by attackers, or snooped by data administrator.
3) Data transmission attack: In SaaS, data will be transmitted through the Internet, and kinds of attackers may get data though the public network.

Problems in data transmission above are consistent with those in data confidentiality of other applied models of Web. Many fully developed schemes such as SSL can be employed directly to solve these problems. And for data processing secure problems we can adopt the trusted calculating environment, and this is a assumed condition in this paper.

Our study mainly starts from solving problems of data confidentiality in data storage under the scene of typical SaaS application.

The intrinsic difference of data confidentiality between SaaS and DAS applications is that business logic operations in DAS applications are processed in the Tenant side, while these operations are calculated in SP side. Though the homomorphic encryption had been prompted, but it's still far away from practical application regarding of its efficiency and realization.

Therefore, another new idea is considered based on practical application, namely operating system and application service system selected as the reliable system, database management system selected as the general business system.

Assumed conditions in the passage:

1) Application server cannot be traced, namely based on trusted application system.
2) Database is not reliable, namely the condition that database is easy to suffer attacks and data administrator is not reliable and so on.

These assumed conditions in practical mean that there's no secret divulging in the mechanism even though the whole database was disclosed. It is helpful when SP is averse from divulging data, however, some data administrator may get personal profit by divulging the data, and attackers break though safeguard in the database to get data. So, these assumed conditions do have practical significance.

4   Main Security Framework

As shown in Fig. 1, our security framework based on a general SaaS application. The Trusted Third Party(TTP) undertakes the key management tasks of our confidential mechanism, in the practical application, it may be Certificate Authority or other Key Management Center based on PKI. Tenant and SP take the same roles defined in section 3.

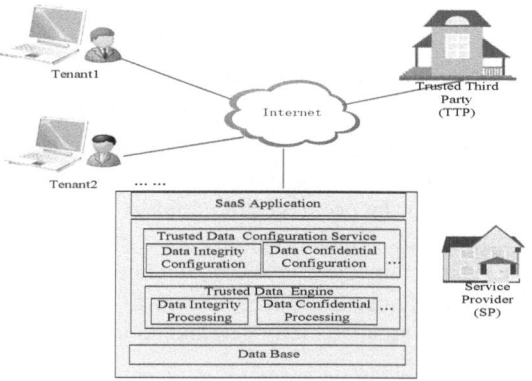

Fig. 1. Security Framework for SaaS

The mechanism includes key management protocols, secure data encryption key transmission and data encryption/decryption when Tenant taking the operation. Here are the main processes of our mechanism.

1) SP applies for its identity key from TTP.
   Under the mechanism, SP must get the identity key used in later confidential process before it offers the services to tenants. The detail process is similar to the traditional certificate application, so we will not describe it in detail in this paper.
2) Tenant applies for its identity key and data encryption key from TTP.
   Tenant should get its identity key and data encryption key before registering in the SP if it wants to protect its data stored at SP.
3) Tenant configures its confidential policy.
   Through the configuration services provided by the mechanism Tenant can set up its confidential policy which determines the tables or attributes needs to be encrypted.
4) Key Agreements Protocol.
   The system will invoke the Key Agreements Protocol when the Tenant login the application server, and the procedure will transfer the data encryption key securely to application server. In practical the data encryption key could be cached, and so get relative high performance.
5) Data Encryption/Decryption.

In the processing procedure, data need protected according to the policy will be encrypted transparently by confidential engine before being stored to physical storage, and decrypted from cipher after reading out from database.

5   Key Agreements and Algorithms

The key management in the initial phase is similar to traditional method under PKI, we will not describe it in detail here, and supposing that Tenant and SP all have obtained their own needed identity keys, and the data encryption key of Tenant here has been generated and stored at TTP. Here are the notations for this paper, in Table 1.

Table 1. Notations used in this paper

Notation	Comments
R^S	Denotes that relation R owned attributes need to be encrypted.
RA^e	Denotes that attribute A in R needs to be encrypted.
T^S	Denotes that tuple T owned encrypted attribute value.
TA^e	Denotes that the attribute value A in T is encrypted.
Ek()	Encrypt using key k, in symmetric encryption mechanism.
Dk()	Decrypt using key k, in symmetric encryption mechanism.
EPpk()	Encrypt using key pk, in asymmetric encryption mechanism.
DPsk()	Decrypt using key sk, in asymmetric encryption mechanism.
Ssk()	Sign using key sk, in asymmetric encryption mechanism.
Vpk()	Verify using key pk ,in asymmetric encryption mechanism.

5.1   Data Confidential Configuration Service

ConfidentialConfigure: Data Confidential Configuration Service supported by the mechanism, which tenants can dispose their confidential policy through it, and the confidential engine will protect data transparently base on the policy. The service can be expressed as:

Input: $R(A_1,...,A_n)$;
Output: $R^S(A_1,...A_i^e,...)$, at least one attribute nominated to be Encrypted. and the service stores policy: $((R^S_{name1}, (A_1^e,...,A_{m1}^e)), ...)$.

5.2   Key Agreements Protocol

Without loss of practical nature, we suppose the initial keys used in the protocol had been dispatched to the Tenant, SP and TTP, as described below.

SP: Asymmetric key pair (sksp,pksp), Symmetric key (k_{sp}) used for encrypting the tenant data encryption key temporary.

Tenant: Asymmetric key pair (skti,pkti) for Tenant i.

TTP: Asymmetric key pair (skttp,pkttp), kti for Tenant i, which be used for encrypting data.

Base on the upper notations we give the detail description of the Key Agreements Protocol in Sequence diagram below. See Fig. 2.

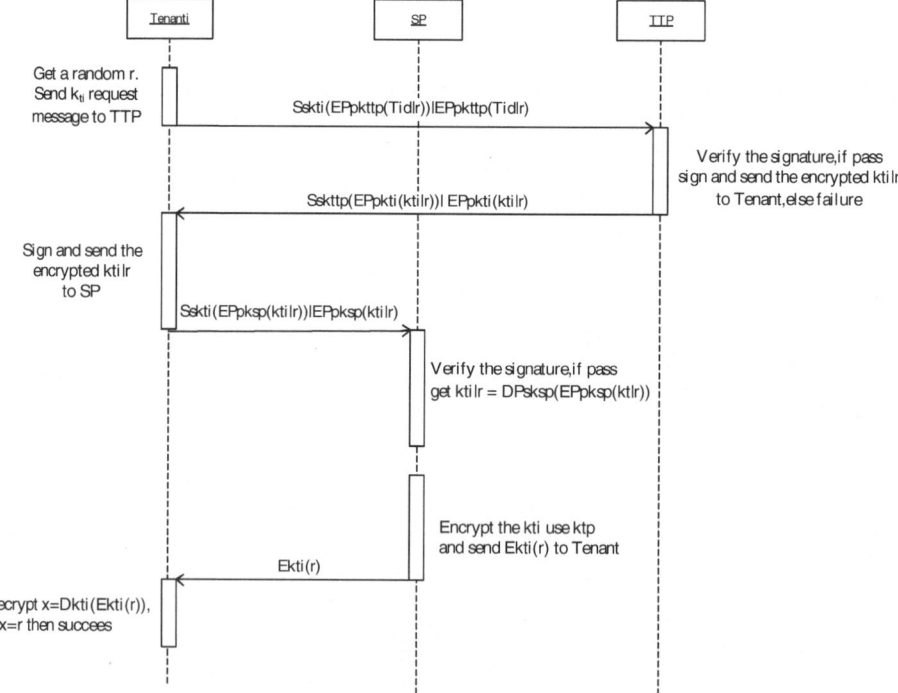

Fig. 2. Key Agreements Protocol for kti Transmission

As shown in Fig. 2, the k_{ti} is encrypted by destination public key in the protocol, and this can ensure its safety. The random number r is used to ensure the process' integrity, also to assure the k_{ti} is available after running the protocol. We use $Ek_{tp}(k_{ti})$ to substitute $EP_{pksp}(k_{ti})$ for higher performance. In the practical applications, the k_{ti} could be cached in the process procedure. This way can keep a higher efficiency.

5.3   Data Encryption/Decryption

In this mechanism, as shown in Fig. 1, the encrypt/decrypt runned by the confidential engine automatically, the detail process is transparent to the application, which imply that application developer can get higher developing efficiency under this Framework.

1) Data Encryption
Data is encrypted before the system storing it to database, and this also occurring before sending SQL for query to database management. The confidential engine invokes the encryption service according to the confidential configuration to encrypt the attribute and substitute corresponding plaintext by the cipher in SQL text. The method is described as follows.

```
sConfig= getConfiditialConfig(Relation,i,SQLText, confidentialConfigure);
if sConfig == NULL then return else
         {
    for all Pj which R, {Aj^e} in sConfig do
             {
               Cj=Ekti (Pj);
               Substitute(SQLText,Pj,Cj);
             }
         }
```

2) Data Decryption
Data is decrypted after the SQL result being returned from the database, and before application computing on data. The confidential engine invokes the decryption service according to the confidential configuration to decrypt the attribute and substitute corresponding cipher in SQL result set by the plaintext. The method is described as follows.

```
sConfig=getConfiditialConfig(Relation,i,SQLResult,
                           confidentialConfig);
if sConfig == NULL then return else
{
   for all Ck which R,{A^e} in sConfig do
       {
         Pk = Dkti (Ck);
         Substitute(SQLResult,Ck,Pk);
       }
}
```

6   Security Analysis

Considered the Key Agreements Protocol shown in Section 5, the sensitive data are only exposed in the memory of the application server, this case implies that the mechanism can ensure the data safety under the assumption that application services run in the trusted computing environment.

For the data encryption key k_{ti}, Fig 2 shows that the key is encrypted by the public key in asymmetric encryption mechanism in the whole transmission procedure, and only the message receiver can disclose it. Attacker can't get the key only if he can break the asymmetric encryption mechanism.

The sensitive data are encrypted in the physical storage, and the key used for encryption is not stored in physical storage of SP, so the data will be kept safety even if the Attacker can steal the cipher from database.

Above all, the mechanism this paper offered can ensure the sensitive data safety under the hypothesis we defined.

7   Performance Experiments

We designed two experiments to compare the cost between query over cipher and query over plain text, one for accurate query, and another for range query. The symmetric encryption mechanism in experiment is TEA.

The data scale in experiments we designed is in Table 2.

Table 2. Data Scale for Experiments

No.	Type	Tenants	Tuples	Result scale
1	Accurate query	$10, 10^2, 10^3$	10^3	10
2	Range query	10^2	$10^2, 10^3, 10^4$	10

7.1   Experiments Configuration

The developing language is Java, the database is Oracle9i, the operating system is Windows Server2003. The memory of computer is 4G, CPU is Intel P8800(2.66GHz).

7.2   Experiments

The experiment result shows that, the costs of the accurate query increase not so much, we can say that it is linear increment according to data magnitude. But for the range query, it shows a sharp increase in costs, the main reason is that the cipher has been disordered entirely in traditional encryption we adapt, so we have to decrypt all the rows of table.

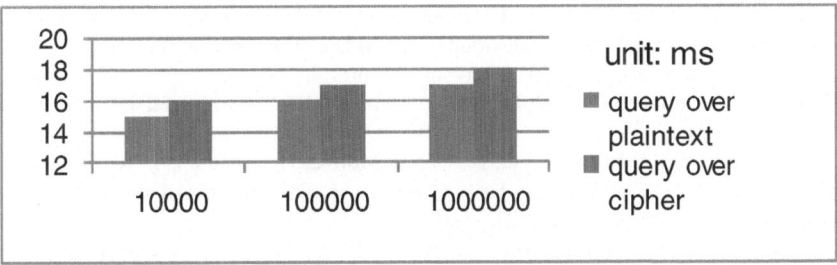

Fig. 3. Costs for Accurate Query

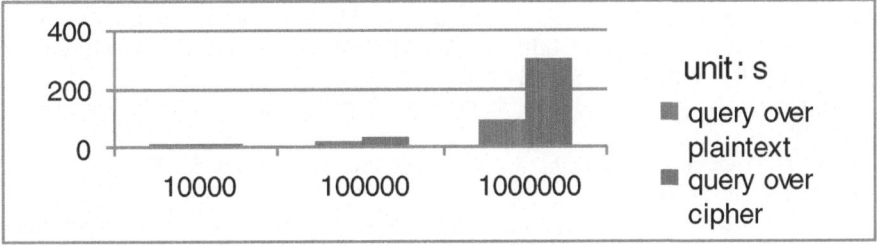

Fig. 4. Costs for Range Query

8   Conclusions and Future Works

In this paper, we give a general confidentiality-guarantee mechanism in practical SaaS applications, the main frame of the mechanism can also be easy used for data integrity protection and data privacy protection. We analyzed the security of our mechanism. The experiments result shows that it keeps high performance when used for the accurate query, but the effectiveness of the mechanism is invalidate when used in range query. Considered the strong security of the symmetric encryption mechanism the mechanism adopted, it fits for the critical and small-scale data, such as metadata and configuration data etc.

We will intend to develop the more practical encryption method in range query, and we will also pay close attention to data integrity and data privacy protection mechanism in our future works.

Acknowledgement. The work is supported by the National Natural Science Foundation of China under Grant No. 61003253; the Natural Science Foundation of Shandong Province of China under Grant No.2009ZRB019YT , ZR2010FM031, ZR2010FQ010 and ZR2010FQ026; Key Technology R&D Program of Shandong Province under Grant No. 2010GGX10105.)

References

1. Hacigumus, H., Hore, B., Iyer, B., Mehrotra, S.: Search on Encrypted Data. IBM Search Report 2007, 385–425 (2007)
2. Feng, D.G., Qin, Y.: Research on Attestation Method for Trust Computing Environment. Chinese Journal of Computers 31(9) (September 2008)

3. KaraBulut, Y., Nassi, I.: Secure Enterprise Services Consumption for SaaS Technology Plataforms. In: IEEE International Conference on Data Engineering (2009)
4. Zwyhun, N.: SaaS Data Security, Microsoft Report
5. Bouganim, L., Pucheral, P.: Chip-Secured Data Access: Confidential Data on Untrusted Servers. In: Proc., of VLDB (2002)
6. Aggarwal, G., Bawa, M., Ganesan, P., Garcia-Molina, H., Kenthapadi, K., Srivastava, U., Thomas, D., Xu, Y.: Two Can Keep a Secret: A Distributed Architecture for Secure Database Service. In: Proc. of CIDR (2005)
7. Goh, E.-J.: Secure Indexes. Technical report 2003/216, in IACR ePrint Cryptography Archive (2003)
8. Song, D., Wagner, D., Perrig, A.: Practical Techniques for Search on Encrypted Data. In: Proc. of IEEE SRSP (2000)
9. Hacigümüg, H., Iyer, B., Mehrotra, S.: Encrypted Database Integrity in Database Service Provider Model. In: Proc. of IFIP 17th World Computer Congress on Certification and Security in E-Services, CSES 2002 (2002)
10. Hacigumug, H., Iyer, B., Mehrotra, S.: Providing Database as a Service. In: Proc. Of ICDE (2002)
11. Hore, B., Mehrotra, S., Tsudik, G.: A Privacy-Preserving Index for Range Queries. In: Proc. of VLDB (2004)
12. Chang, Y.-C., Mitzenmacher, M.: Privacy Preserving Keyword Searches on Remote Encrypted Data. In: Ioannidis, J., Keromytis, A.D., Yung, M. (eds.) ACNS 2005. LNCS, vol. 3531, pp. 442–455. Springer, Heidelberg (2005)
13. Golle, P., Staddon, J., Waters, B.: Secure Conjunctive Keyword Search over Encrypted Data. In: Jakobsson, M., Yung, M., Zhou, J. (eds.) ACNS 2004. LNCS, vol. 3089, pp. 31–45. Springer, Heidelberg (2004)
14. Guo, C.J., Sun, W., Huang, Y., Wang, Z.H., Gao, B.: A Framework for Native Multi-Tenancy Application Develoment and Management. In: The 9th IEEE International Conference on E-Commerce
15. Reiner, S., Zhang, X.-L., Trent, J., Van Doorn, L.: Design and implementation of a TCG-based intergrety mesurement architecture. In: Proceeding of the 13th Usenix Security Symposium, San Diego, California, pp. 223–238 (2004)
16. Reiner, S., Van Doorn, L., Ward, J.P.: The role of TPM in enterprise security. IBM Research Report RC23368 (October 2004)
17. Agrawal, R., Kiernan, J., Srikant, R., Xu, Y.: Order Preserving Encryption for Numeric Data. In: SIGMOD 2004, Paris, France, June 13-18 (2004)
18. Wang, Z., Wang, W., Shi, B.: Efficient method of querying encrypt data. Computer Engineering and Applications 44(12), 29–33 (2008)
19. Lilin, M., Hong, L.: A Permission Model of SaaS System Based on RBAC. Computer Applications and Software 27(4), 42–44 (2010)

A QoS-Aware Hyper-graph
Based Method of Semantic Service Composition

Cui Lizhen and Xu Meng

School of Computer Science and Technology, Shandong University, Jinan, China
Shandong Provincial Key Laboratory of Software Engineering
clz@sdu.edu.cn

Abstract. Semantic service composition is an important issue in web service based systems. It is about how to build a new, reusable and value-added service by combining existing semantic web services. In this paper we propose a new hyper-graph based method supporting semantic service composition, which model the service composition problem as a hyper-graph. Then the hyper-graph based service composition algorithm has been implemented and evaluated. The evaluation results have shown that the method can effectively reduce the composition time and has good robustness, especially in the case of large number of web services and concepts.

Keywords: QoS-aware, Hyper-graph, Service Composition.

1 Introduction

Service-oriented computing (SOC) has been widely accepted as the next generation programming paradigm. The web services are loosely coupled reusable and self-describing software components that encapsulate discrete functionality and are distributed and programmatically accessible over standard internet protocols [1]. It is an alternative and promising approach to development web-based application or system rapidly to combine the existing Web Services. But with the number of Web Service on the internet over the last few years increasing sharply, it is difficult and time consuming to combine web services manually [2]. Therefore, semantic web is introduced into Web Service technologies to support dynamic and automated tasks such as discovery, composition and execution. In recent years, how to composite services automatically have drawn lots of research attentions [3-9].

In this paper we proposed a QoS(Quality of Service)-aware hyper-graph based method for semantic Web Service Composition. We model the service composition problem as two hyper-graphs. And by pruning the vertexes and the link between two hyper-graphs, the composite service is built effectively.

The main contributions of this paper are as follows:

(1) Show how the problem of service composition can be modeled as a hyper-graph transversal problem.
(2) Tackle the problem of automatic service composition and QoS-aware service selection problem together with an algorithm that both efficient and 100% precise.

The original version of this chapter was revised: The copyright line was incorrect. This has been corrected. The Erratum to this chapter is available at DOI: 10.1007/978-3-642-33068-1_20

M. van Sinderen et al. (Eds.): IWEI 2012, LNBIP 122, pp. 81–91, 2012.
© IFIP International Federation for Information Processing 2012

The rest of the paper is organized as follows: Section 2 reviews related work and motivates this work. Section 3 shows how to model the service composition problem as a hyper-graph transversal problem. Section 4 discusses the detail of the approach. Section 5 evaluates the performance of the proposed QoS-aware hyper-graph based method of semantic service composition in this paper, and finally Section 6 concludes.

2   Related Work

Since it is very difficult and time consuming to find composite service manually from huge amount of services, automatic service composition is proposed to enable automatic building composition for a given request. Some approaches, such as [5, 6], tackle Web service composition problem via AI planning. On the other hand, some other researches [4, 10] regards it as a graph search problem and solves it by shortest path, A*, etc. algorithms.

To guarantee local or global QoS requirements of service composition, the QoS-aware service composition has attracted a lot of attention in recent years. Different from automatic service composition, it assumes that a work plan is predefined and has a set of "abstract" tasks and the objective is to select service for each task from its candidate services to meet local or global QoS constraints. Zeng [12] uses two service selection approaches based on Multiple Criteria Decision Making. In [13], the authors model the problem as a multi-choice 0-1 knapsack problem or a multi-constraint optimal path problem, and then compute optimal result according to the objective function. In addition, a genetic algorithm is proposed to address the problem in [3]. Although it is more inefficient than Integer Programming, it can deal with non-linear constraints.

In one words, all the methods above for automatic service composition or QoS-aware service composition only consider one aspect of QoS-aware automatic service composition, which is to search work plans for a given request or to guarantee global QoS requirements. Furthermore, Some researchers have proposed approaches to address the QoS-aware automatic service composition problem, such as [14-16]. Peter [11] proposes a fast approach by some index tables stored in database to fit the competition CEC'09[11]. But it cannot provide 100% precision and its efficiency are not good enough when the scale of services is big.

In [17], Zhu modeled the problem of computing cost constrained collections of Web services as a constrained hyper-graph transversal problem. But it only can compute a set of services to fulfill some functions. Out method can find a composite service which can satisfy a user request.

3   Definition and Problem Model

We now provide the necessary definition about hyper-graphs and the semantic service composition. Then a formal description of the problem will be given.

Definition 1. A hyper-graph H is a pair H = <E, V> where V is a finite set of vertices V = { v_1, v_2,...,v_m } and E is a family of (hyper) edges, E ={ e_1, e_2,..., e_t } where each e_i is a subset of V, $1 \leq i \leq t$. We assume V = { $\cup e_i$ | $e_i \in E$, $1 \leq i \leq t$ }.

Definition 2. The candidate service is a service which can be used in the service composition process. The candidate service set is a finite set of services S={s_i|s_i is a cadidate service}. And s_i=<p(s_i)$_{in}$, p(s_i)$_{out}$, QoS>, where p(s_i)$_{in}$ is the input parameters set of s_i, p(s_i)$_{out}$ is the output parameters set of s_i, QoS is the QoS property of s_i.

In this paper, we only consider the response time as the QoS property of web service. And the computing method can be find in [18].

Definition 3. The composition request is a request of user which can be represent as R= {Pin,Pout} , P_{in} is the set of input parameters and P_{out} is the set of output parameters.

We now describe the reduction of the semantic service composition problem to the problem involving hyper-graphs. We will model the problem to two hyper-graphs. One is called output parameters hyper-graph, which is represented by H_o. And the other is called input parameters hyper-graph, which is represented by H_i. Each Web Service in S is modeled as a vertex both of H_o and H_i. Furthermore, a virtual service (vertex) is added in H_o and H_i respectively. The virtual service which is added in H_o is called input_service I_s={φ,R.P_{in}, 0} whilst the virtual service which is added in H_i is called output_service O_s={R.P_{out}, φ, 0}. Then we will add edges in H_o and H_i. Each edge in H_o(H_i) corresponds to a set of vertices (web services) which have a particular output(input) parameter. The transversals of the two hyper-graphs now correspond to two sets of services that cover all the services requested by the user.

Example 1. Let us consider a example. S={s_1, s_2, s_3, s_4, s_5, s_6}. The input and output parameters of all services are listed in Table 1. The request of user is R={{a,b,e}, {f,g}}.

Table 1. Candidate Services

Service Name	input	output	QoS
s1	a, b	c, d	10
s2	c	g	20
s3	d, e	f	15
s4	c	g	25
s5	c, d	f, g	30
s6	f, g	h	20
s7	h, i	j	15

The request of user is R={{a,b,e},{f,g}}.

According to the R, we add two virtual services I_s={{φ,{a,b,e}} and O_s={{f,g},φ}. Then the H_o and H_i are drawn in Fig. 1.

$$H_o = \begin{matrix} e1: I_s^0 \\ e2: I_s^0 \\ e3: I_s^0 \\ e4: s_1^{10} \\ e5: s_1^{10} \\ e6: s_2^{30} \quad s_4^{35} \quad s_5^{40} \\ e7: s_3^{25} \quad s_5^{40} \\ e8: s_6^{60} \end{matrix}$$

$$H_i = \begin{matrix} e1: s_1^{10} \\ e2: s_1^{10} \\ e3: s_3^{15} \\ e4: s_2^{30} \quad s_4^{35} \quad s_5^{40} \\ e5: s_3^{25} \quad s_5^{40} \\ e6: s_6^{60} \quad O_s^{30} \\ e7: s_6^{55} \quad O_s^{25} \\ e8: s_7^{75} \end{matrix}$$

Fig. 1. Hi and Ho

4   Hyper-graph Based Service Composition Algorithm

In this section, we will describe the hyper-graph based service composition algorithm. We will use the example shown in Fig. 1. Response time of every service is shown using superscripts. Fig. 2 illustrates the basic outline of the algorithm.

First, the two hyper-graphs are generated according to the request and candidate service set. During the process of generating hyper-graphs, the complete time is calculated for every service. Then a pruning strategy is applied to delete the useless service and edge. At last, a solution generation algorithm is used to create the composite service.

Input: User Request R, Candidate Service Set S
Output: Composite Service CS

---

1. $H_o = \varphi$, $H_i = \varphi$
2. HG_Generate(R, S, H_o, H_i)
3. Prune(H_o, H_i)
4. CS=Solution_Generate(H_o, H_i)
5. Return CS

Fig. 2. Hyper-Graph Based Service Composition Algorithm

4.1   Generating the Hyper-graphs

Fig. 3 shows how to generate the hyper-graphs. First, two virtual services, I_s and O_s, is created. The output of I_s is the input of request R.P_{in} and the input of O_s is the output of request R.P_{out}, while the input of I_s and the output of O_s isφ (line 0). After the creation of the virtual services, the I_s is added into H_o and its complete time is computed. And an edge is added into H_o for every output parameter of I_s. Moreover, all parameters of I_s.output is put into a queue Q (line 2-6). If the queue Q is not null, it suggests that there are parameters which are not processed. So we get the parameter and find the services whose input parameters include it. Then the service is added into

H_i and its complete time is calculated. At that time, it is decided whether the edge need to be added into H_i (line 9-17). If all of the input parameters of the service is in H_o, the service is added into H_o. Repeat that until the queue is null. After doing all this, we get two hyper-graph H_i and H_o. Fig. 1 shows the H_i and H_o which is generated by the algorithm.

	HG_Generate
	Input: User Request R, Candidate Service Set S
	Output: Hyper-Graphs H_o, H_i
1.	create virtual service $I_s=\{\varphi, R.P_{in}, 0\}$, $O_s=\{R.P_{out}, \varphi, 0\}$
2.	set I_s.complete_time=0
3.	for each $p \in I_s$.output do
4.	add e_p to H_o
5.	add I_s to $H_o.e_p$
6.	EnQueue(Q,p)
7.	end for
8.	while Q!=NULL
9.	p= DeQueue(Q)
10.	while $\exists$ service s which input includes p
11.	if s.complete_time<s.response_time+min($H_o.e_p$.s.complete_time)
12.	s.complete_time=s.response_time+min($H_o.e_p$.s.complete_time)
13.	end if
14.	if e_p not in H_i
15.	add e_p to H_i
16.	end if
17.	add s to $H_i.e_p$
18.	if all $p \in$s.input exist e_p in H_o
19.	for each $p \in$s.output do
20.	add e_p to H_o
21.	add s to $H_o.e_p$
22.	EnQueue(Q,p)
23.	end for
24.	end if
25.	end while
26.	end while

Fig. 3. Hyper-Graph Generating Algorithm

4.2   Pruning Strategy

After the hyper-graphs is generated, they should be pruned to remove the useless vertexes and edges. Fig. 4 shows the pruning strategy. By this way, the search space and the time of composition time can be reduced. Before the pruning strategy is applied, the redundant vertexes of H_i should be deleted and the edge order of the H_i should be adjusted first. We arrange the edges which contain the service O_s at last (line 1-2). By doing this, the pruning strategy can be applied from the last to first of

Hi. The edges of Hi which contain Os should be reserved and all vertexes except Os in the edge should be deleted. On the other hand, the edges of Hi which do not contain Os will only reserve the vertex which has the minimal complete time and all other vertexes will be deleted. After the edge of Ho is pruned, the edge of Hi which has the same subscript will be pruned. Then we will get two pruned hyper-graphs after Ho and Hi are pruned. Fig. 5 shows the pruned hyper-graphs of Fig. 1.

Prune
Input: Hyper-Graphs H_o, H_i
Output: Hyper-Graphs H_o, H_i after pruned

---

1.   delete all vertexes from H_i which not in H_o
2.   sort the edges $H_i.e$ to make all edges $e \supseteq O_s$ have max subscript
3.   for i=number of edges in H_i to 1 do
4.   if $H_i.e_i = \varphi$
5.   delete $H_i.e_i$
6.   delete $H_o.e_i$
7.   continue
8.   end if
9.   if $H_i.e_i \supseteq O_s$
10. $s_i = O_s$
11.   else
12. $s_i = \text{min\_complete\_time}(H_i.e_i)$
13.   end if
14.   delete all vertexes except s_i which in $H_i.e_i$ from $H_i.e_i$
15. $t = s_i.\text{complete\_time} - s_i.\text{response\_time}$
16. $s_o = s$ whose complete_time=t and $s \in H_o.e_i$
17.   delete all vertexes except s_o which in $H_o.e_i$ from $H_o.e_i$
18.   delete all vertexes except s_o which in $H_o.e_i$ from H_i
19. end for

Fig. 4. Pruning Algorithm

$$
\begin{array}{ll}
e1: I_s^0 & e1: s_1^{10} \\
e2: I_s^0 & e2: s_1^{10} \\
e3: I_s^0 & e3: s_3^{15} \\
H_o = e4: s_1^{10} \quad H_i = e4: s_2^{30} \\
e5: s_1^{10} & e5: s_3^{25} \\
e6: s_2^{30} & e6: O_s^{30} \\
e7: s_3^{25} & e7: O_s^{25}
\end{array}
$$

Fig. 5. Pruned Ho and Hi

4.3   Solution Generation

Solution Generation is used to generate the composite service of the request. After applying the pruning strategy to H_o and H_i, we get two pruned hyper-graph. The every edge of pruned H_o and H_i must have and only have one vertex. Furthermore, the number of edges of H_o and H_i is equal. So we can get the ith edge of H_o and the ith edge of H_i, and then link the vertexes of two services in the edges. This is an edge in composite service. Combining all edges which we get, the composite service is generated. Fig. 6 shows the solution generating algorithm and Fig. 7 gives the composite service of Example 1.

	Solution_Generate Input: Hyper-Graphs H_o, H_i Output: Composite Service CS
1.	Graph CS=φ, temp=φ
2.	for i=1 to number of edges in H_o do
3.	get s_o from $H_o.e_i$
4.	get s_i from $H_i.e_i$
5.	add s_o to temp
6.	add s_i to temp
7.	add edge $<s_o, s_i>$ to temp
8.	CS=combine(CS, temp)
9.	temp=φ
10.	end for
11.	return CS

Fig. 6. Solution Generating Algorithm

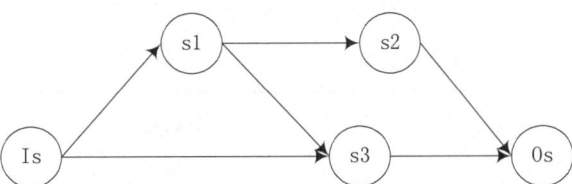

Fig. 7. Composite Service

5   Experiments and Results

To evaluate the performance of our method, we have developed some experiments. And our evaluation consists of two parts. First, we compare SUTB [4] with our method by the precision and composition time. Then we carry out some experiments on the test sets which are generated by the WSC 2009 Testset Generator to evaluate the method furthermore. This generator has three input parameters: concept number, service number and solution depth. In order to prove the scalability and efficiency of our algorithm in different and even extreme conditions, we generate five groups of test sets which have solution depth 10, 15, 20, 25 and 30 respectively. And each group contains three subgroup of different ratio of concept number and service number.

We generate service number of test sets from 4000 to 20000 to make sure that our method has good scalability. Furthermore, we conduct experiments on each test set several times to get the average values. All experiments were performed on a PC platform with a Intel® Core™2 Duo 2.33GHz CPU, Windows XP, and 2 GB RAM and all algorithms were implemented in Java.

5.1   Compare with SUTB

We use the 5 Testsets of WSC'09[19] to evaluate the precision and composition time of SUTB and HGSC(Hyper-Graph based Service Composition). The composition time is shown in Fig. 8. The composition time of SUTB is increased sharply from Testset01 toTestset05. But it is not true for HGSC. The composition time of HGSC has little changed. On the other hand, from Table 2, the precision of HGSC is 100% while SUTB is only 20%. So we can conclude that HGSC has a better scalability and precision.

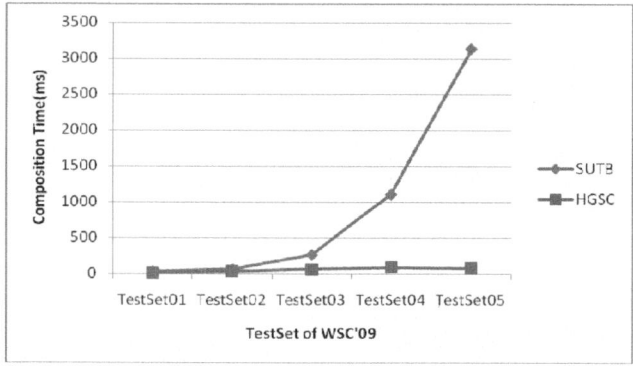

Fig. 8. Composition Time of WSC'09 TestSet

Table 2. Pricision of SUTB and HGSC

TestSets	SUTB	HGSC	Optimal QoS
TestSets01	780	500	500
TestSets02	2100	1690	1690
TestSets03	760	760	760
TestSets04	2070	1470	1470
TestSets05	4500	4070	4070

5.2   Experiments with Other Testsets

We use WSC 2009 Testset Generator to generate more testsets and evaluate HGSC furthermore. Fig. 9 shows the experiment results with different service number (4000-20000), concept number (8000-200000) and solution depth (10-30). From Fig. 9, we can find that the maximum composition time of HGSC is less than 180ms. In addition, with the change of service number, concept number and solution depth, the composition time varied little. So the HGSC has good scalability and can be applied in large number of service and concept.

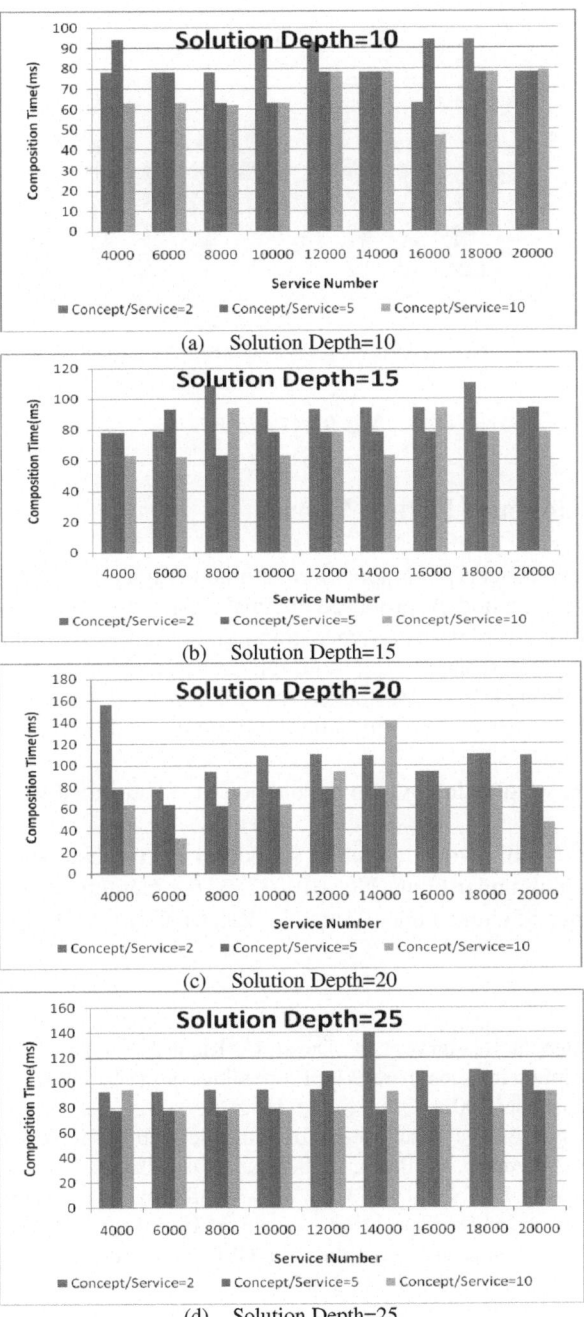

(a)   Solution Depth=10

(b)   Solution Depth=15

(c)   Solution Depth=20

(d)   Solution Depth=25

Fig. 9. Composition Time of our method

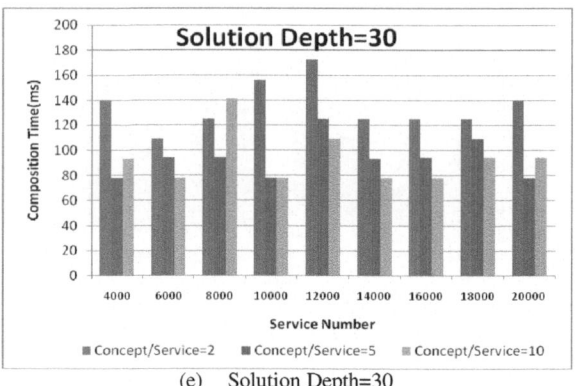

(e)   Solution Depth=30

Fig. 9. (*Continued*)

6   Conclusion and Future Work

To handle QoS-aware service composition automatically and efficiently, a QoS-aware hyper-graph based method is proposed in this paper. We show how to model the service composition problem as a hyper-graph and give the algorithms of generating hyper-graph, pruning strategy and solution generating. At last, to address the scalability, precision and performance of our method, some experiments are conducted and results show that our method has good scalability, efficiency and 100% precision.

In future work, we plan to develop the method in a distributed way.

Acknowledgment. This work has been supported by the National Natural Science Foundation of China under Grant No. 61003253; the Natural Science Foundation of Shandong Province of China under Grant No. ZR2010FM031,ZR2010FQ010.

References

[1] Tsur, S., Abiteboul, S., Agrawal, R., Dayal, U., Klein, J., Weikum, G.: Are Web services the next revolution in e-commerce? In: Proceedings of the VLDB Conference, Rome, pp. 614–617 (September 2001)

[2] Lécué, F., Léger, A.: A Formal Model for Semantic Web Service Composition. In: Cruz, I., Decker, S., Allemang, D., Preist, C., Schwabe, D., Mika, P., Uschold, M., Aroyo, L.M. (eds.) ISWC 2006. LNCS, vol. 4273, pp. 385–398. Springer, Heidelberg (2006)

[3] Canfora, G., Penta, M.D., Esposito, R., Villani, M.L.: An approach for qos-aware service composition based on genetic algorithms. In: GECCO, pp. 1069–1075 (2005)

[4] Hashemian, S.V., Mavaddat, F.: A graph-based framework for composition of stateless web services. In: ECOWS, pp. 75–86 (2006)

[5] McIlraith, S., Son, T.: Adapting golog for composition of semantic web services. In: KR 2002, Toulouse, France, April 22-25, pp. 482–493 (2002)

[6] Sirin, E., Parsia, B., Wu, D., Hendler, J., Nau, D.: Htn planning for web service composition using shop2. Web Semantics: Science, Services and Agents on the World Wide Web 1(4), 377–396 (2004)

[7] Yu, T., Zhang, Y., Lin, K.-J.: Efficient algorithms for web services selection with end-to-end qos constraints. ACM Trans. Web 1(1), 6 (2007)

[8] Zeng, L., Benatallah, B., Ngu, A., Dumas, M., Kalagnanam, J., Chang, H.: Qos-aware middleware for web services composition. IEEE Transactions on Software Engineering 30(5), 311–327 (2004)

[9] Zhou, A., Huang, S., Wang, X.: Bits: A binary tree based web service composition system. Int. J. Web Service Res. 4(1), 40–58 (2007)

[10] Milanovic, N., Malek, M.: Search strategies for automatic web service composition. Int. J. Web Service Res. 3(2), 1–32 (2006)

[11] Bartalos, P., Bielikova, M.: Semantic web service composition framework based on parallel processing. In: CEC 2009, Vienna, Austria (2009)

[12] Zeng, L., Benatallah, B., Ngu, A., Dumas, M., Kalagnanam, J., Chang, H.: Qos-aware middleware for web services composition. IEEE Transactions on Software Engineering 30(5), 311–327 (2004)

[13] Yu, T., Zhang, Y., Lin, K.-J.: Efficient algorithms for web services selection with end-to-end qos constraints. ACM Trans. Web 1(1), 6 (2007)

[14] Liu, J., Gu, N., Zong, Y., Ding, Z., Zhang, S., Zhang, Q.: Web services automatic composition based on qos. In: ICEBE 2005, pp. 607–610 (2005)

[15] Wang, X., Huang, S., Zhou, A.: Qos-aware composite services retrieval. J. Comput. Sci. Technol. 21(4), 547–558 (2006)

[16] Naseri, M., Towhidi, A.: Qos-aware automatic composition of web services using ai planners. In: ICIW 2007, p. 29 (2007)

[17] Zhu, Z., Bailey, J.: Fast Discovery of Interesting Collections of Web Services. In: IEEE/WIC/ACM International Conference on Web Intelligence (WI 2006), pp. 152–160 (2006)

[18] Ardagna, D., Pernici, B.: Adaptive Service Composition in Flexible Processes. IEEE Transactions on Software Engineering 33(6), 369–384 (2007)

[19] Kona, S., Bansal, A., Brian Blake, M., Bleul, S., Weise, T.: WSC-2009: A Quality of Service-Oriented Web Services Challenge. In: IEEE Conference on Commerce and Enterprise Computing, CEC, pp. 487–490 (2009)

Towards Information Customization and Interoperability in Food Chains

Kai Mertins, Frank-Walter Jaekel, and Quan Deng

Fraunhofer Institute Production Systems and Design Technology,
Pascalstr. 8-9, D-10587 Berlin, Germany
{Kai.Mertins,Frank-walter.Jaekel,Quan.Deng}@ipk.fraunhofer.de

Abstract. Food supply chain networks are characterized by clouds of various partners providing required products or services to meet customer demands. The coordination of the SMEs (small and medium-sized enterprise) is a major challenge that food chain networks are facing. Delivering the right information to partners and providing semantic interoperability play key roles in effective coordination. This paper proposes an efficient framework to help these SMEs to easily negotiate and shape the profiles of the traceability information products. It tries to involve various tools to model the contexts of SMEs, and then adopt the concepts of mass customization to suggest optimal profiles for the desired information. In supply chain level, agents and governance boarders are supposed to negotiate and determine the profiles of needed information products. The customized information profiles are then employed to map and integrate various information sources to produce the required information products.

Keywords: food supply chain network, cloud enterprise, traceability, information product, semantic interoperability, ontology, mass customization, Constraint satisfaction, quality management.

1 Introduction

Food supply chain networks are characterized by clouds of various partners providing required products or services to meet customer demands. Most of the partners in food chain networks are SMEs [1]. With limited resources and knowledge, these SMEs usually have problems to adapt dynamic changes in environment. With the equipment of cloud computing, as shown in Fig. 1, SMEs have chances to collaborate with a large number of other partners and services. The various companies distributed among different countries could dynamically choose the partners or services to meet their particular demands. Meanwhile, they have to adapt themselves to meet their own specific contexts, objectives as well as the requirements from other partners. Considering traceability in food chain networks, many SMEs do not have precise knowledge on the required traceability information that best satisfy their own contexts. For the cooperation with other partners in the cloud environment, it is difficult for them to negotiate and then determine the profiles of their desired/exchanged information products.

The original version of this chapter was revised: The copyright line was incorrect. This has been corrected. The Erratum to this chapter is available at DOI: 10.1007/978-3-642-33068-1_20

M. van Sinderen et al. (Eds.): IWEI 2012, LNBIP 122, pp. 92–103, 2012.
© IFIP International Federation for Information Processing 2012

The SMEs in the clouds of food chain networks are supposed to work collaboratively to provide high-quality food to customers. However, in the last few years, food-safety issues were frequently discussed, such as avian flu, EHEC food-safety crisis. Meanwhile, the clear awareness of sustainability and healthy regarding food products is increasing importance. Traceability which is usually referred as following the movement of entities throughout a whole supply chain is often taken as an essential tool to increase food quality [2]. Not only movement information, but also much other information related to food products, such as animal warfare, GMO (genetically modified organisms), impact of ingredients to customer's health (e.g. too much sugar in food is not healthy for a patient with diabetes), could be kept as traceability information. The collected traceability information is possible to be used for addressing un-safe food products in case of incidents as well as verification of food quality with respect to safety, healthy and sustainability [3]. There are many other benefits related to traceability information, for instance, increasing transparency, increasing customers' satisfactions, verification of regulation compliance, etc. But setting up associated systems as well as gathering, processing, storing and sharing of the information is costly. For efficient coordination of the SMEs with respect to traceability, delivering the right information to partners and providing semantic interoperability play key roles. For instance, suppose information regarding GMO is critical important for a specific customer group, then all partners in the supply chain would be required to provide and exchange GMO-related information. However, for other customers, GMO information could be ignored to save cost. Customization of the information profiles which are expressed in ontologies would help SMEs to specify what information should be gathered /delivered with respect to their own contexts, objectives and constraints. And the customized information profiles then provide guidelines for information collection. However, to the best knowledge of the authors, currently there is no suitable framework available to help the users in SMEs to easily negotiate and get the food traceability information related ontologies that could best satisfy their particular business strategies, contexts, objectives and constraints.

With respect to delivering the right information to partners and providing semantic interoperability in food chain networks, some requisites should be satisfied by a proposed framework:

- Framework should provide tools and methodologies to help SMEs specify their own contexts, objectives and constraints with respect to traceability.
- Based on the provided information from SMEs, the framework should be able to propose optimal information profiles (expressed in ontologies) which could best satisfy SMEs' contexts, objectives and constraints.
- Distinctive information profiles should be provided for diversity products under different environments (e.g. different customer demands).
- In case of dynamic changes in business environment, SMEs should be able to easily get their own suitable information profiles.
- Semantic interoperability between information products should be guaranteed, so that SMEs could freely exchange information with other potential partners.

- Partners in the same supply chain should be coordinated to comply with a common information profiles to support all necessary traceability scenarios. For instance, if GMO information at broiler rearing stage is required in a supply chain, then all broiler farms in the supply chain are expected to provide GMO information.

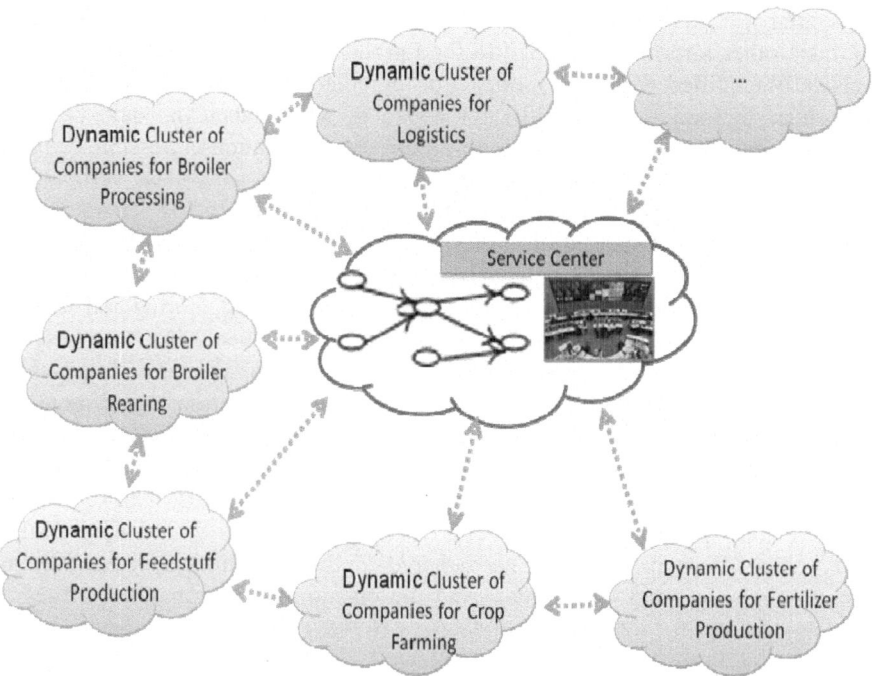

Fig. 1. Sample Cloud Environment for Broiler Supply Chains

The following section provides a review on related areas. And then, section 3 briefly described the proposed approaches. Finally, conclusion and future work to be done are presented.

2   Related Works

Traceability was first clearly described by Kim in the context of the TOVE (Toronto Virtual Enterprise) project [4]. Since then, numerous researches were conducted in this area. Traceability systems evolving from centralized to distributed "one step up, one step down", are becoming more distributed, interoperable and intelligent. More and more technologies, e.g. RFID (Radio), Frequency Identification), SOA (Service Oriented Architecture), web service, TraceCoreXML, ebXML (Electronic Business using extensible Markup Language), EDI (Electronic Data Interchange) etc. are used to facilitate integration and interoperability in food traceability. In the process of setting up an effective traceability system, one of the most important things is to determine the information to be recorded [5]. However, Partners are usually not sure, what the optimal traceability level is and what the exactly data that should be gathered is. Depends on traceability objectives, product characteristics, production processes, consumers' expectations and regulations, etc., the needed traceability data elements are different from one to another. There is no common accepted standard regarding the needed traceability data elements, and there is no single best way to introduce traceability because of the differences in product attributes and motivation of traceability etc. [6]. Partners usually collect only limited traceability information for regulation compliance. But for many other purposes, e.g. sustainability verification, the information is usually not sufficient enough to bring maximum benefit. The SMEs are difficult to be coordinated to provide all necessary information for various traceability scenarios.

To standardize the traceability data elements, some reference data models on traceability, such as the model from von Drop [7], and Bechini et al [8], were proposed. But they seem to be in a high general level, which cannot easily be customized or configured for partners in a food chain network under a specific environment. The detailed needed data elements cannot be easily derived from the models. Many constraints such as customers' expectations on traceability, regulations are not considered. Partners worldwide with varying regulations and business restrictions, have different markets and traceability expectations from consumers. Some consumers with some diseases, like diabetes or obesity, would have more interest in the traceability information related to nutrition and healthy. Others who concern more on the sustainability aspects (e.g. carbon emission) would be more interested in traceability information regarding sustainability. Besides, foods supply chain networks are becoming more demand driven and dynamical [9]. These dynamics in networks imply corresponding changes in the traceability needs, as well as the desired traceability data elements.

Information customization is to tailor information to meet special customer demands [10]. It is usually helpful to personalize information and avoid information overload. Abidi and Han presented an information customization framework which applied constraint satisfaction methods to select the hypermedia documents that conform to the user model [11]. Related to identifying the to be recorded traceability information, Diogo M. Souza-Monteiro et al. propose a framework based on vertical control and agency theory to model three dimensions of traceability systems: depth, breadth, and precision [12]. They model and analysis voluntary traceability system in a supply chain producing multi-ingredient foods from the point view of economic implications. However, their assumptions simplified the real supply chain networks, and many other factors besides economic implications such as production process, traceability motivations, products' characteristics, and regulations etc., which influence the determination of the information profiles, are not considered. For the products/ingredients that result more risk than others, more detailed information should be recorded. Thakur et al. present a soybean value chain and model the information that should be captured by three links in the chain [13]. On the basis of process models, they specify the data elements that should be included in the traceability information. Based on the information profiles, related information is then gathered, integrated to produce needed traceability information products. For information integration and semantic interoperability, the information profiles of SMEs are expressed as local ontologies that represent SMEs' own perspectives on traceability. Then the problem could be transformed into customization of optimal local ontologies that satisfy various constraints and objectives.

Ontology construction is one of the central research issues in the ontology area. There are lots of tools available for ontologies development, such as Protégé [14]. Regarding methodologies for ontology construction, it could trace back to the Cyc Project, in which the experience in the Cyc ontology development process is recorded [15]. Some years later, in the enterprise modelling domain, the experience in development TOVE ontology [4] is gathered. And then many other methodologies such as METHONTOLOGY [16], On-To-Knowledge [17] are presented. To support collaborative and distributed ontology construction, some methodologies like DOGMA [18], DILIGENT [19], Onto-Agent [20] were presented. In DOGMA and Onto-Agent methodologies, ontology resources are explicitly decomposed into ontology bases and ontological commitment. In ontology base, intuitive concepts and relationships between concepts within a domain are kept. In the ontology commitment layer, a set of constraints and rules are contained to allow agents to specify commitment ontology from their own point of view. In DILIGENT methodology, an initial shared ontology is first constructed, and then users could locally adapt the shared ontology for their own purposes. However, in the DOGMA, DILIGENT and Onto-Agent methodologies, users should have enough knowledge on ontology and know clearly about their desired ontology in order to reuse and construct their own ontologies. Farqahar et al. introduced Ontolingua Server for Collaborative Ontology Construction [21]. It supports ontologies reuse through an ontologies library, although the supports for ontology development in a distributed and collaborative environment are still limited [22]. To provide better supports for collaborative and argumentative ontology development as well as on the building of ontology networks, NeOn Methodology was then proposed [22] [23]. It considers the reuse and possible subsequent reengineering of knowledge resources as one of the key aspects.

Ontology selection is the process to identify one or more ontologies or ontology modules that satisfy certain criteria [24]. In the process, Ontologies could be searched based on specific keywords, logic query, ontology or some more complex query mechanism [24]. Some ontology search engines were presented in last few years, such as Swoogle [25] and OntoSelect [26]. Some of them like OntoSelect are ontology libraries that offer the ability of ontology selection. The SAIQL (Schema And Instance Query Language for OWL DL) proposed in NeOn project, is a sample language well suited for to extract a domain oriented sub-ontology [27].On the ontology selection, sub-ontology extraction and ontology pruning process, users usually need to input the related concepts either by manual input or extraction from other documents/knowledge sources. Some approaches such as TEXT-TO-ONTO [28] generate ontology based on the concepts discovered from texts or other resources. Lonsdale et al. take natural language (NL) documents and source ontologies as input, and then select/discovery related concepts etc. from source ontologies on the basis of descriptions in NL documents [29]. The main focus in these approaches are discovery/select concepts etc. based on documents for ontology generation, but understanding the contexts of SMEs and then proposing optimal ontologies to best satisfy SMEs' contexts is not the advantage of their approaches.

Although in the construction process, lots of the reuse processes are supported by semantic web technologies like ontology searching, selecting, merging, evaluation, but these technologies are still immature. Most of the processes still need lots of manual interventions. Moreover, they are mostly based on a hidden assumption that users know which the right ontologies considering their particular contexts are, and then users are able to understand, select and reuse ontologies for their own ontology construction. However, when the ontologies as well as application contexts and constraints become increasing complex, for instance, in the traceability context, users (e.g. users in SMEs) usually have no clear ideas about what the optimal traceability level and optimal information profiles (optimal ontologies) for them are. They do not know exactly whether a concept or property should be encompassed. The users in SMEs do have much knowledge on their own process models, motivations of traceability and complied regulations etc., but have little knowledge regarding ontology construction, as a result, the existing approaches for ontology construction would be unsuitable or a great challenge for them.

The term of Mass customization coined by Davis [30] was defined as "producing goods and services to meet individual customer's needs with near mass production efficiency" [31]. As the definition states, the goals of mass customization are to best server various customers' needs while at the same time maintain high efficiency. Production configuration for generating a product variant for a rapid response of customers' individual demands is one of the key approaches to enable mass customization. Considering the diversities in business environments and dynamics in traceability needs, the concept of mass customization used in manufacturing is possible to be applied in the customization of "local ontologies" (information profile) for traceability in SMEs.

3   Proposed Approaches

In order to answer aforementioned challenges, a framework which adopts the concepts of mass customization to shape the right information profiles will be presented. The core components for ontology customization in the framework are shown in the Fig. 2.

The service side provides toolkits for domain experts to maintain generic ontology structures, modularized reference ontologies and associated knowledge bases. In the repositories, the ontology modules are kept and the interoperability between ontology modules is pre-analyzed. For reusing and mass customization, related context information is attached to the ontology modules. The context information of ontology modules will be then associated with models of SMEs to help to select the right modules. In the knowledge base, the knowledge related to food traceability as well as the knowledge related to ontology customization like generic ontology structure are kept. Meanwhile, toolkits for SMEs are provided to support them model their own contexts, constraints etc. With the help of the toolkits, the factors like regulations, customer requirements and process models, etc., which would drive the selection of traceability data elements and customization of ontologies, could be clearly modelled.

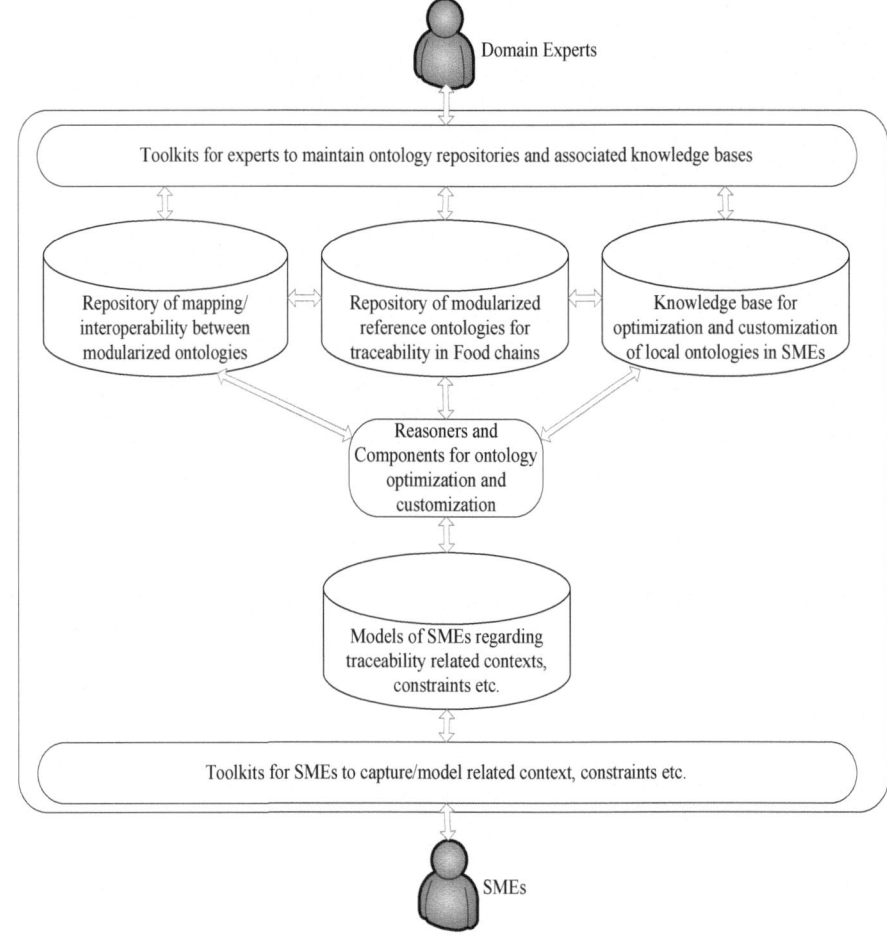

Fig. 2. Basic Structure in Framework for Ontology Customization

For instance, the following or toolkits could be included:

- Toolkits for business process model. Business process models represent processes, resources, products, etc. of an enterprise. Based on the process models, the potential information capture points as well as related costs and constraints are identified. The toolkits could be based on available tools like MO²GO [32].
- Toolkits for capturing customer requirements. In order to satisfy customer needs, requirements from customers should be captured and reflect in the information profiles. For example, if health impact of the foods with respect to special customer groups is critical importance, then collection, processing and evaluation health associated information (e.g. nutrition) would be in a relative high priority. Some toolkits from quality management areas like Quality Function Deployment (QFD) are possible to be equipped in the framework.

After the reference modularized ontologies, knowledge bases and the environments of SMEs etc. are specified within the framework, the methodologies used in mass customization, e.g. constraint satisfaction approach, will be employed to propose optimal local ontologies. In the customization process, ontology modules which satisfy the requirements and targets of SMEs' contexts are selected and then merged. For example, if the models of a SME show that sustainability information of a food product is demanded only by a few consumers and is costly to be gathered, then the ontology modules related to sustainability information would not be selected. In the local contextualized ontologies, the data elements/concepts which the SMEs really interested in are displayed. Based on customized ontologies, information dispersed in many other systems is then integrated to produce the needed traceability information products, as shown in Fig. 3. Besides, it provides guidance for the SMEs to collect and prepare the required but missed data elements. Since the customized local ontologies of SMEs are generated on the basis of the repository of modularized ontologies, the semantic interoperability between information products is then supported by the pre-specified interoperability of the reference modularized ontologies.

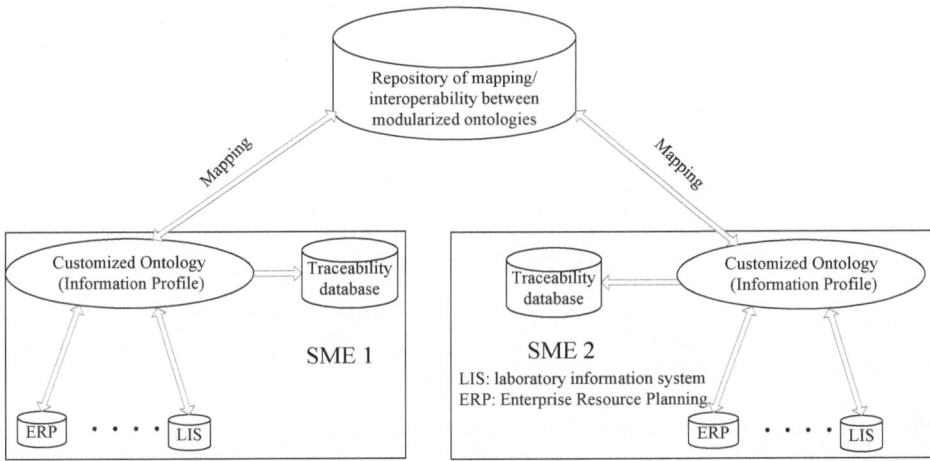

Fig. 3. Interoperability between SMEs

To ensure that the required traceability data supporting necessary scenarios are available within all partners of a supply chain, the partners producing the same ingredients in the same supply chain should negotiate to have a customized common shared ontology. In the ontology, the traceability information that needs to be exchanged in the supply chain is explicit expressed. Fig. 4 shows a mechanism for the coordination and determination of the common shared ontology in a sample supply chain. For each specific kind of partners (e.g. broiler farm), a high-level agent is initialized. The high-level agent will first coordinate with its sub-level agents i.e. agents of SMEs, as well as with other high-level agents to get necessary information. The information is then transformed and used as input for the aforementioned ontology customization approach to suggest common shared ontologies for the supply chain. At last, a governance boarder will make some modifications and determine the customized common shared ontology in the supply chain. The common shared ontologies describe the traceability information that will be exchanged and provided by partners. When there are some dynamic changes in business environment (e.g. Changes in partnership or customer demands), the ontologies could be easily re-customized to adapt to the new environment. For instance, imagine sustainability related information is currently missed in a food supply chain, but when this kind of information is required by regulations, and at the same time their target consumers are willing to pay for it, then the common shared ontology as well as local ontologies of the partners need to be quickly re-customized to encompass the sustainability related data elements/concepts.

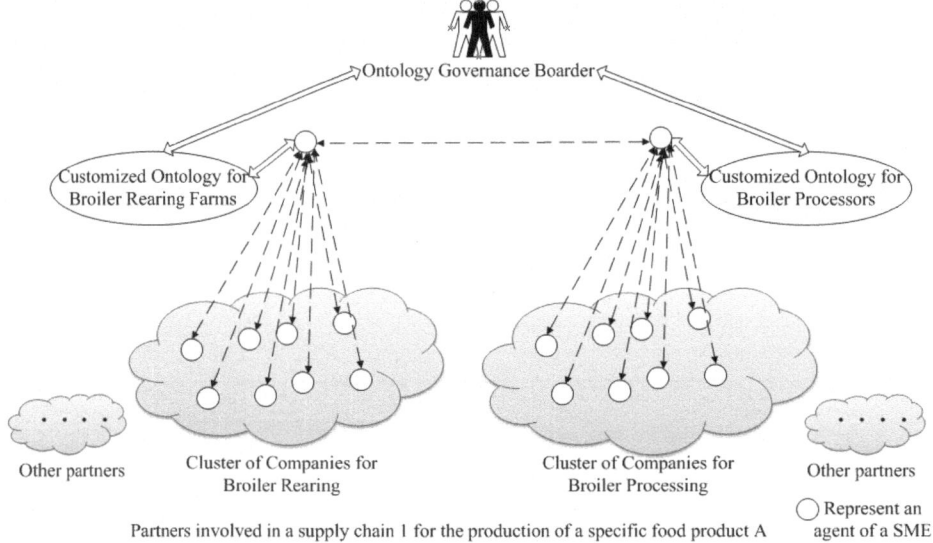

Fig. 4. Coordination Mechanism for Determination of Common Ontologies in a Sample Broiler Supply Chain

4   Conclusions

Identifying the list of data elements to be recorded is significant important for an efficient supply chain traceability systems. Depending on product characteristics, process model, customers' demands, motivation of traceability etc., the optimal information profiles which specify the needed traceability information are usually different from one to another. For information integration and semantic interoperability, the information profiles are expressed as local ontologies that represent SMEs' own perspectives on traceability information. Considering the dynamics in business environments and diversities in traceability needs, the paper adopts the concept of mass customization into the customization of these local ontologies /information profiles. An efficient framework to help these SMEs to negotiate and shape the right traceability information products is briefly presented. It involves the toolkits to help SMEs to model traceability relevance factors, such as business process models, customer demands, etc. With the pre-specified interoperability between modularized reference ontologies, semantic interoperability of the traceability information between various SMEs is also guaranteed. To ensure that the traceability data required to support necessary traceability scenarios are available within all partners of a supply chain, multi-agents and ontology governance boarder are introduced in the coordination mechanism. In traceability areas, this paper is supposed to provide a methodology for the determination of the to be recorded traceability information. In ontology construction area, it tries to adopt the concepts of mass customization to help the users who do not know clearly what right ontology for their purposes is and the ones who are not familiar with ontology technologies to easily get the customized ontologies that could satisfy their particular contexts. For the collaboration of the SMEs in food chain networks, a coordination mechanism is simply introduced.

In future work, we will start detailing the components, associated toolkits and building the framework described in the paper. Definitely, there are many challenges to build the system and run successfully in food industry. Because the ontologies in SMEs are customized through reusing modularized ontologies, the quality and granularity of ontology modules will certainly affect the quality of customized ontologies. The context information of ontology modules should be carefully designed, so that the modules could be correctly reused. With respect to context models of SMEs, some issues like how to model the driving factors and then use them effectively for the selection of traceability data elements as well as customization of related ontologies still need to be further detailed. For the negotiation of common shared ontologies, the cooperation and communication between agents will be further specified. And then the approach is expected to be experimented in food industry to evaluate how well it works in real business scenarios.

References

1. Food industry, EU food market overview, http://ec.europa.eu/enterprise/sectors/food/eu-market/index_en.htm
2. ISO: ISO 22005:2007, Traceability in the feed and food chain — General principles and basic requirements for system design and implementation, 1st edn., Switzerland (2007)
3. Hobbs, J.E.: Information asymmetry and the role of traceability systems. Agribusiness 20, 397–415 (2004)
4. Kim, H.M., Fox, M.S., Gruninger, M.: An ontology of quality for enterprise modeling. In: Proceedings 4th IEEE Workshop on Enabling Technologies: Infrastructure for Collaborative Enterprises (WET ICE 1995), pp. 105–116 (1995)
5. Regattieri, A., Gamberi, M., Manzini, R.: Traceability of food products: general framework and experimental evidence. Journal of Food Engineering 81, 347–356 (2007)
6. Golan, E., Krissoff, B., Kuchler, F., Calvin, L., Nelson, K., Price, G.: Traceability in the U. S. Food Supply: Economic Theory and Industry Studies Library Cataloging Record. Economic Theory (830) (2004)

7. van Dorp, C.: Reference-data modelling for tracking and tracing. Wageningen University (2004)
8. Bechini, A., Cimino, M.G.C.A., Lazzerini, B., Marcelloni, F., Tomasi, A., Elettronica, I.: A General Framework for Food Traceability. In: Proceedings of the 2005 Symposium on Applications and the Internet Workshops, pp. 366–369 (2005)
9. Verdouw, C.: Business process modelling in demand-driven agri-food supply chains: a reference framework. Wageningen University (2010)
10. Berleant, D., Berghel, H.: Customizing Information: Part I - IEEE Computer, 27(9), 96–98 (1994); Part II - IEEE Computer, 27(10), 76–78 (1994)
11. Abidi, S.S.R., Chong, Y.: An adaptive hypermedia system for information customization via content adaptation. IADIS Intl. Journal of WWW/Internet 2(1), 79–94 (2004)
12. Souza-monteiro, D.M., Caswell, J.A.: The Economics of Voluntary Traceability in Multi-Ingredient Food Chains. Agribusiness 26(1), 122–142 (2010)
13. Thakur, M., Donnelly, K.A.-M.: Modeling traceability information in soybean value chains. Journal of Food Engineering 99(1), 98–105 (2010)
14. The Protégé Ontology Editor and Knowledge Acquisition System, http://protege.stanford.edu/
15. Elkan, C.: Building Large Knowledge-Based Systems:Representation and Inference in the Cyc Project book review 1 Comments on the Cyc project. Readings, pp. 1–11 (1989)
16. Ferndndez, M., Gmez-Perez, A., Juristo, N.: METHONTOLOGY: From Ontological Art Towards Ontological Engineering. Assessment, pp. 33–40 (1997)
17. Staab, S., Schnurr, H.-P., Studer, R., Sure, Y.: Knowledge Processes and Ontologies. Knowledge Creation Diffusion Utilization (2000)
18. Jarrar, M., Meersman, R.: Formal Ontology Engineering in the DOGMA Approach. In: Meersman, R., Tari, Z. (eds.) CoopIS 2002, DOA 2002, and ODBASE 2002. LNCS, vol. 2519, pp. 1238–1254. Springer, Heidelberg (2002)
19. Pinto, S., Staab, S., Tempich, C., Sure, Y.: DILIGENT: Towards a fine-grained methodology for Distributed, Loosely-controlled and evolvInG Engineering of oNTologies. In: N.N. (eds.), ECAI. IOS Press (2004)
20. Hadzic, M.: Onto-agent methodology for design of ontology-based multi-agent systems. Computer Systems Science and Engineering 34(3), 358–364 (2008)
21. Farquhar, A., Fikes, R., Rice, J.: The ontolingua server: A tool for collaborative ontology construction. International Journal of Human-Computer Studies (1996)
22. del Carmen Suárez, M., de Baonza, F.: NeOn Methodology for Building Ontology Networks: Specification, Scheduling and Reuse. Doctoral Thesis in Building (2010)
23. NeOn Project, http://www.neon-project.org/
24. Sabou, M., Lopez, V., Motta, E., Uren, V.: Ontology Selection: Ontology Evaluation on the Real Semantic Web, Victoria (2006)
25. Ding, L., et al.: Swoogle: a search and metadata engine for the semantic web. In: Proceedings of the Thirteenth ACM International Conference on Information and Knowledge Management, pp. 652–659 (2004)
26. Buitelaar, P., Eigner, T., Declerck, T.: OntoSelect: A Dynamic Ontology Library with Support for Ontology Selection. In: The OntoSelect Ontology Library. Research Management, pp. 3–6 (2003)
27. Kubias, E., Schenk, S., Staab, S., Pan, J.Z.: OWL SAIQL-an OWL DL query language for ontology extraction. In: Proc. of OWLED 2007 (2007)
28. Maedche, E., Staab, S.: The TEXT-TO-ONTO Ontology Learning Environment. In: Software Demonstration at ICCS 2000 - Eight International Conference on Conceptual Structures (2000)

29. Lonsdalea, D., Embley, D.W., et al.: Reusing Ontologies and Language Components for Ontology Generation. Journal Data & Knowledge Engineering 69(4), 318–330 (2010)
30. Davis, S.M.: From 'future perfect': Mass customizing. Strategy & Leadership 17(2), 16–21 (1989)
31. Tseng, J., Jiao, M.M.: Mass customization. In: Handbook of Industrial Engineering, 3rd edn., New York (2001)
32. Mertins, K., Jochem, R.: MO^{2}GO. In: Handbook on Architectures of Information Systems. Springer, Berlin (1998)

A Value-Oriented Iterative Service Modeling Process

Xiaofei Xu, Chao Ma, and Zhongjie Wang

Research Center of Intelligent Computing for Enterprises and Services (ICES),
School of Computer Science and Technology, Harbin Institute of Technology, Harbin, China
{xiaofei,rainy}@hit.edu.cn, machao8396@163.com

Abstract. In order to help service designers build high-quality service models quickly and accurately, this paper presents a value-oriented iterative service modeling process. This modeling process combines service business perspective and service value perspective together, and it is executed interactively between service model space and service value space, simultaneously, some value-awareness activities (e.g. value proposition, value analysis, value optimization, etc) are executed iteratively among different layers in the whole model process, so as to make service models can support the implementation of the expected values to a great extent. At last the rationality of the modeling process is explored.

Keywords: business perspective, value perspective, value-awareness, expected values, rationality.

1   Introduction

In recent years modern service industry was developing fast, and it has become the new economic growth point. The accurate execution of service business needs to be supported by service systems. Service engineering methodology is used to help service designers and service developers define, describe, design, optimize and implement the high-quality service systems accurately and quickly, which is viewed as a focus of research in service engineering field [1]. Service modeling process is an important part of service engineering methodology [2]. Service modeling process is used to carry on requirement analysis, business design, model transformation and mapping for service systems.

IBM SSME research group believes "service is the interactive process and behaviors between service providers and customers to create and share value" [3]. According this, various tangible and intangible values are regarded as the output of service systems [4]. Service values are an important characteristic of service systems. Service systems can be gradually transformed from service models by utilizing model-driven approach, so the quality of service models determines the quality of the service systems. The sole criterion for evaluating the quality of a service model is whether and to what degree the model can support the implementation of the values that are expected by both customers and providers [5]. Therefore, it is necessary to carry on value-awareness activities in the whole service modeling process, so as to obtain a high-quality model.

The original version of this chapter was revised: The copyright line was incorrect. This has been corrected. The Erratum to this chapter is available at DOI: 10.1007/978-3-642-33068-1_20

M. van Sinderen et al. (Eds.): IWEI 2012, LNBIP 122, pp. 104–116, 2012.

Value-awareness means that "the value is regard as the basis of the service model design and decision-making in each phase of service life cycle, and before moving to the next phase, the value-oriented service model analysis must be executed to insure the implementation of all the expected values". In service modeling process, the corresponding value-awareness activities include value proposition, value expressing, value keeping, value decomposition, value analysis and value optimization. In order to better carry on value-awareness activities, this paper presents a value-oriented iterative service modeling process.

In this modeling process, not only service functional modeling from business perspective is needed, but also service value modeling from value perspective is needed, and this modeling process is executed interactively between service model space and service value space to insure the consistency in service models and value models. Service systems may refer to various stakeholders. At the beginning of the modeling process, these stakeholders understand the service systems partially and simply, therefore value-oriented model analysis, model optimization and feedback need to be executed iteratively to modify and deepen the understanding of service system incessantly.

The remainder of this paper unfolds in the following manner. Section 2 introduces service modeling theory. Section 3 presents a value-oriented iterative service modeling process. And then the rationality of the modeling method is explored in section 4, followed by conclusions in the last section.

2 Service Modeling Theory

For now, there are lots of study results of service modeling method from different perspectives (e.g. traditional software engineering, model-driven, domain analysis, semantics-driven).

From the traditional software engineering perspectives, the typical methods include SOMA [6], SODA [7] and SOUP [8]. By means of some methods such as domain decomposition, target service modeling, SOMA built service models, and then identified a set of self-existent service. And aiming at each service, some aspects (e.g. component specification, service interface specification, information, etc.) of the service are designed. At last a specific technique is selected to implement the services and combine these services tighter to realize a service system according to the layered structure. SODA can carry on various analysis and verification for service models, and support the flexible reuse, the reverse engineering, the automatic code generation, and so on. SOUP is a software method that is used to built and manage SOA project by utilizing RUP and XP. RUP is used to initially build the new service systems, and XP is used to analyze, assemble, reuse and optimize the existing service systems.

From the model-driven perspectives, the typical methods include the model driven service engineering process [9], the service model driven architecture (SDMA) [10]. In the model driven service engineering process, the requirement model, the enterprise model, the execution model and the IT management model are respectively built for service systems. The service system is composed of the high level goals, the low level service components and the sensors embedded during runtime. Various phases are connected by utilizing model-driven approach. In SMDA, the service requirement model, the service behavior/capability model and the service execution model are respectively built for service systems. By means of model-driven approach, the three models are gradually built layer by layer, and the whole modeling process is top-down.

From the domain analysis perspectives, the typical methods include the SOA domain analysis method [11], the framework-based IT service engineering [12] and the rule-based configuration approach [13]. In the SOA domain analysis method, the VINCA business model is built and instantiated from top to down by utilizing domain analysis approach, simultaneously, the web services are virtualized from bottom to up, at last in the middle the VINCA business model and the web services are combined together. In the framework-based IT service engineering, service templates are used as a model specification to describe service. In rule-based configuration approach, a configurative service system is built to meet the requirements of the group customers by embedding a set of variable parameters into service models and service systems. On this basis, the individual requirements of each customer are taken into consideration, and the concrete values of various parameters in service systems are confirmed, at last the service systems that can meet service requirements are built by utilizing the automatic configuration in combination with manual configuration.

From the semantics-driven perspectives, the agent-based service system design method (Tropos) is a typical method [14]. In Tropos, the semantics of service business requirements (e.g. knowledge, rules) are defined by means of formal methods, and the requirements are mapped into the concrete service design and service orchestration by carrying on semantics transformation, at last the corresponding service systems is built.

Besides, Gordijn and others presented a multi-perspective service modeling method [15] [16] [17]. The method refers to three perspectives: a value perspective, a process perspective, and an information systems perspective. The first two perspectives belong to the requirements analysis and business design phase. The last one belongs to the systems implementation phase. During service modeling, firstly, a value network is built from the value perspective, and it is used to analyze the future economic profit of service business. And then from the process perspective the service tasks are decomposed from top to down and those tasks are described by utilizing UML-like language, at last the service process model is obtained. MDA approach is used to build service systems.

In the above methods, the most ones are the multi-perspective or hierarchical modeling methods. They only focus on the traditional functional and quality characteristic of service systems, and ignore the value characteristic. But the value is the most characteristic of service systems. The method presented by Gordijn takes the value characteristic into consideration. It carrying on the economic values calculation in the strategy layer, but it did not take the value as the constraint for the whole service modeling. The value-oriented iterative service modeling process can solve the above problem. It has the three advantages: 1) it focus on value characteristic, and combines service business perspective and value perspective together; 2) it is interactive; 3) it is iterative.

3   Service Modeling Process

Value-oriented iterative service modeling process is shown in figure 1. From transverse look, this process carries on interactively between service model space and service value space. From fore-and-aft look, this process carries on iteratively among different layers. The goal of this modeling process is take the expected values as the constraints for service modeling, so as to make service model can support the implementation of the expected values. The quantitative analysis of the expected values is taken as the basis of policy-making of various phases in this service modeling process.

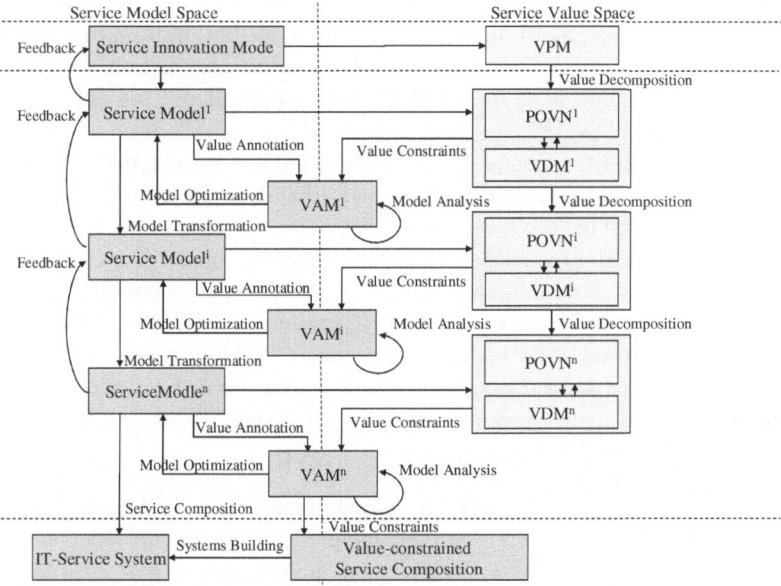

Fig. 1. Schematics of the service modeling process

3.1   Service Model and Value Model

As is shown in figure 1, in service model space, service models are built layer by layer from coarse-grained elements into fine-grained ones. Service model is composed of service functional elements and the relationships among the various elements. It can be denoted as SM=(SE, R), where SE is service functional elements including two kinds: 1) service behaviors; 2) sub-process that is composed of a set of service behaviors. Service behaviors can be denoted as se= (PA, Fe, AO, ST, RES, QoS), where:

- PA is the set of participants of se;
- Fe is the farter behaviors of se, Fe is transformed into a set of fine-grained behaviors, and se is one of them;

- *AO* is the set of action objects which are manipulated by *se* and whose state are changed by the effect of *se*;
- *ST* is a set of *ao*'s state transitions. In $\forall st \in ST$, $\exists ao \in AO$ makes $st = ao.s_i \rightarrow ao.s_j$.
- *RES* is a set of necessary resources of *se*;
- *QoS* is a set of quality parameters that are attached to *se*.

In the beginning of service modeling process, some service business can not be directly described as a service behavior, and only can be described as a sub-process. In the subsequent service modeling process, the sub-processes are gradually refined, until all the sub-processes are transformed into the service behavior that can be implemented by service component (e.g. web service).

In service value space, the four kinds of value models are used in the iterative and interactive service modeling process. They are value proposition model (VPM), participant oriented value network (POVN), value dependency model (VDM) and value annotation model (VAM).

VPM is used to identify various end-customers and end-providers in the top service that will be designed and implemented, and identify which service values they expected to obtain from the top service.

It is denoted as VPM=(*TS*, *EPA*, *TV*), where *TS* is the top service composed of the attribute *name* and the attribute *description*, *TS* would be decomposed into a series of sequential sub-services and service behaviors during service modeling; *EPA* is the set of end-participants composed of the end-customers set *EC* and the end-providers set *EP*; *TV* is the set of the top value, $\forall v_i \in TV$, service value v_i can be denoted as $v_i=(BA, CA)$, where:

BA is the set of basic attributes of v_i, $BA=\{v\_ID, Name, Producer, Receiver, View, State, rc, rc.Type, rc.s^I, rc.s^O, Fv\_ID, B, C, E, CON\}$:

- v_ID, *Name* are respectively the unique identification and name of v_i;
- *Producer, Receiver* are respectively the producer set and the receiver set of v_i;
- *View* is the type of v_i's *Receiver*, *View* includes two types: customers *C* and service providers *P*;
- *State* is the granularity of v_i, *State* includes the root value *RV*, the interim value *IV* and the atomic value *AV*;
- *rc* is the realization carrier that v_i is attached to. It means that v_i's effect is exhibited as the improvement of *rc*.
- *rc.Type* is the type of v_i's *rc*, *rc.Type* includes *ECV*, *TIV*, *RUV* and so on;
- $rc.s^I$, $rc.s^O$ are respectively the initial state and expected final state of *rc*;
- Fv_ID is the farter behaviors of v_i, Fv_ID is decomposed into a set of fine-grained values, and v_i is one of them;
- *B, C, E* are respectively the direct benefits, the direct cost and the indirect profits of v_i;
- *CON* is the value profit constraint. $\forall q_j \in CON$, q_j can be used to evaluate the a specific characteristic of the service in which v_i's receiver is participating.

CA is the set of constraint attributes of v_i, $CA=\{e(B), e(C), e(E), e(CON)\}$, where $e(B)=\{B_{best}, min(B)\}$, B_{best} is the value of *B* during v_i's receiver accepts the best service, $min(B)$ is the worst value of B that v_i's receiver can accept; (C), $e(E)$ are similar to $e(B)$; $\forall econ \in e(CON)$, $econ$ is the constraint set of some quality parameter q_j, $econ$ include basic constraint, comparative constraint and conditional constraint.

POVN is used to identify which enablers that are needed to import so as to realize service. POVN is also used to describe how the various values are exchanged among the participants (customers, providers, enablers).

POVN is denoted as POVN=$\{N, E\}$, where N is the node set in POVN, $\forall node \in N$, $node$ is a participant. $N=C \cup P \cup EN$, where C is the customer subset, P is the provider subset and EN is the enabler subset. E is the edge set in POVN, $\forall edge \in E$, $edge=(se, v)$, $\exists participant_i$, $participant_j \in N$, $participant_i$, $participant_j$ are two endpoints of $edge$, se is the service functional elements that $participant_i$ and $participant_j$ refer to, and v is the corresponding value of se.

VDM is used to describe the relationships among the various edges in POVN. The relationships are the dependency relationships among the various service values in POVN. VDM is denoted as VDM = (N, SN, E^D, E^I), where:

- $N=\{node_1, node_2,\ldots, node_n\}$, $\forall node_i \in N$, $\exists edge_i \in$ POVN.E, $node_i=edge_i =(se_j, v_i)$;
- $SN=\{super\_node_1, super\_node_2,\ldots, super\_node_m\}$, $super\_node_k \subseteq N$, | $super\_node_k|>1$, where $super\_node_k$ is a set of edges in POVN, and its constitutive rules: 1) to take the set of edges $\{(se_j, v_p),\ldots, (se_l, v_q)\}$ as $super\_node_k$, and the participants of any two edges are same; 2) to take the set of edges $\{(se_j, v_p),\ldots, (se_j, v_q)\}$ as $super\_node_k$, and the service functional element of any two edges is same;
- $\forall e^D \in E^D$, e^D is a directed super edge, it is denoted as $e^D=(a(e^D), c(e^D))$, where $a(e^D)$, $c(e^D)$ may be the super node, and may also be node. $E^D = CDE \cup ADE \cup SDE \cup TSDE$, where CDE is the set of composition dependency edges, ADE is the set of aggregation dependency edges, SDE is the set of support dependency edges, $TSDE$ is the set of timing sequence dependency edges;
- $\forall e^I \in E^I$, e^I is an undirected super edge, $e^I \subseteq N$, $|e^I|>1$. $E^I = DPDE \cup SPDE$, where $\forall d \in DPDE$, $d=$DiffProducer$(v_1,v_2,\ldots,v_n)$, $\forall d \in SPDE$, $d=$SameProducer$(v_1,v_2,\ldots,v_n)$, and let $pset=\{v_1,v_2,\ldots,v_n\}$.

VAM is used to describe the corresponding relationships between service values and service functional elements. It is denoted as VAM= $(SM, VAT, R(se, vat))$, where VAT is the set of value annotation tables, $\forall vat_k \in VAT$, vat_k is a set of values, and their corresponding service functional element is same; $R(se, vat)$ is the set of the corresponding relationships between se and vat. $\forall v_i \in vat_k$, $v_i= (BA, CA, DA)$, where DA is the set of impendency attributes of v_i, $DA= E^D \cup E^I$.

For more details of value models please refer to the references [18][19].

3.2   Detailed Modeling Process

The detailed value-oriented iterative service modeling process is shown in figure 2. This modeling process include 13 phases, and each phase is composed of serval steps.

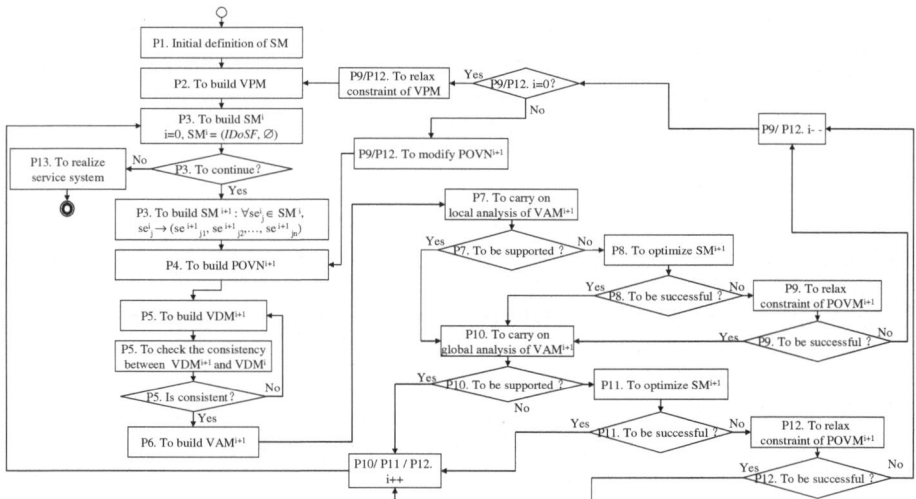

Fig. 2. Detailed modeling process

The detailed modeling process is as follows:

Phase1: To give initial definition of service model, denoted as *IDoSM*= (*IDobss*, *IDoSP*, *IDoSV*, *IDoSF*);

Step1. To initialize *IDobss*, *IDobss* is the business scope of the service;

Step2. To initialize *IDoSP*, *IDoSP* is the service participant set in the service;

Step3. To initialize *IDoSV*, *IDoSV* is the service value set provided by the various service participants in *IDoSP*;

Step4. To initialize *IDoSF*, *IDoSF* is the service function set supporting the realization of *IDobss*;

Phase2: To build VPM, denoted as VPM= (*TS*, *EPA*, *TV*);

Step1. To let *TS.name = IDobss*, and assign values to *TS.description*;

Step2. To identify end-customer set *EC* and end-provider set *EP* from *IDoSP*, and let *EPA= EC ∪ EP*;

Step3. To initialize *TV*=∅, *n*=|*EC*|+|*EP*|, and add *n* service values into *TV*;

Step4. $\forall c_i \in EC$, to assign values to *BA* of service value v_i that end-customer c_i expects to obtain according to *IDoSV* and the domain knowledge;

Step5. $\forall p_j \in EP$, to assign values to *BA* of service value v_j that end-provider p_j expects to obtain according to *IDoSV* and the domain knowledge;

Step6. $\forall c_i \in EC$, end-customer c_i would consult with the corresponding end-providers, and then to assign values to *CA* of service value v_i ;

Step7. $\forall p_j \in EP$, end-provider p_j would consult with the corresponding end-customers, and then to assign values to *CA* of service value v_j;

Phase3: To build service model, denoted as SM^i= (*SE*, *R*); SM^i would be gradually transformed layer by layer by means of MDA;

Step1. If *i*=0, to initialize SM^i= (*SE*, *R*), let SM^i= (*IDoSF*,∅);

Step2. To judge whether or not all the service elements se^i_j belonging to $SM^i.SE$ can be realized by service components (e.g. web service);

Step3. If it can be, then go to Phase13;

Step4: $\forall se^i_j \in SM^i.SE$, if se^i_j can not be realized, to decompose se^i_j into $(se^{i+1}_{j1}, se^{i+1}_{j2}, \ldots, se^{i+1}_{jn})$, and then SM^i is transformed into SM^{i+1};

Phase4: To build POVN^{i+1} corresponding to SM^{i+1}, denoted as POVN$^{i+1} = (N, E)$;

Step1. $\forall se^{i+1}_j \in SM^{i+1}.SE$, to identify the customer set C, the provider set P and the enabler set EN from $se^{i+1}_j.PA$, and to let POVN$^{i+1}.N = C \cup P \cup EN$;

Step2. $\forall (se^i_j, v^i_h) \in POVN^i.E$ (if $i=0$, $\forall v^i_h \in VPM.TV$), according to the decomposition relationships between se^i_j and the corresponding service elements of SM^{i+1}, by utilizing some decomposition method of service value, to decompose v^i_h into $v^{i+1}_{h1}, v^{i+1}_{h2}, \ldots, v^{i+1}_{hm}$, and then to identify all the corresponding relationships $(se^{i+1}_{jk}, v^{i+1}_{hk})$, and add $(se^{i+1}_{jk}, v^{i+1}_{hk})$ into POVN$^{i+1}.E$;

Step3. $\forall (se^{i+1}_j, v^{i+1}_h) \in POVN^{i+1}.E$, according to se^{i+1}_j, to assign values to BA of service value v^{i+1}_h;

Step4. $\forall (se^{i+1}_j, v^{i+1}_h) \in POVN^{i+1}.E$, according to $v^{i+1}_h.Fv$, to divide all the service values of POVN^{i+1} into a group of subsets $\{subV_1, subV_2, \ldots, subV_n\}$, Fv of any two service values in each subset is same;

Step5. $\forall subV_k \in \{subV_1, subV_2, \ldots, subV_n\}$, $\forall v^{i+1}_h \in subV_k$, according to CA of $v^{i+1}_h.Fv$, by utilizing some decomposition method of service values constraint, to assign values to CA of v^{i+1}_h;

Phase5: To build VDM^{i+1} corresponding to POVN^{i+1}, denoted as VDM$^{i+1} = (N, SN, E^D, E^I)$;

Step1. $\forall edge^{i+1}_h \in POVN^{i+1}.E$, to let VDM$^{i+1}.node^{i+1}_h = edge^{i+1}_h = (se^{i+1}_j, v^{i+1}_h)$;

Step2. $\forall subE \subset POVN^{i+1}.E$, to let VDM$^{i+1}.super\_node^{i+1}_k = subE$, and $subE = \{(se^{i+1}_j, v^{i+1}_p), \ldots, (se^{i+1}_j, v^{i+1}_q)\}$, or $subE = \{(se^{i+1}_j, v^{i+1}_p), \ldots, (se^{i+1}_l, v^{i+1}_q)\}$;

Step3. If $i=0$, to skip this step; $\forall node^{i+1}_h \in VDM^{i+1}.N$, according to $v^{i+1}_h.Fv$, to identify CDE and ADE, and then add CDE and ADE into E^D;

Step4. To identify SDE, $TSDE$, $SPDE$ and $DPDE$ between various service values of VDM^{i+1}, and to add SDE, $TSDE$ into E^D, to add $SPDE$, $DPDE$ into E^I;

Step5. To judge whether or not all the consistency between SDE, $TSDE$, $SPDE$, $DPDE$ of VDM^{i+1} and the corresponding ones of VDM^i is maintained;

Step6. If it is, then go to Phase6;

Step7. If it is not, then go back to Phase5_Step 4;

Phase6: To build VAM^{i+1}, denoted as VAM$^{i+1} = (SM^{i+1}, VAT, R(se^{i+1}_j, vat))$;

Step1. $\forall (se^{i+1}_j, v^{i+1}_h) \in POVN^{i+1}.E$, according to the corresponding relationship between v^{i+1}_h and se^{i+1}_j, to divide all the service values of POVN^{i+1} into a group of subsets $\{subV_1, subV_2, \ldots, subV_m\}$, the corresponding service element of any two service values in each subset is same; each subset is related to one vat;

Step2. $\forall subV_k \in \{subV_1, subV_2, \ldots, subV_m\}$, $\forall v^{i+1}_h \in subV_k$, $\forall d \in SDE \cup TSDE$, if $v^{i+1}_h \in cons(d)$, then add d into $v^{i+1}_h.DA$; $\forall d \in SPDE \cup DPDE$, if $v^{i+1}_h \in pset(d)$, then add d into $v^{i+1}_h.DA$; $\forall d \in CDE \cup ADE$, if $v^{i+1}_h \in ante(d)$, then add d into $v^{i+1}_h.DA$;

Phase7: To carry on the local analysis of VAM^{i+1} [20];

Step1. $\forall v^{i+1}{}_h \in VAM^{i+1}$, to calculate $v^{i+1}{}_h$ based on the Qos of the corresponding service functional elements;

Step2. To judge whether or not the implementation of all the values can meet the constraints;

Step3. If there are the constraints of some values (represented by *UnmetVset*) that can not be met, then go to Phase8;

Step4. If the constraints of all the values can be met, then go to Phase10;

Phase8: To optimize SM^{i+1};

Step1. To modify the QoS of the corresponding service functional elements of the values belonging to *UnmetVset* by utilizing some heuristic optimization method;

Step2. If the gaps between the implementation and the constraints of the values belonging to *UnmetVset* can be eliminated, then go to Phase10;

Step3. If the gaps can not be, then go to Phase9;

Phase9: To eliminate the gaps by relaxing the constraints of the values of $POVN^{i+1}$;

Step1. To relax the constraints of the values belonging to *UnmetVset*;

Step2. To judge whether or not the gaps can be eliminated;

Step3. If the gaps can be, then go to Phase10;

Step4. If the gaps can not be, then let $i=i-1$:

Step4.1. If $i==0$, to relax the constraints of the values in VPM which are the father value of the values belonging to *UnmetVset*, then go back to phase2;

Step4.2. If $i\neq 0$, to relax the constraints of the values in $POVN^{i+1}$ which are the father value of the values belonging to *UnmetVset*, and then go back to phase4;

Phase10: To carry on the global analysis of VAM^{i+1};

Step1. FV^{i+1} is the set of the Fv of all the values in VAM^{i+1}, $\forall v^i{}_k \in FV^{i+1}$, to calculate all the values of FV^{i+1};

Step2. To judge whether or not the implementation of all the values can meet the constraints;

Step3. If there are the constraints of some values (represented by *UnmetFVset*) that can not be met, then go to Phase12;

Step4. If the constraints of all the values can be met, then $i=i+1$, and go to Phase3;

Phase11: To optimize SM^{i+1};

Step1. To modify the QoS of the corresponding service functional elements of the values decomposed from the values belonging to *UnmetFVset* by utilizing some heuristic optimization method;

Step2. If the gaps between the implementation and the constraints of the values belonging to *UnmetFVset* can be eliminated, then $i=i+1$, and go to Phase3;

Step3. If the gaps can not be, then go to Phase12;

Phase12: To eliminate the gaps by relaxing the constraints of the values of $POVN^{i+1}$;

Step1. To relax the constraints of the values decomposed from the values belonging to *UnmetFVset*;

Step2. To judge whether or not the gaps can be eliminated;

Step3. If the gaps can be, then $i=i+1$, and go to Phase3;

Step4. If the gaps can not be, then let $i=i-1$;

Step4.1. If $i==0$, to relax the constraints of the values belonging to *UnmetFVset* in VPM, and then go back to phase2;

Step4.2. If $i\neq0$, to relax the constraints of the values belonging to *UnmetFVset* in $POVN^{i+1}$, and then go back to phase4;

Phase13: To realize service system by utilizing service composition approach;

Step1: To carry on the quantitative evaluation on the value-oriented priority of service functional elements in SM^n [21];

Step2: To carry on VOP based service composition.

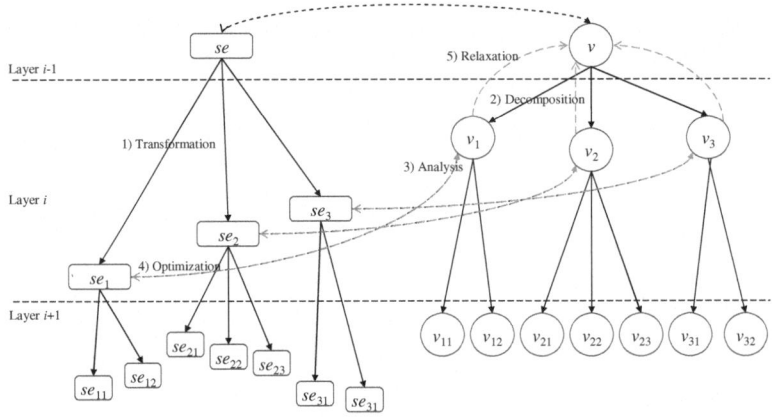

Fig. 3. An example of the modeling process

In order to better explain the above modeling process, a simple example is given in figure 3. It is assumed that there is a service functional elements *se* in the layer *i*-1, its corresponding value is *v*, and the implementation of *v* can meet *v*'s own constraints. In the layer *i*, firstly , *se* is transformed into <*se₁, se₂, se₃*>; secondly, *v* is decomposed into $\{v_1, v_2, v_3\}$, and there is a corresponding relationship between se_1 and v_1; the next phase is to analyze whether or not the constraints of v_1 can be met by v_1's implementation that is under the support of se_1. If the constraints of v_1 can not be met, the next phase is optimize se_1 by modifying its QoS; If the gaps between v_1's implementation and v_1's constraints can not be eliminated by optimizing se_1 or by relaxing v_1's own constraints, the next phase is to go back to the layer *i*-1 to relax *v*'s constraints. If all the constraints of se_1, se_2 and se_3 can be met, then go to the layer *i*+1.

4   Rationality of Modeling Process

The iteration and interactive are two key characteristics of the modeling process. The rationality of them is respectively discussed below.

There are various stakeholders in service system, their requirements are different and their degree of the understanding for service system is also different. Each stakeholder only can understand service system from their own point of view, and then pursue their own goal. Therefore, the stakeholder that can understand service system from a global perspective is impossible to exist. During service system designing, it is necessary to interactively carry on modeling process among various stakeholders, and to combine those understandings for service system together, so as to make service system can meet the requirements of all the stakeholders. As is shown in figure 4, the different stakeholders have different perspectives, and their range of the cognition for service and service system is different, but there are the intersections among various cognitive ranges, it is rational to interactively carry on modeling process among various stakeholders.

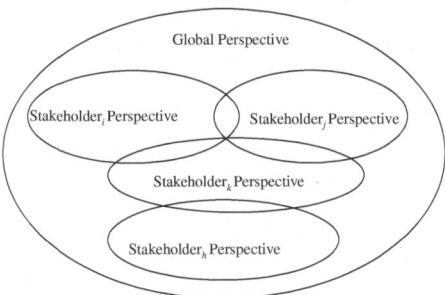

Fig. 4. Different perspectives of the different stakeholders

In this paper, the modeling process includes two perspectives: values perspective and business perspective. The modeling process is executed interactively between service model space and service value space. From business perspective, service functional model is gradually built; the model designers only focus on the functional and quality requirements, and ignore the expected values. From value perspective, several corresponding value models is built along with service functional model, the value designers mainly focus on the expected values, and did not understand much service business. But the value designers and the model designers can know what relationship between the expected values and service functional elements. Therefore, it is rational to interactively carry on modeling process between the value designers and the model designers.

The people's cognition for new things is progressive. The same goes for the cognition of the stakeholders for service systems. At the beginning of modeling, the stakeholders' degree of the understanding for service system is not high because their perspectives are local and the information obtained is few. As the stakeholders obtain some new information from others, their degree of the understanding for service system become higher, they may found some previous understanding for service system is wrong, so it is necessary to go back to adjust. It is similar to the backtracking method in software engineering.

In this paper, at the beginning of modeling, the cognition of the value designers and the model designers for service systems is limited. The cognition is constantly deepened by carrying on iteratively modeling process. For example, the model designers built SM^i, but it is founded that SM^i can not support the sufficient implementation of the expected values by model analysis, so it is necessary to go back to modify SM^i. For another example, the value designers set the constraints of the expected values in $POVN^i$, but the gaps can not be eliminated by utilizing model optimization or relaxing the constraints of the expected values in $POVN^i$, so it is necessary to go back to relax the constraints of the corresponding values in $POVN^{i-1}$. Therefore, it is rational to iteratively carry on modeling process among different layers.

5 Conclusion

This paper presents a value-oriented iterative service modeling process. On the one hand, it combines the service business perspective and service value perspective together. The expected values are taken as constraints for service models. The value characteristic of service system is focused on. On the other hand, it makes service models can support the implementation of the expected values to a great extent by carrying on interactively between service model space and service value space and by carrying on iteratively among different layers. The modeling process can be used to help service designers to build the high-quality service model, and the service system that is built based on this service model can deliver the service values to providers and customers to a great extent.

Acknowledgment. Research works in this paper are supported by the National Natural Science Foundation (NSF) of China (No. 61033005, 70971029).

References

1. Papazoglou, M., Traverso, P., Dustdar, S., Leymann, F., Krämer, B.: Service-Oriented Computing Research Roadmap (March 2006),
   http://infolab.uvt.nl/pub/papazogloump-2006-96.pdf
2. Xu, X., Wang, Z., Mo, T.: Methodology for service engineering. Computer Integrated Manufacturing Systems 13(8), 1457–1464 (2007)
3. Jim, S., Paul, M., John, B., Daniel, G.: Steps toward a Science of Service Systems. IEEE Computer 40(1), 71–77 (2007)
4. Ma, C., Xu, X., Wang, Z.: Preliminary Discussions on Several Characteristics of Service Value. International Journal of Service Science, Management, Engineering and Technology 1(3), 50–62 (2010)
5. Xu, X., Wang, Z.: Value-Aware Service Model Driven Architecture and Methodology. In: IFIP: E-Government ICT Professionalism and Competences Service Science, vol. 280, pp. 277–286. Springer, New York (2008)
6. Arsanjani, A., Ghosh, S., Allam, A., et al.: SOMA: A method for developing service-oriented solutions. IBM System Journal 47(3), 377–396 (2008)

7. Nigam, S.: Service Oriented Development of Applications (SODA) in Sybase Workspace. Sybase Inc. whitepaper, Sybase Inc. (2005), http://www.sybase.com/detail?id=1036164
8. Mittal, K.: Service Oriented Unified Process (SOUP), http://www.kunalmittal.com/html/soup.html
9. Anaby-Tavor, A., Amid, D., Sela, A., et al.: Towards a Model Driven Service Engineering Process. In: IEEE Congress on Services 2008 - Part I, pp. 503–510 (July 2008)
10. Xu, X., Mo, T., Wang, Z.: SMDA: A Service Model Driven Architecture. In: Goncalves, R.J., Muller, J.P., Mertins, K., Zelm, M. (eds.) Proceedings of the 3rd International Conference on Interoperability for Enterprise Software and Applications, Madeira Island, Portugal. Enterprise Interoperability II: New Challenges and Approaches, March 28-30, pp. 291–302, ISBN: 978-1-84628-857-9
11. Wang, J.W., Yu, J., Han, Y.B.: A Service Modeling Approach with Business-Level Reusability and Extensibility. In: IEEE International Symposium on Service-Oriented System Engineering, pp. 23–28 (2005)
12. Specht, T., Spath, D., Weisbecker, A.: Framework-based IT Service Engineering. In: ITI 3rd International Conference on Information and Communications Technology, pp. 19–38 (2005)
13. Becker, J., Beverungen, D., Knackstedt, R., Matzner, M.: Configurative Service Engineering - A Rule-Based Configuration Approach for Versatile Service Processes in Corrective Maintenance. In: Proceedings of the 42nd Hawaii International Conference on System Sciences, pp. 1-10 (January 2009)
14. Lau, D., Mylopoulos, J.: Designing Web Services with Tropos. In: International Conference on Web Services, pp. 306–313 (2004)
15. Gordijn, J., Eck, P.V., Wieringa, R.: Requirements Engineering Techniques for e-Services. In: Georgakopoulos, D., Papazoglou, M.P. (eds.) Service-Oriented Computing. The MIT Press, Cambridge (2009)
16. Gordijn, J., Yu, E., van de Raadt, B.: E-Service Design Using i* and e3value Modeling. IEEE Software 23(3), 26–33 (2006)
17. Gordijn, J., Akkermans, H.: E3-value: Design and Evaluation of e-Business Models. IEEE Intelligent Systems 16(4), 11–17 (2001)
18. Wang, Z., Xu, X.: Multi-Level Graphical Service Value Modeling Method. Computer Integrated Manufacturing Systems 15(12), 2319–2327 (2009)
19. Wang, Z., Xu, X.: Service value dependency model based on layered hyper-graph. Computer Integrated Manufacturing Systems 17(8), 1837–1846 (2011)
20. Ma, C., Xu, X., Wang, Z.: A Process Algebra based Method for Value Analysis on Service Process Model. Chinese Journal of Computers 33(11), 2177–2189 (2010)
21. Ma, C., Xu, X., Wang, Z.: The Quantitative Evaluation on the Value-Oriented Priority of Service Elements. In: 2011 International Joint Conference on Service Science (IJCSS 2011), Taipei, Taiwan, China, May 25-27, pp. 257–261. IEEE Computer Society (2011)

Principles of Servitization and Definition of an Architecture for Model Driven Service System Engineering[*]

Yves Ducq, David Chen, and Thècle Alix

University of Bordeaux - IMS/LAPS
351 cours de la Libération
33405 Talence cedex
david.chen@ims-bordeaux.fr

Abstract. European manufacturing enterprise will progressively migrate from traditional product-centric business to product-based service-oriented virtual enterprise and ecosystems However, the changes in this servitization process must be accompanied using specific techniques. This paper aims at presenting the principles of migration from traditional tangible product company to a set of virtual organisations ensuring the various steps of a Product2service life cycle as well as a preliminary result to develop service modelling architecture. The proposed Model Driven Service Engineering (MDSE) architecture is adapted from MDA/MDI approaches as developed in INTEROP Network of Excellence. This architecture defines the various modelling levels and the related constructs to model based on servitization principles. The potential modelling languages to represent these constructs at each level of MDSE will be presented at the same time. Conclusions are given in the end of the paper.

Keywords: Service system modelling, Enterprise modelling, MDI/MDA approaches.

1 Introduction

European manufacturing enterprise will progressively migrate from traditional product-centric business to product-based service-oriented virtual enterprise and ecosystems [1]. In this sense, traditional companies have to cooperate in one or several virtual enterprises, considered as service systems dedicated to support the service design, development, and implementation. During this migration process, service system that will provide desired services around the product will have to be modelled, designed, implemented, tested and managed along its entire lifecycle in order to ensure the correct migration of the company.

This paper presents some preliminary result of a research work performed in the frame of the FP7 MSEE Integrated Project [2]. Particularly, the goal of this work is to

---

[*] This paper is elaborated on the basis of MSEE deliverable D11.1: Service concepts, models and method: Model Driven Service Engineering, WP1.1, MSEE consortium, 2012.

The original version of this chapter was revised: The copyright line was incorrect. This has been corrected. The Erratum to this chapter is available at DOI: 10.1007/978-3-642-33068-1_20

M. van Sinderen et al. (Eds.): IWEI 2012, LNBIP 122, pp. 117–128, 2012.
© IFIP International Federation for Information Processing 2012

develop service system modelling language to support service system engineering and implementation. The approach adopted is to use Enterprise Modelling techniques as a basis under the Model Driven Service Engineering Architecture extended from Model Driven Interoperability approach developed in INTEROP Network of Excellence [3].

So, in a first part, the servitization process and the definition of what a service system is will be developed as well principles of system modelling. Then, the Model Driven Service Engineering Architecture will be presented insisting on its interest for the implementation of a coherent and complete virtual enterprise based on business models and on the description of each modelling level. The various levels of the architecture will be detailed as well as the required constructs to represent at each level based on the previous servitization principles. Then, enterprise modelling languages will be proposed to represent the constructs at each level. Finally, the perspectives of this work will be proposed.

2   Servitization and Virtual Organization as a Service System

The studies and researches in the domain of Service have been mostly devoted to support tertiary sector domains (e.g. banking & finance, tourism, trade, public administration), with an obvious focus on ICT. At the end of the nineties, the concept of Service in Manufacturing appeared and the evolution from an economy of products towards an economy of services round the products becomes more and more important in manufacturing: this evolution is called **Product Service System (PSS)** or **Servitization.**

According to Wikipedia "a service is to make available a technical or intellectual capacity" or "to supply a work which will be useful for the user without material transformation".

Most of the time a service is opposed to a good. The following list characterizes a service [4]:

- A service is not owned, but there is a restricted access,
- Services have intangible results,
- Customers are involved in the service production process,
- Other persons than the customers can be involved in the service process as stakeholders, sub-contractors, etc....
- Quality in service is difficult to control while increasing productivity and also difficult to apprehend
- Service cannot be stored.
- Service delivery delay is crucial.
- Service delivery integrates physical and electronic way.

Since a decade, new research thinking has been emerging, trying to systematize the multi-disciplinary knowledge involved in service systems. On their web page, IBM describes service science as "a growing multi-disciplinary research and academic effort that integrates aspects of established fields like computer science, operations research, engineering, management sciences, business strategy, social and cognitive sciences, and legal sciences" [5].

In the computer science domain, Service Oriented Architectures (SOA), have revolutionized information systems, by providing software engineers with powerful methodologies and tools for decomposing complex systems into autonomous components. The final aim of such evolution is to support enterprise vital processes and workflows, by simple orchestrations and compositions in the hand of business specialists.

Clearly the servitization of manufacturing companies covers different levels of service provision and consequently different stages can be followed to evolve.

In servitization, the product is considered as the core element of the service to deliver to customers and subsequently we follow a manufacturing approach taking into account the market pressure that oblige to create new models in order to meet the servitization challenge. An appropriate concept to link products, product related services and the needs of the users is the "Extended Product" (EP) [6].

The Extended Product concept belongs to the category of Product-Service System. The Extended Product-Service is characterized by a layer model based on manufacturing product and defining the process extensions (Figure 1). The Extended Product is a complex result of tangible and intangible components.

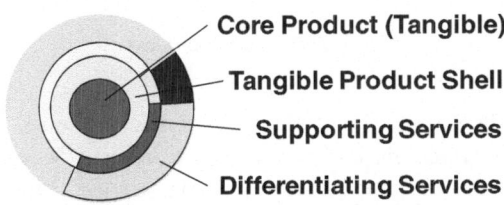

Fig. 1. The Extended Product Concept, adopted from [6]

The Core Product is the physical product that is offered to the market; while the Product Shell describes the tangible "packaging" of the product (e.g. one enterprise sells machine-tools and will add the maintenance which can be done by another company). Supporting Services are intangible additions, which facilitate the use of the product (e.g. maintenance plans or mobility guarantees). Differentiating Services provide individualization of the Extended Product on the market.

Then product extensions are described by the tangible and intangible aspects of a "utility package" to satisfy the customers' needs. They can be used to gain competitive advantage by offering added value to the customer. While in the past production costs, marketing, quality and reliability or time to market have been key success factors, nowadays innovation is the decisive characteristic [7].

The resulting Extended Product would be the specific solution satisfying the customers demand. As the solution can become very complex, several business partners may be collaborating for the provision of the EP in the frame of an Ecosystem.

Customers are looking for solutions and benefits (not only to acquire products) or even more they are requesting intangibles like leadership on the market, success, fame, etc. Manufacturers need to package their core products with additional services to make them more attractive.

The different stages of service provision are shown in Figure 2.

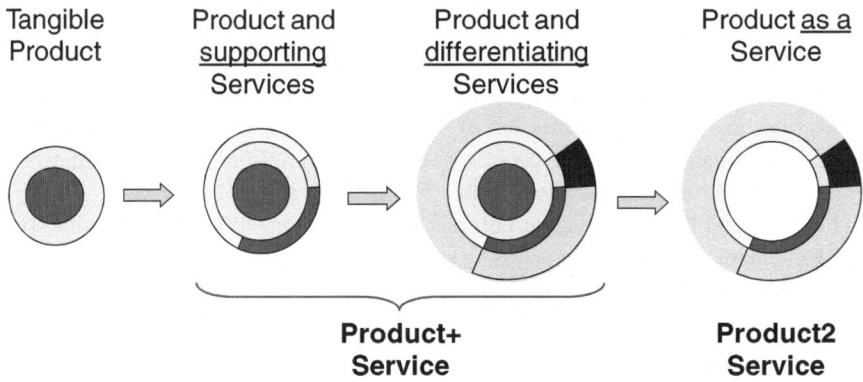

Tangible Product   Product and supporting Services   Product and differentiating Services   Product as a Service

Product+ Service   Product2 Service

Fig. 2. Servitization process

The first stage is the selling of a product (e.g. a machine tool).

The second stage which initializes the servitization process and the evolution toward Product+Service, start by adding a simple service (Product and supporting service) (e.g. the company will add a device on the machine-tool allowing to check continuously the running of the machine etc).

The third stage (Product and differentiating service) is an evolution of the previous one. The service is more elaborated and increases the differentiation (e.g. the company can propose to sell the machine plus a service which guaranties a high percentage of availability of this machine).

The fourth stage, Product2Service scenarios are in contrast sharply decoupling manufacturing of goods and selling of services, where in most cases physical goods remain the property of the manufacturer and are considered as investment, while revenues come uniquely from the services (e.g. the company doesn't sell the machine-tools but sells hours of running of the machine-tool).

However, in this context, this is difficult for most of the companies to work alone in the Product2Service scenario but need to be associated to other companies all along the service life cycle. Working together in design and production networks results in an extension of companies' "ability to reach" e.g. wider markets and knowledge spheres, a higher level of the companies agility, as well as the possibility to share risks and resources. An industrial model for collaboration to exploit the various opportunities is a Virtual Organisation (VO) (figure 3).

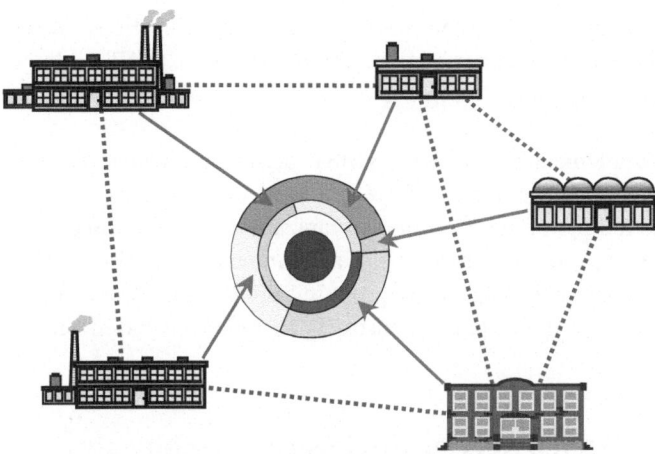

Fig. 3. Virtual Organisation

A virtual organisation is an enterprise that marshals more resources than it currently has on its own, using collaborations both inside and outside of its boundaries, presenting itself to the customer as one unit. It is a set of (legally) independent organizations that share resources and skills to achieve a mission/goal.

However, such a virtual organization must be implemented differently in the different phases of a service life cycle in order to support the service system as shown in figure 4 below.

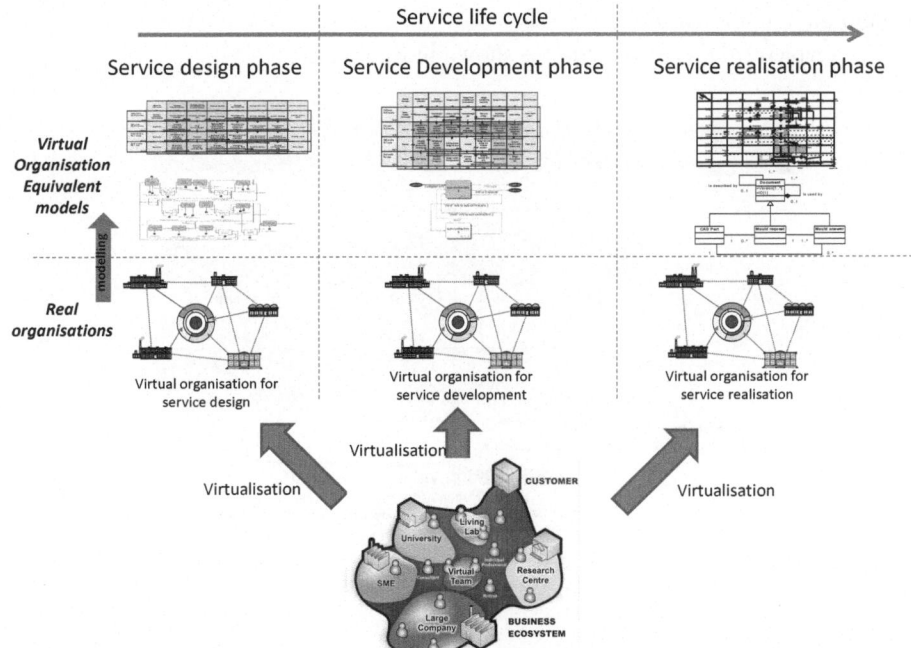

Fig. 4. Virtualisation of enterprises and modelling for each phase the service life cycle

So from a common Ecosystem (Service Manufacturing Ecosystem) composed of several kinds of companies as research centres, SME's, lerge companies, consultants…, it is possible to select the companies which will be virtualized for each stage of the life cycle.

Then, the implementation of each virtual organization must be done with agility and without spending too much cost, reaching an interoperable organisation. In order to do so, modelling of each virtual organization will be done through a set of modelling languages used in the frame of a common model driven architecture. In this sense, the next part will present the proposed architecture, describing in detail each modelling level and the required constructs to represent based on the servitization principles.

3   Model Driven Service Engineering Architecture

The proposed Model Driven Service Engineering (MDSE) Architecture is elaborated as an adaptation and an extension of MDA/MDI [8],[9] for the engineering of product related services in virtual enterprise environment. Although MDA/MDI approached are more focused on IT system deployment, MDSE architecture aims to allow supporting the needs of modelling the three types of service system components (IT, Human and Physical Means). The main benefits of this model driven approach is to allow a continuum in the modelling from the business to the realisational level and to specify and implement a set of component coherent with the chosen strategy of collaboration in the virtual enterprise.

The adapted MDSE architecture is shown in figure 5.

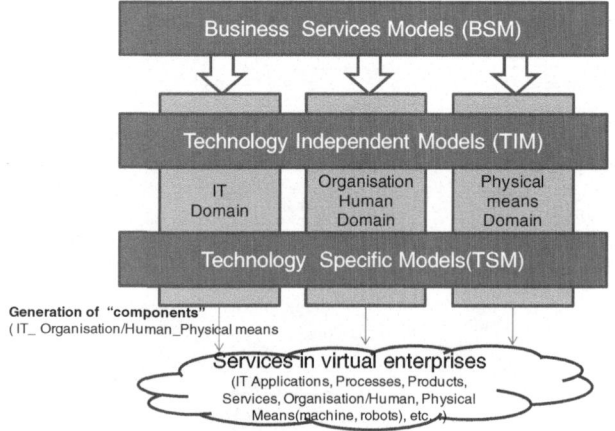

Fig. 5. MDSE architecture

Similar to MDA/MDI, the proposed MDSE defines a framework for service system modelling around three abstraction levels: Business Service Modelling, Technology Independent Modelling and Technology Specific Modelling.

3.1 The Business Service Modelling Level and Related Constructs and Languages

The Business Service Modelling (BSM) aims to model the service system, at the global level, describing the running of the virtual enterprise, i.e. the running of the collaboration between the considered enterprises. The models at the BSM level must be independent to the future technologies that will be used for the various resources. In this sense, it's useful, not only as an aid to understand a problem, but also it plays an important role in bridging the gap between domain experts and the development experts that will build the service system (adapted [9]). In fact we develop the BSM in two sub-levels: the Top BSM and the Bottom BSM. The Top BSM sub level models the enterprise and its environment at a global level in order to analyse the possibilities to develop the System Service (the GRAI modeling could be used). The Bottom BSM will allow to model in details the domain concerned by the servitization process (we can use the languages defined by the local modeling). Based on this first analysis, the service system will be decomposed in the various components domains (IT, Organisation/Human and Physical Means) with a detailed description. For instance, at the BSM level (top and bottom), the decisions are listed but not the related decision makers are related decision support systems. Similarly, the type of resources doing the activities is listed but not the precise name or location of these resources. The concepts identified on the basis of the principles of servitization and virtual organization as presented previously are listed below:

- o   Service
- o   Product
- o   Value
- o   Customer
- o   Partner
- o   Stakeholder (provider, intermediary, designer,...)
- o   Functionality
- o   Resource (Human type, Physical mean type, IT type)
- o   Process (business)
- o   Organization (responsibility, authority)
- o   Decision
- o   Decision structure
- o   Performance indicator

This list of concepts is considered as a list of core concepts.

Based on these concepts, several modelling languages can be used to represent the virtual organization at the BSM level as indicated in the figure 6 below:

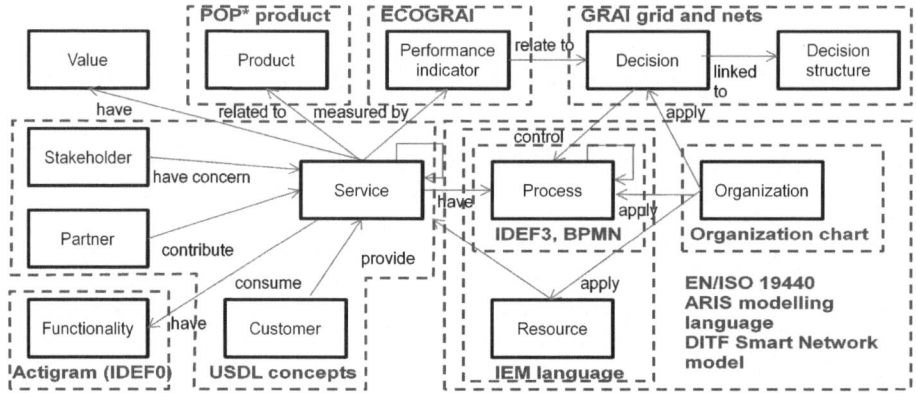

Fig. 6. Modelling languages at the BSM level

3.2   The Technology Independent Modelling Level and Related Constructs and Languages

Technology Independent Modelling (TIM), aims to represent the models at a second level of abstraction independent from the technology used to implement the system. It gives detailed specifications of the structure and functionality of the service system that do not propose technological details. More concretely, it focuses on the operation details while hiding specific details of any particular technology in order to be suitable for use with several different technologies. At TIM level, the detailed specification will be elaborated with respect to the components in the domains of IT, Organisation and Human and Physical means for a service system. So, the IT related modelling part aims at detailing the model of the enterprise application, but mainly in terms of functionalities which will be implemented and without defining which application will be chosen. The functionalities will be of course derived from the models at the BSM level. These functionalities will be classified according to their importance in order to prepare the future selection at the lower level. The functionalities can also cover the requirements in terms of interoperability with other systems implemented in one company of the ecosystem. The Physical mean part will be related to the means to add value to the product and to support the service production. At this level, the functionalities of a specific machine and the expected performances can be proposed but no name of specific machine is proposed. As for the IT part, the functionalities can be prioritized and synthetized in order to propose a questionnaire that would be sent to the various machine providers. This is obvious that the functionalities are derived from the models, in particular the models of the physical system and business processes. The human resource part aims at defining the kinds of skills that are required according to the models. At this level, the name of a specific resource is not given but his/her place in the organization, his/her role in this organization and performance to reach must be detailed. This is obvious that this information can be derived, mainly from the decisional modelling and the business process modelling as well as from the physical models mainly for the persons directly involved in the product manufacturing and the service distribution. Moreover, this information will be sued for the recruitment or the move of specific human resource as well as for the planning of the training of existing resource.

Based on these principles, the following constructs are proposed to be represented in the models at this level:

- o Service
- o Process
- o Organisation
- o Resource
- o Organisation unit
- o Enterprise Application
- o Information
- o Human
- o Physical mean,

Based on these concepts, several modelling languages can be used to represent the virtual organization at the TIM level as indicated in the figure 7 below:

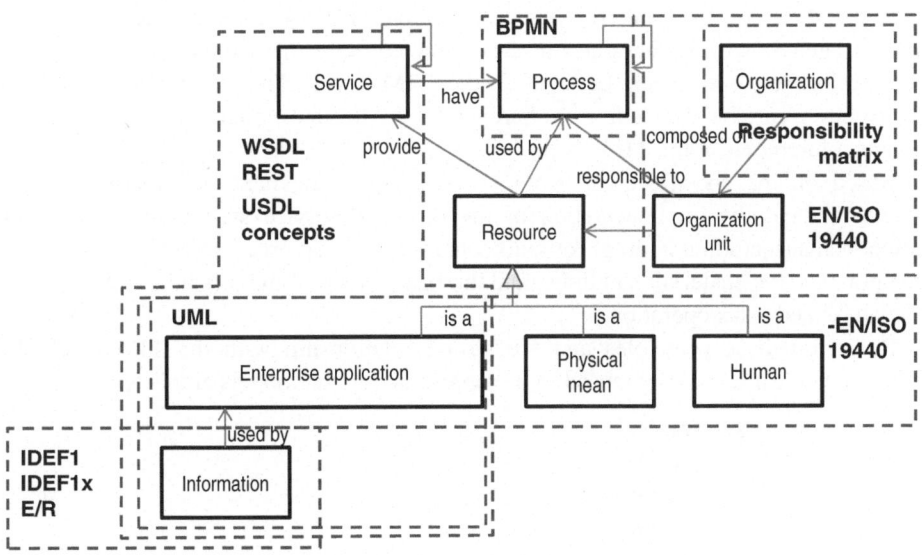

Fig. 7. Modelling languages at the TIM level

3.3   The Technology Specific Modelling Level and Related Constructs and Languages

Technology Specific Modelling (TSM) aims to combine the specification in the TIM model with details that specify how the system uses a particular type of technology (such as for example IT platform, Physical Means or Organisation with Human profile). At TSM level, modelling and specifications must provide sufficient details to allow developing or buying software/hardware components, recruiting human operators / managers or establishing internal training plans, buying and realizing machine devices, for supporting and delivering services in interaction with customers. For instance for IT component, TSM adds to the TIM, technological details and implementation constructs that are available in a specific implementation platform, including middleware, operating systems and programming languages. So, the IT related modelling part aims at detailing the model of the enterprise application, but mainly in terms of detailed functionalities which will be bought or developed in the chosen enterprise application. The functionalities will be of course derived from the functionality modelling at the TIM level. The detailed functionalities can also cover the requirements in terms of interoperability with other systems implemented in one company of the ecosystem. The Physical mean part will be related to the choice of a specific physical mean. At this level, the functionalities of a specific machine and the expected performances will be verify and tested. As for the IT part, the functionalities will be very detailed and detailed actigrams could be used. This is obvious that the functionalities are derived from the models at the TIM level. The human resource part aims at defining the specific resource which will be selected, to verify the appropriateness with his/her place in the organization, his/her role in this organization and performance to reach defined at the TIM level. This is obvious that this information can be derived, in coherence with the decisional modelling and the organization moels at the TIM level.

Based on the specifications given at TSM level, the next step consists in the realization and the implementation of the designed service system in terms of IT components (including coding) for automated information processing, machine/device components for material handling, and human resource and organization ensuring human related tasks/operations.

Based on these principles and the strong relationship with the TIM level, the following constructs are proposed to be represented in the models at this level:

- o Service
- o Process
- o Organisation
- o Resource
- o Organisation unit
- o Enterprise Application
- o Information
- o Human
- o Physical mean,
- o Layout

Based on these concepts, several modelling languages can be used to represent the virtual organization at the TSM level as indicated in the figure 8 below:

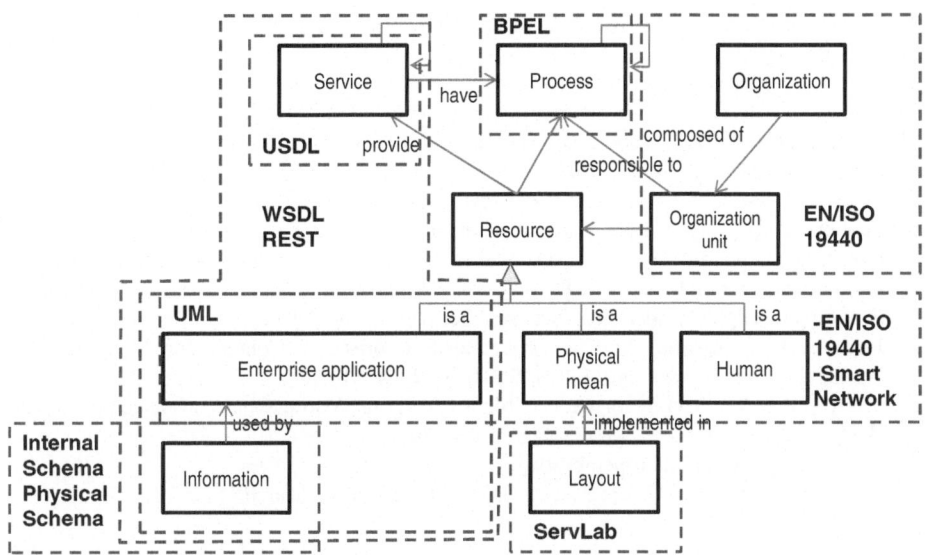

Fig. 8. Modelling languages at the TSM level

4   Conclusion

In order to face the competitiveness, companies must progressively migrate from traditional product-centric business to product-based service-oriented virtual enterprise and ecosystems. In order to do so, they must create different virtual organization all along the service life cycle. To support the migration, enterprise modelling must be used to allow a progressive implementation of these virtual organizations in the frame of a common architecture as MDSE architecture proposed in this work with ensuring a continuum in the modelling, coherent from the business to the technological level. The related constructs required to represent at each modelling levels are derived from the servitization and virtual organization principles. Potential modelling languages are proposed at each modelling level.

The main perspective of this work is to perform a first application to a real case study in order to validate the architecture and the various concepts. Of course, some modelling languages are already chosen at each level as the extended actigrams and BPMN 2.0 at the top and bottom BSM levels for the process modelling or GRAI Grid at the BSM level for the decisional modelling and the transformation mechanisms are in progress. But this application could be fruitful for this validation.

References

[1] Thoben, K.-D., Jagdev, H., Eschenbächer, J.: Extended Products: evolving traditional product concepts. In: Thoben, K.-D., Weber, F., Pawar, K.S. (eds.) Proceedings of the 7th International Conference on Concurrent Enterprising: Engineering the Knowledge Economy through Co-operation, Bremen, Germany (June 2001)

[2] FP7 – FoF-ICT-2011.7.3 - Manufacturing SErvice Ecosystem Project- Annex 1 description of work, July 29 (2011)

[3] MDI: Model Driven Interoperability, http://www.modelbased.net/mdi/ (accessed on: March 15 2010)

[4] Lovelock, C., Wirtz, J., Lapert, D.: Marketing des Services, 2nd edn., p. 619. Prentice Hall, Paris (2004) ISBN 2-7440-7026-2

[5] http://www.ibm.com/developerworks/spaces/ssme

[6] Thoben, K.-D., Jagdev, H., Eschenbächer, J.: Extended Products: evolving traditional product concepts. In: Thoben, K.-D., Weber, F., Pawar, K.S. (eds.) Proceedings of the 7th International Conference on Concurrent Enterprising: Engineering the Knowledge Economy through Co-operation, Bremen, Germany (June 2001)

[7] Jagdev, H.S., Browne, J.: The Extended Enterprise. A Context for Manufacturing. Production Planning & Control 9(3), S.216–S.229 (1998)

[8] MDA - The Architecture of Choice for a Changing World. Object Management Group (January 2008), http://www.omg.org/mda/

[9] MDI: Model Driven Interoperability, http://www.modelbased.net/mdi/ (accessed on: March 15, 2010)

Control-Flow Pattern Based Transformation from UML Activity Diagram to YAWL

Zhaogang Han[1], Li Zhang[1], Jiming Ling[1], and Shihong Huang[2]

[1] School of Computer Science & Engineering, Beihang University, China
[2] Department of Computer Science&Engineering, Florida Atlantic University, USA
hanzhaogang@gmail.com, lingjimin@126.com, lily@buaa.edu.cn,
shihong@fau.edu

Abstract. Business process verification is an important topic in business process management (BPM). The verification of standard UML Activity Diagram is not easy due to lack of mature tools. YAWL (yet another workflow language) has a formal semantics based on Petri net; verification of YAWL model seems easier than other modeling languages such as UML-AD. A series of mature verification tools has been released (Woflan, WofYAWL, ProM) based on YAWL to find structural errors, such as deadlocks in the model. These tools can be used for verifying UML-AD models if they can be transformed to YAWL models.

The most challenging problem is that some control-flow patterns in UML-AD can't be transformed via an element-to-element mapping. To solve this problem we provide a control-flow pattern based method for transforming a UML-AD model to YAWL. We regard these patterns that need to be transformed as whole model segments, pick them out from the UML-AD model and transform the left part using an element-to-element mapping as well as an object flow transforming method. We subsequently transform the picked-out patterns via patterns-based transformation and combine all the transformed YAWL segments to a new YAWL net.

Categories and Subject Descriptors: D.2.1 [Requirements]: Requirements –
Methodologies.

General Terms: Theory.

Keywords: Business Process Verification, UML Activity Diagram, YAWL, Transformation, Control-flow Pattern.

1   Introduction

Business process verification is an important topic in business process management [1-5]. This involves identifying structural conflicts in the business process definition. UML Activity Diagram[1] is intended for modeling computational and business

---

[1] The formal UML 2.0 specification was published in July 2005, and the latest UML specification version is 2.3, which is published in May 2010. Since there is not much difference between version 2.0 and version 2.3 when concerning the activity diagram, we call these two versions of UML activity diagram "UML 2.x Activity Diagram".

The original version of this chapter was revised: The copyright line was incorrect. This has been corrected. The Erratum to this chapter is available at DOI: 10.1007/978-3-642-33068-1_20

M. van Sinderen et al. (Eds.): IWEI 2012, LNBIP 122, pp. 129–145, 2012.
© IFIP International Federation for Information Processing 2012

processes [6-9]. UML Activity Diagram (UML-AD for short) has a wide usage in business process modeling and lots of research work have been done concerning its verification [10-12][2], but these work usually take a subset of UML-AD as a verification basis and some advanced control structures (for example, cancel activity and cancel region) has been excluded from this subset.

YAWL [13-15] is a BPM system having a formal semantics based on Petri net. Because of its foundation on Petri net, its verification seems easier than other modeling languages such as UML-AD. There are lots of research works [16-19] and a series of mature tools [20-24] concerning the verification of YAWL. And YAWL models with advanced control structures like or-join and cancel region can be verified using these mature tools. In order to benefit from these mature tools, a transformation from UML-AD to YAWL is needed. In [25], the first step has been taken but only a small subset of UML-AD has been taken into account. So it is a good start but far from enough. In this paper we try to give a deep analysis of this transformation.

Some key questions in such a transformation are "Can we keep all the control aspect informations without being lost in the transforming procedure" and "what technology should be taken to guarantee a "correct" transformation". In this paper a method based on control-flow patterns is proposed to solve these problems.

We propose a three-step method to implement this transformation. Based on a rigorous analysis, numerous results are drawn on how UML-AD and YAWL support all the 43 control-flow patterns, control information of which patterns will lose during the transformation, which pattern need to be transformed as a model segment and which pattern can be transformed by element-to-element method. After picking out the model segments that need to be transformed by pattern-based way in the first step, we transform the rest parts of model based on an element-to-element mapping rule. In the second step we transform UML-AD object nodes and object flows into YAWL data and control flow since UML-AD object flows also contain control informations. In the third step we transform the picked-out model segments via patterns-based method and combine all the transformed YAWL segments to a whole YAWL net.

The rest of the paper is organized as follows. Section 2 provides background information regarding model transformation and UML activity diagram. In section 3 based on the assumption that the model segments that need to be transformed by pattern-based way have been picked out, we transform the rest parts of model based on UML-AD and YAWL meta-models. An element-to-element mapping is used first followed by transformation of UML-AD objects node and objects flow into YAWL data and control flow. Section 4 illustrates which patterns need to be transformed as a model segment by a pattern-based method and which patterns can be transformed by an element-to-element transformation based on a rigorous analysis. We then pick out the patterns (model segments) that need a pattern-based transformation and transform them via patterns-based method and combine all the transformed YAWL segments to a whole YAWL net. After presenting an example to illustrate our method (Section 5), we draw a conclusion and present future research issues in section 6.

---

[2] We have excluded the UML verification research and tool since they are not specific to UML activity diagram, and we have also excluded the research that extends the standard UML-AD and verifies it.

2   Preliminaries

2.1   Model Transformation

Model transformation technology is first used in Model-Driven Software Development and now it has a widely application in many research domains [26]. Two kind of model transformation methods have been identified in [27]: Horizontal transformation where the source and target models reside at the same abstraction level and vertical transformation where the source and target models reside at different abstraction levels. The key point of model transforming is the definition of transformation rules. Traditional model transformation methods usually define their transformation rules based on the meta-models of the source model and the target model. Transformation rules are the mapping relations between the elements in the meta-models of the source and target model in majority of cases.

Model transformation is used to bridge the gaps between different business process languages on a different level of abstraction in BPM. Lots of research work has been done to transform other business process modeling languages to YAWL [25, 28-31]. In [28, 29] BPMN (business process modeling notation) has been transformed into YAWL. In [30] EPC (Event-driven Process Chains) has been transformed into YAWL. In [31] BPEL has been transformed into YAWL. These transformations all aiming at the benefits from the verification tools based on YAWL since these modeling languages support advanced control-flow patterns such as or-join and cancel region and YAWL verification tools can verify these patterns[32].

Pattern-based model transformation is not a novel technique. Some researchers have earlier proposed the pattern-based transformation. They suggested selecting some certain model segment in the source model and transforming them to model segment in the target model. But how to determine these model segments (patterns) remains an unsolved problem. Most of current existing researches use design patterns to conduct the pattern-based model transformation when transforming PIM model to PSM model in a MDA environment. Graphic pattern was also used to transform a source graphical model to a target graphical model. This kind of pattern-based method only enlarges the operating granularity during the transformation (from element to model segment), it has no advantage in enhancing the conversion accuracy and ensuring the transforming correctness compared to the element-to-element method. Using the control-flow pattern based method proposed in this paper, we can expect a more precise and more "correct" result than the element-to-element method.

2.2   UML Activity Diagram

A business process model usually includes four parts of information: control aspect, data aspect, resource aspect and exception handling aspect. Since Woflan, WofYAWL and ProM mainly verify the control structures of YAWL model and our purpose is to check structural errors in UML-AD model (deadlock and etc.), we only show an analysis on how to transform control-flow aspect information to YAWL, other issues such as resources and exception handling is beyond this paper's scope.

Figure 1 is a simplified UML-AD meta-model that contains necessary meta-classes that are needed to model business processes and we will exclude the resource (the

ActivityPartation meta-class) and exception handling (the ExecptingHandler meta-class) aspects informations since they have no effects on the control structure correctness of business process model.

3   Meta-model Based Transformation

3.1   UML-AD Meta-model

In order to   define the element-to-element transformation rule, UML-AD meta-model and YAWL meta-model is needed. UML is a language defined under the MOF framework, UML-AD meta-model is described in [33] (chapter 11 and chapter 12). The meta-model is, however, scattered in many small segments and some meta-classes solve no purpose for transformation. In this paper we illustrate in Figure 1the recommended subset of UML-AD notation for process definition. Meta-classes in light color rectangles stand for meta-classes having no graphic notations and used as classifier. Meta-classes in dark color rectangle stand for meta-classes having graphic notations which are used in modelling. The details of attributions can be found in [33].

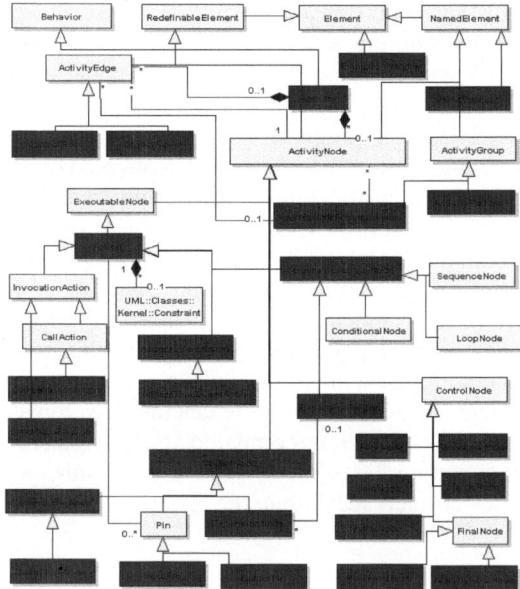

Fig. 1. UML-AD meta-model

3.2   YAWL Meta-model

Unlike UML-AD, YAWL is defined basing on a formal semantic of Petri net and it has no meta-model that fits the MOF framework. The YAWL graphic notations are shown in Figure 2.

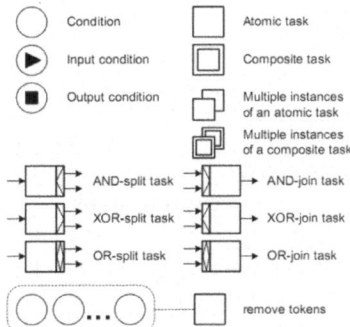

Fig. 2. YAWL notations

After a careful study of paper [13, 34] and the YAWL 2.1 system, we come up with a YAWL meta-model that includes all the notations and meta-classes (without graphic notation) as shown in figure 3. Meta-classes in light color rectangles stand for meta-classes having no graphic notations which are used as classifier. Meta-classes in dark color rectangle stand for meta-classes having graphic notations which are used in modeling. Due to the limitation on space, the attributions have been left out.

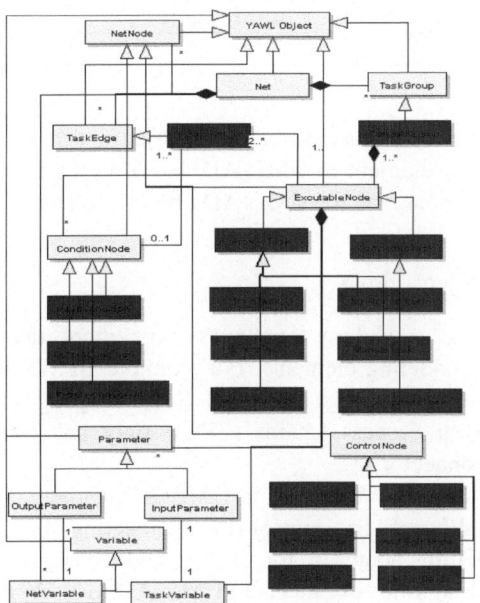

Fig. 3. YAWL meta-model

3.3   Element-to-Element Transformation Rule

Based on UML-AD meta-model and YAWL meta-model given in previous section, we can define an element-to-element mapping rule as shown in table 1.

Table 1. Element-to-element mapping rule

UML-AD Notation	YAWL Notation
StartNode&FinishNode	
InitialNode	InputCondition
ActivityFinalNode	OutputCondition
ExecutableNode	
Action	AtomicTask
SendSignalAction	AtomicTask
AcceptEventAction	EventTask
AcceptTimeEventAction	TimeTask
CallBehaviorAction	CompositeTask
ExpansionRegion	MultiInstanceCompositeTask
ControlNode	
ForkNode	And-SplitNode
JoinNode	And-JoinNode
DecisionNode	Xor-SplitNode
MergeNode	Xor-JoinNode
Edge(Flow)	
ControlFlow	ControlFlow
Containment	
Activity	Net

Not all notations have been listed in table 1. Note that there are no direct mapping relations between every element in UML-AD and YAWL. For example there are no corresponding YAWL notations for UML-AD object node and its subclasses.

3.4   Transform Object-Flows

Some business process modeling languages have more than one kind of flows connecting the basic modeling elements. For example BPMN has two types of flow namely sequence flow and message flow [35]. Some languages have only one kind of flow. The Event-driven Process Chains (EPCs) only has control flow connecting event, function and connector.

There are two kinds of activity edges in UML-AD, namely control flow and object flow [33]. While YAWL only has control flow connecting condition and task. YAWL has no graphic modelling notations for objects and object flow. How to transform object flow and different kinds of objects in UML-AD to YAWL is a big problem.

Objects and object flow are very important in UML-AD and there are several different kinds of object notations. These notations have been listed in figure 4. For more details about these notations refer to [33]. Not all object aspect informations will be transformed into YAWL since the majority of them have nothing to do with the control aspect informations.

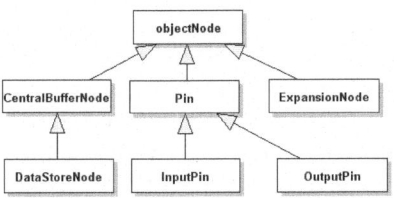

Fig. 4. Object notations in UML-AD

As a business process modeling language, YAWL has provided modeling mechanism to describe objects and data, as well as the movement of objects and data transfer. In YAWL, data-aspects information is modeled as variables. There are two types of variables namely net variable and task variable, both of which can have a variable type pre-defined or defined by the user. Task can have input parameters and output parameters, an input parameter defines a data transformation from a net variable to a task variable and an output parameter defines a data transformation from a task variable to a net variable. For more information about data aspect of YAWL, refer to [36], chapter 5.

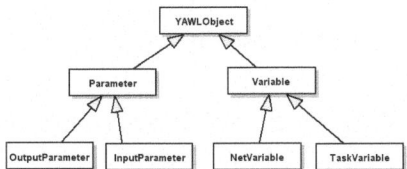

Fig. 5. Data aspect meta-classes in YAWL

When transforming object flows in UML-AD to YAWL, we first transform all the object nodes to the "pin" form and then we transform pins attached to actions and object flow related with them to YAWL data attached to tasks and control flow between the tasks. Object flow attributes like weight and effect have been omitted during the transformation since they have nothing to do with the control-flow information contained in object flows.

As an example, consider a UML-AD segment with object flow shown in figure 6.

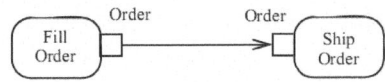

Fig. 6. UML-AD object flow example

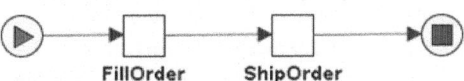

Fig. 7. Corresponding YAWL notations of figure 6

We can model this UML-AD segment in YAWL editor. The graphic notations have been shown in figure 7. And in order to model the object "order" between tasks "FillOrder" and "ShipOrder", we need to define a data type named "OrderType" in the YAWL net that contains these two actions as shown in figure 8 and a net variable named "Order" with that data type.   Then we define a task variable of task "FillOrder" and a task variable of task "ShipOrder" with the same name "Order", both of which have a data type of "OrderType". The transformation of "Order" then can be illustrated by two task parameters. One parameter is defined under task "FillOrder" with a parameter type "Out" to illustrate the flow of "Order" from the task "FillOrder" to the net and the other parameter is defined under task "ShipOrder" with a parameter type "In" to illustrate the flow of "Order" from the net to the task "ShipOrder".

```
<xs:schema xmlns:xs="http://www.w3.org/2001/XMLSchema">
  <xs:complexType name="OrderType">
   <xs:sequence>
     <xs:element name="OrderState" type="xs:enumeration{normal,final,pending}" />
   </xs:sequence>
  </xs:complexType>
</xs:schema>
```

Fig. 8. Data type definition of OrderType

4   Control-Flow Pattern Based Transformation

4.1   An Introduction to Control-Flow Pattern

Workflow pattern was first proposed by Van Aalst in 2003. In [37] Aalst systemically defined 20 workflow control-flow patterns. In 2006 Russell put forward a revised version of workflow control-flow patterns [38]. Shortly after the proposal of control-flow pattern, other workflow patterns like workflow data pattern [39, 40], workflow resource pattern [41, 42] and workflow exception pattern [43, 44] have also been identified.   For   more   information   about   workflow   patterns,   refer   to http://www.workflowpatterns.com/.

The research of workflow patterns have provided a thorough examination of various perspectives (control flow, data, resource, and exception handling) that need to be supported by a workflow language or a business process modeling language. The examined results can be used to evaluate the suitability of a particular process language or workflow system for a particular project, implement certain business requirements in a particular process-aware information system, and serve as a basis for language and tool development.

43 control-flow patterns are used to "guarantee" a "correct" transformation and enhance the precision of the transformation in this paper.   Control-flow patterns are divided into eight categories, the first and the most simple category is the basic control-flow patterns, which includes sequence, "Parallel Split", "Synchronization", "Exclusive Choice" and "Simple Merge". Figure 9 illustrates these five patterns in UML-AD. For detail description of these control-flow patterns, refer to [45].

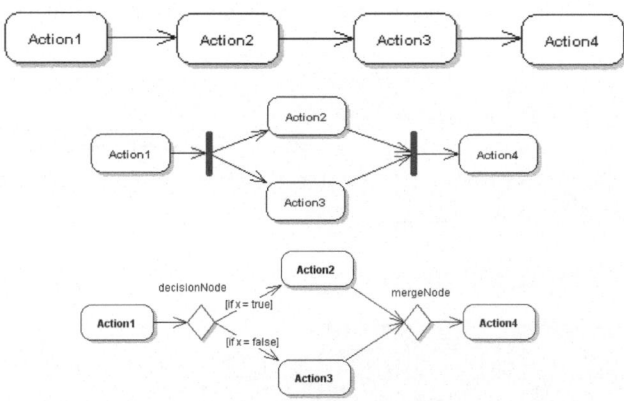

Fig. 9. Basic control-flow patterns in UML-AD

4.2 Control-Flow Patterns in UML-AD and YAWL

Neither YAWL nor UML-AD supports all the 43 control-flow patterns. For the patterns that are supported only by UML-AD, the control aspect informations that they stand for will be lost during the transformation, since they can't be described in YAWL. These patterns mainly belong to the categories of advanced branching and synchronization and trigger patterns; these patterns are colored as red in table 2. This implies the limits of YAWL when describing control aspect informations of business process model. An improved version of YAWL language has been proposed in [46], this new YAWL supports all the 43 control-flow patterns.

There are 10 patterns that are not supported by UML-AD though YAWL supports them. These patterns mainly belong to the category of advanced branching and synchronization and the category of state-based patterns. These are colored as light green in table 2. State-based patterns are not well supported since there are no notations representing state changing like a condition in YAWL.

Patterns that supported by both UML-AD and YAWL can be and should be transformed from UML-AD to YAWL without losing the control aspect information. But how to transform them properly remains a problem. After a thorough study of these patterns in UML-AD and YAWL, we identify 6 patterns that need to be transformed by a pattern-based way and 2 patterns that in some certain cases need to be transformed by a pattern-based way which are colored as orange in table 2. The patterns colored as green in table 2 represent those patterns that can be easily transformed using an element to element transformation. Detailed analysis will be given in the next section.

Besides these patterns, there are 3 patterns colored as blue in table 2 namely Pattern 22("Recursion"), Pattern 27("Complete Multiple Instance Activity"), and Pattern 36("Dynamic Partial Join for Multiple Instances") which are not supported by either UML-AD or YAWL.

Table 2. Control-flow pattern based evaluation of UML-AD and YAWL

No	Pattern	AD	YAWL	No	Pattern	AD	YAWL
	Basic Control			34	Static Partial Join for MI	-	+
1	Sequence	+	+	35	Cancelling Partial Join for MI	-	+
2	Parallel Split	+	+	36	Dynamic Partial Join for MI	-	-
3	Synchronization	+	+		**State-based Patterns**		
4	Exclusive Choice	+	+	16	Deferred Choice	+	+
5	Simple Merge	+	+	17	Interleaved Parallel Routing	-	+
	Advanced Branching & Synchronization			18	Milestone	-	+
6	Multi-Choice	+	+	39	Critical Section	-	+
7	Structured Synchronizing Merge	-	+	40	Interleaved Routing	-	+
8	Multi-Merge	+	+		**Cancellation and Force Completion**		
9	Structured Discriminator	+/-	+	19	Cancel Task	+	+
28	Blocking Discriminator	+/-	-	20	Cancel Case	+	+
29	Cancelling Discriminator	+	+	25	Cancel region	+	+
30	Structured Partial Join	+/-	-	26	Cancel MI Activity	+	+
31	Blocking Partial Join	+/-	-	27	Complete MI Activity	-	-
32	Cancelling Partial Join	+	-		**Iteration Patterns**		
33	Generalised AND-Join	-	+	10	Arbitrary Cycles	+	+
37	Local Synchronizing Merge	+/-	+	21	Structured Loop	+	+
38	General Synchronizing Merge	-	+	22	Recursion	-	-
41	Thread Merge	+	-		**Termination Patterns**		
42	Thread Split	+	-	11	Implicit Termination	+	+/-
	MI Patterns			43	Explicit Termination	+	-
12	MI without Synchronization	+	+		**Trigger**		
13	MI with a Priori Design-Time Knowledge	+	+	23	Transient Trigger	+	-
14	MI with a Priori Run-Time Knowledge	+	+	24	Persistent Trigger	+	-
15	MI without a Priori Run-Time Knowledge	-	+				

To achieve a + rating (direct support) or a +/- rating (partial support) the language should satisfy the corresponding evaluation criterion of the pattern. Otherwise a - rating (no support) is assigned. We use color gray to identify the 8 pattern categories. Blue color stands for patterns that not supported by both UML-AD and YAWL. Light green is used for patterns that UML-AD doesn't support. Red color represents the patterns that YAWL doesn't support. Green color stands for patterns that can be transformed by element-to-element mapping. Orange color stands for patterns that need to be transformed by pattern-based transformation.

4.3   Patterns Should Be Transformed by Pattern-Based Transformation

There are five basic control patterns that are supported by all BPM languages. Due to their simplicity it seems unnecessary to transform them by the complex pattern-based way. But a careful study reveals that this is not the case. If parallel split (pattern 2) and synchronization (pattern 3) is modeled in UML-AD in the way shown in figure 10 (a), there will be no problem if we transform these two patterns by an element-to-element mapping: action in UML-AD to atomic task in YAWL, ForkNode in UML-AD to And-Split Node in YAWL and JoinNode in UML-AD to And-Join Node in YAWL. Then we will get a YAWL net as shown in figure 10 (c). The YAWL net we obtained is correct as it is in "accordance" with the YAWL "syntax". We only need to first merge the Atomic Task 1 and AndJoin Task and then merge the AndSplit Task and Atomic Task 2 to finally get a result as shown in figure 10 (d).

UML-AD language grammar allows another form of these two patterns. Consider a model segment shown in figure 10 (b). This is another form of parallel split (pattern 2) and synchronization (pattern 3) and they can't be transformed via an element-to-element mapping to YAWL model segment as figure 10 (c) since the ForkNode and JoinNode has been omitted and we can't get the "AndJoinTask" and "AndSplitTask" in figure 10 (c). And only after we have got figure 10 (c) can we simplify it to figure 10 (d). So we can draw a conclusion that parallel split and synchronization in figure 10 (b) can't be transformed to figure 10 (c) by element-to-element mapping and a pattern-based transformation is needed. We need to first recognize parallel split and synchronization in this form and then transform them as a whole to YAWL segment as shown in figure 10 (d).

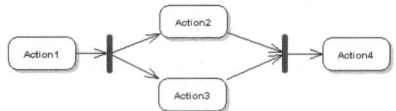

(a) Standard form of parallel split and synchronization in UML-AD

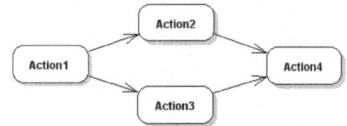

(b) Simplified form of parallel split and synchronization in UML-AD

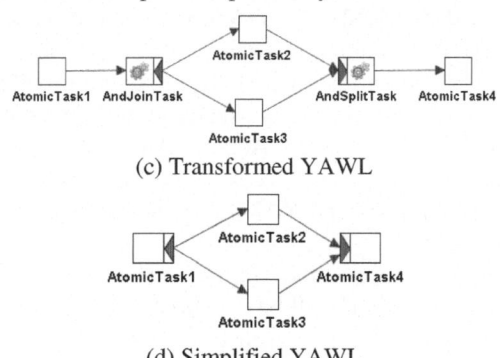

(c) Transformed YAWL

(d) Simplified YAWL

Fig. 10. Different forms of parallel split and synchronization in UML-AD and YAWL

Another pattern that needs a pattern-based transformation is the multi-choice pattern (pattern 6). This pattern provides the ability for the thread of execution to be diverged into several concurrent threads on a selective basis. The decision as to whether to pass the thread of execution to a specific branch is made at runtime. This pattern is essentially an analogue of the Exclusive Choice pattern (pattern 4) in which multiple outgoing branches can be enabled [47]. Since there is no specialized notation for multi-choice in UML-AD, ForkNode is used to achieve this pattern as shown in figure 11(a). It is different from the parallel split pattern since there are guards on each of the output control flows. In the example of figure 11, after execution Action1 will output a ValuePin named "x" and the value of x has been determined during the execution of Action1. It is passed to the ForkNode and the routing is then determined by the value of x. If x>10 Action2 and Action3 will be executed and if x<10, Action4 will be executed. This is different from Exclusive Choice (Pattern 4) since in Exclusive Choice the guards on each of the outgoing control flows after ForkNode must be mutually exclusive. This pattern also needs a pattern-based transformation to get a result YAWL net as shown in figure 11(b) because if we use an element-to-element mapping the ForkNode notation in Multi-Choice pattern will be mapped to a YAWL And-JoinTask resulting in a wrong output.

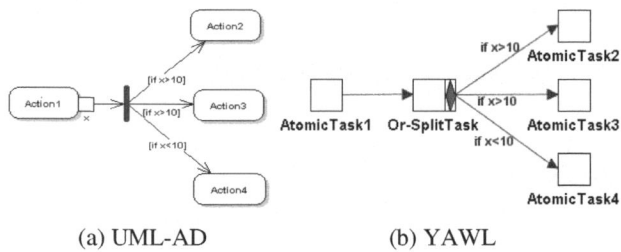

(a) UML-AD   (b) YAWL

Fig. 11. Multi-Choice (Pattern 6) in UML-AD and YAWL

Figure 12 is the multi instance without synchronization (pattern 12) in UML-AD and YAWL (refer to [6] and [36]). After Action1 (AtomicTask1), a multi-instance action namely "MIActionWithoutSychronization" (a MIAtomicTask named "MITaskWithoutSychronization") is created. The MI action (MITask) will create 10 instances of itself, leaving these instances executing and give the control-flow token to Action2(AtomicTask2) which means Action2(AtomicTask2) will start execution without the synchronization of any instances of the MI action (MI Task). Pattern 12 has a different form in UML-AD and YAWL due to the lack of specialized notation for MI actions in UML-AD.

As shown in figure 12(a), the initial value of x is 0, the action "MIActionWithoutSychronization" will be executed if x<10 so it will be executed 10 times and Action2 will not wait for the finish of its ten instances to start execution. The corresponding YAWL net is shown in figure 12(b). There is a specialized notation for MI actions in YAWL called MIAtomicTask having 4 parameters. The first parameter "10" means the task "MITaskWithoutSychronization" will have a minimum instance number of 10; the second parameter "10" means the task will have a maximum instance number of 10. So these two parameters define the instance number to be 10. The third parameter "0" means 0 instance of this MIAtomicTask needs to be synchronized and the last parameter "s" (short for static) indicates that new instances can not be created dynamically during the execution of any instances. For more information of MIAtomicTask, refer to [36].

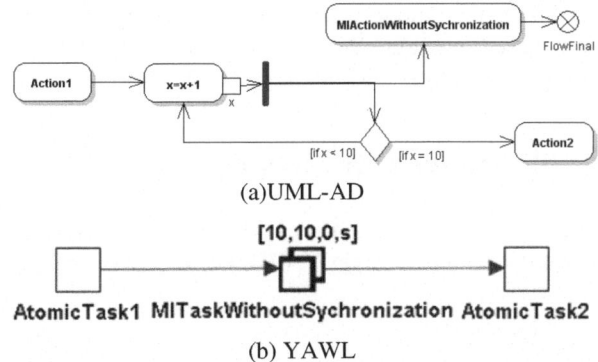

(a)UML-AD

(b) YAWL

Fig. 12. Multiple Instances without Synchronization (Pattern 12) in UML-AD and YAWL

InterruptibleActivityRegion can be used to model cancel-related patterns in UML-AD [6], whereas in YAWL CancelRegion is used to model these patterns. Element to element mapping transformation of these patterns will be troublesome. Due to the limited space we take cancel task (pattern 19) as an example to illustrate why a pattern-based transformation is needed and the other cancel patterns may be treated as same as cancel task pattern.

As shown in the UML-AD diagram of figure 13(a), the InterrruptibleActivityRegion has two actions in it: Action2 and Action3. Whereas in the corresponding YAWL net in figure 13(b), AtomicTask3 has a cancel region with only one task (AtomicTask2) in it (this is illustrated by the red point in the top right corner of the notation of AtomicTask3 and the red outline of AtomicTask2). So a pattern based transformation is also needed when transforming this pattern.

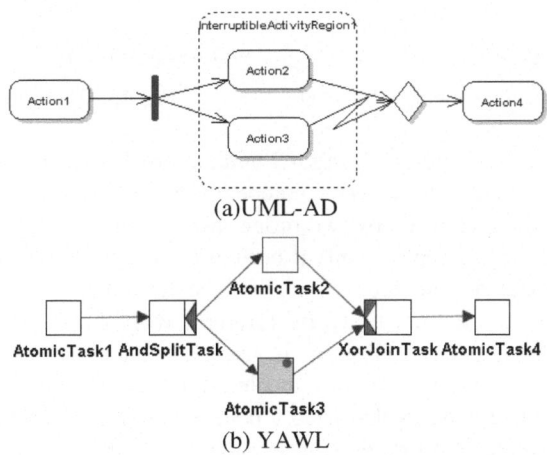

(a)UML-AD

(b) YAWL

Fig. 13. Cancel Task (Pattern 19) in UML-AD and YAWL

After patterns that need to be transformed by pattern-based method have been identified, we can pick them out of the source UML-AD model, transform the left parts to YAWL using a meta-model based method and then transform the pick-out parts via a pattern based method. We subsequently combine all the transformed YAWL segments together and get a whole target YAWL model.

5   Example Illustrating Our Method

In order to illustrate our methods we take a UML-AD model shown in figure 14 as a source model and transform it to a target YAWL net as shown in figure 15.

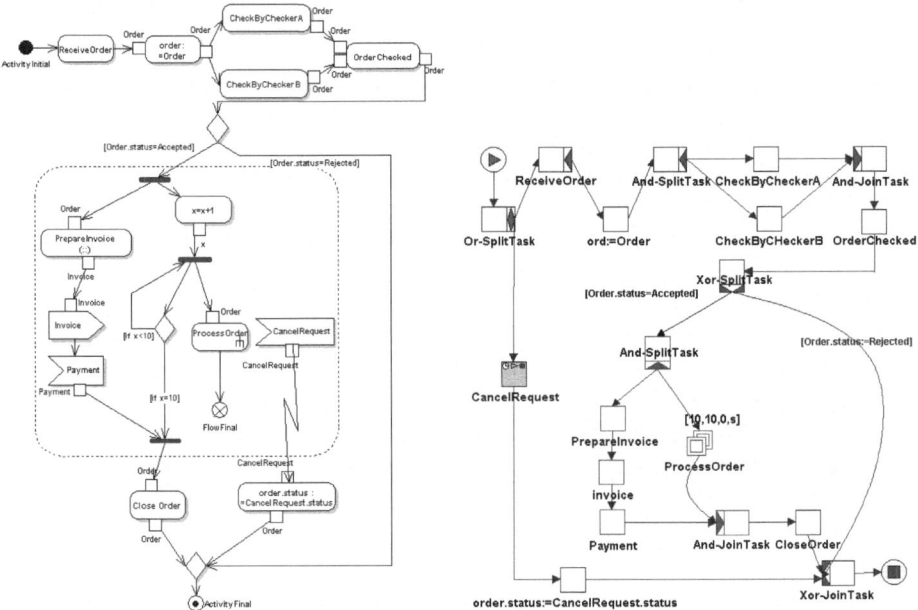

Fig. 14. An order process model in UML-AD   **Fig. 15.** The target YAWL net

On top left corner of figure 14, pattern 2 and pattern 3 are used in a form shown in figure 10 (b) except that there are pins attached to actions and the flow type is object flow. Orders need to be checked by two order checkers namely checker A and B. The status of Order will be "Accepted" only if both of the checkers accept it, otherwise the status will be "Rejected" and the activity will be terminated. The "ProcessOrder" action will be executed for ten times by different workers so it is a multi-instance action. An InterruptableActivityRegion is used as cancel region (pattern 25), the whole order-processing process can be canceled if a "CancelRequest" is received.

Since there are three patterns that need a pattern based transformation in the source UML-AD model, we have to first pick these patterns out and transform the left parts of the model to YAWL via a meta-model based meethod, that is, an element-to-element mapping and a transformation of object flow. Note that we have omitted the data aspect of the target YAWL net due to a limited space. Then we transform the picked-out patterns using a pattern based transformation. Element-to-element mapping and object flow transformation may also be used during this procedure. The final target YAWL net is as shown in figure 15. Note that there is an additional Or-Split Task in the target YAWL net connecting the InputConditon and the TimeTask "CancelRequest". This signifies a problem caused by the multi-start phenomenon in UML-AD. For details about this problem, refer to [25].

6   Conclusion and Future Work

In order to benefit from the mature verification tools (Woflan, WofYAWL, ProM) based on YAWL, UML Activity Diagrams need to be transformed to YAWL nets. Since our goal is to verify UML-AD model and to check if it contains structural errors like deadlock and lack of synchronization, therefore our study has been limited to transformation of control-flow aspect information only. A transformation method that transforms all information that can be transformed to YAWL is beyond our discussion.

Based on a proposed YAWL meta-model, this paper has solved the UML-AD to YAWL transformation problem by a three step method. First UML-AD object nodes and object flows are transformed into YAWL control flows by adding necessary data to the corresponding task nodes. Secondly all control-flow patterns that UML-AD supports are analyzed and classified based on their transformation either by element-to-element mapping or by pattern to pattern methods. Finally the remaining model segments are transformed by element-to-element mapping based on UML-AD meta-model and the proposed YAWL meta-model. Since this method is more precise than the method proposed in [25], we can expect a better result when verifying UML-AD models using YAWL verification tools.

The future work includes applying this control-flow pattern based transformation method to transform other business process modeling languages to YAWL to check if we can get better transformation results than other transformation methods [28-31]. More over we aim to use this transformation method to convert the large amount of UML-AD process models to YAWL and analyze them with verification tools such as Woflan, WofYAWL and ProM.

Acknowledgments. This work is supported by the National Basic Research Program of China 973 project No. 2007CB310803 and the National Natural Science Foundation of China under Grant No. 90818017.

References

1. Burlton, R.: Business process management: profiting from process, 1st edn. Sams, Indianapolis (2001)
2. ter Hofstede, A., et al.: Business Process Management: A Survey, p. 1019 (2003)
3. Hepp, M., et al.: Semantic Business Process Management: A Vision Towards Using Semantic Web Services for Business Process Management. In: IEEE International Conference on E-Business Engineering, pp. 535–540 (2005)

4. Smith, H., Fingar, P.: Business Process Management: The Third Wave. Meghan-Kiffer Press (2006)
5. Weske, M.: Business Process Management: Concepts, Languages, Architectures. Springer-Verlag New York, Inc., Secaucus (2007)
6. Russell, N., et al.: On the suitability of UML 2.0 activity diagrams for business process modelling. In: APCCM 2006. Australian Computer Society, Inc., Darlinghurst (2006)
7. Dong, Y., ShenSheng, Z.: Using π - calculus to Formalize UML Activity Diagram. In: IEEE International Conference on the Engineering of Computer-Based Systems, p. 47 (2003)
8. List, B., Korherr, B.: A UML 2 Profile for Business Process Modelling, pp. 85–96 (2005)
9. Korherr, B., List, B.: Extending the UML 2 Activity Diagram with Business Process Goals and Performance Measures and the Mapping to BPEL, pp. 7–18 (2006)
10. Eshuis, R., Wieringa, R.: Verification support for workflow design with UML activity graphs. In: ICSE 2002. ACM, New York (2002)
11. Baldan, P., Corradini, A., Gadducci, F.: Specifying and Verifying UML Activity Diagrams Via Graph Transformation, pp. 18–33 (2005)
12. Eshuis, R.: Symbolic model checking of UML activity diagrams. ACM Trans. Softw. Eng. Methodol., 1–38 (2006)
13. van der Aalst, W.M.P., ter Hofstede, A.H.M.: YAWL: yet another workflow language. Inf. Syst., 245–275 (2005)
14. van der Aalst, W.M.P., et al.: Design and Implementation of the YAWL System, pp. 281-305 (2004)
15. Hofstede, T.A.A., et al.: Modern business process automation: YAWL and its support environment. Springer (2010)
16. Verbeek, H.M.W., van der Aalst, W.M., ter Hofstede, A.H.: Verifying Workflows with Cancellation Regions and OR-joins: An Approach Based on Relaxed Soundness and Invariants (2007)
17. Wynn, M.T., van der Aalst, W.M.P., ter Hofstede, A.H.M., Edmond, D.: Verifying Workflows with Cancellation Regions and OR-Joins: An Approach Based on Reset Nets and Reachability Analysis. In: Dustdar, S., Fiadeiro, J.L., Sheth, A.P. (eds.) BPM 2006. LNCS, vol. 4102, pp. 389–394. Springer, Heidelberg (2006)
18. Wynn, M.T., van der Aalst, W.M.P., ter Hofstede, A.H.M., Edmond, D.: Verifying Workflows with Cancellation Regions and OR-Joins: An Approach Based on Reset Nets and Reachability Analysis. In: Dustdar, S., Fiadeiro, J.L., Sheth, A.P. (eds.) BPM 2006. LNCS, vol. 4102, pp. 389–394. Springer, Heidelberg (2006)
19. Wynn, M.T., et al.: Business Process Verification - Finally a Reality! Business Process Management Journal (2010)
20. Verbeek, H.M.W., van der Aalst, W.M.P.: Woflan 2.0 A Petri-Net-Based Workflow Diagnosis Tool. In: Nielsen, M., Simpson, D. (eds.) ICATPN 2000. LNCS, vol. 1825, pp. 475–484. Springer, Heidelberg (2000)
21. van der Aalst, W.M.P., van Dongen, B.F., Günther, C.W., Mans, R.S., Alves de Medeiros, A.K., Rozinat, A., Rubin, V., Song, M., Verbeek, H.M.W., Weijters, A.J.M.M.: ProM 4.0: Comprehensive Support for *Real* Process Analysis. In: Kleijn, J., Yakovlev, A. (eds.) ICATPN 2007. LNCS, vol. 4546, pp. 484–494. Springer, Heidelberg (2007)
22. Verbeek, H.M.W., Basten, T., van der Aalst, W.M.P.: Diagnosing Workflow Processes Using Woflan. The Computer Journal, 2001 (1999)
23. van Dongen, B.F., et al.: The ProM Framework: A New Era in Process Mining Tool Support, pp. 444–454 (2005)
24. Verbeek, E.: WofYAWL. Technical report (2005),
    http://home.tm.tue.nl/hverbeek/wofyawl03.pdf

25. Han, Z., Zhang, L., Ling, J.: Transformation of UML Activity Diagram to YAWL, pp. 289–299 (2010)
26. Sendall, et al.: Model transformation: The heart and soul of model-driven software development, p. 4 (2003)
27. Mens, T., Van Gorp, P.: A Taxonomy of Model Transformation. Electronic Notes in Theoretical Computer Science, 125–142 (2006)
28. JianHong, Y., et al.: Transformation of BPMN to YAWL. In: International Conference on Computer Science and Software Engineering (2008)
29. Decker, G., Dijkman, R., Dumas, M., García-Bañuelos, L.: Transforming BPMN diagrams into YAWL nets. In: Dumas, M., Reichert, M., Shan, M.-C. (eds.) BPM 2008. LNCS, vol. 5240, pp. 386–389. Springer, Heidelberg (2008)
30. Mendling, J., Moser, M., Neumann, G.: Transformation of yEPC business process models to YAWL. ACM, New York (2006)
31. Brogi, A., Popescu, R.: From BPEL Processes to YAWL Workflows. In: Bravetti, M., Núñez, M., Zavattaro, G. (eds.) WS-FM 2006. LNCS, vol. 4184, pp. 107–122. Springer, Heidelberg (2006)
32. Wynn, M.T., et al.: Business Process Verification - Finally a Reality! Business Process Management Journal (2010)
33. The Unified Modeling Language™(UML) specification version 2.3. 2010, Object Management Group.
34. van der Aalst, W.M.P., et al.: Design and Implementation of the YAWL System, pp. 281–305 (2004)
35. Business Process Modeling Notation (BPMN) Version 2.0, Object Management Group/Business Process Management Initiative (2009)
36. ter Hofstede: YAWL User Manual Version 2.0 (2009)
37. van der Aalst, W.M.P., et al.: Workflow Patterns. In: Distributed and Parallel Databases, pp. 5–51 (2003)
38. Russell, N., ter Hofstede, A.H.M., Mulyar, N.: Workflow ControlFlow Patterns: A Revised View (2006)
39. Russell, N., ter Hofstede, A.H.M., Edmond, D.: Workflow data patterns (2004)
40. Russell, N., et al.: Workflow Data Patterns: Identification, Representation and Tool Support, pp. 353–368 (2005)
41. Russell, N., et al.: Workflow resource patterns, Technische Universiteit Eindhoven, BETA (2005)
42. Russell, N., et al.: Workflow Resource Patterns: Identification, Representation and Tool Support, pp. 216-232 (2005)
43. Russell, N., ter Hofstede, A.H.M., van der Aalst, W.M.P.: Workflow Exception Patterns (2006)
44. Russell, N., ter Hofstede, A.H.M.: Exception Handling Patterns in Process-Aware Information Systems
45. Russell, N., ter Hofstede, A.H.M., Mulyar, N.: Workflow ControlFlow Patterns: A Revised View (2006)
46. Russell, N., van der Aalst, W.M.P., ter Hofstede, A.H.M.: New YAWL: designing a workflow system using coloured Petri Nets. Xidian University (2008)
47. Russell, N., ter Hofstede, A.H.M., Mulyar, N.: Workflow ControlFlow Patterns: A Revised View (2006)

MDA-Based Interoperability Establishment
Using Language Independent Information Models

Carlos Agostinho[1], Jaroslav Černý [1], and Ricardo Jardim-Goncalves[1,2]

[1] Centre of Technology and Systems, CTS, Uninova, 2829-516 Caparica, Portugal
[2] Departamento de Engenharia Electrotécnica, Faculdade de Ciências e Tecnologia, FCT,
Universidade Nova de Lisboa, 2829-516 Caparica, Portugal
{ca,rg}@uninova.pt

Abstract. Nowadays, more and more enterprises realize that one important step to success in their business is to create new and innovative products. Many times the solution to do that is to abandon the idea of an enterprise as an "isolated island", and get collaboration with others: worldwide non-hierarchical networks are characterized by collaboration and non-centralized decision making. This paper proposes a conceptual model common to the entire business network, in a framework that enables the abstraction of individual models at their meta-level and increase language independency and interoperability, keeping all the enterprise software's integrity intact. The strategy presented allows an incremental mapping construction, to achieve growing integration.

Keywords: MDA, MDE, Enterprise Interoperability, Model-Morphisms, Model and Data Transformations, Language Independent Information Models.

1   Introduction

Interoperability is a property directly related with the heterogeneity of model languages, communication capabilities, databases and semantics. Differences in these hide a great barrier to achieve the time-to-market symbiosis that can unleash a solution more valuable than the sum of its creators. Interoperability is more than just a communication support: it is a software approach to maximize the benefits of diversity, rather than to integrate the different system into one. Such diversity leads to more fruitful results than by just integrating different systems into one. Since many organizations developed and purchased software solutions based on their own needs, the required cooperation with others is not a trivial activity and business partnerships are less effective, evidencing low level of interoperability.

To solve this problem, instead of adopting a paradigm that obligates every organization to migrate their systems, or develop complex mappings in a single step to comply with these advanced practices, one can act at the communication module, where the data is exchanged. The authors propose Model Driven Architecture (MDA) based technologies for the development of transformations and execution of automatic and executable Model Morphisms (MoMo), also providing traceability and repeatability on them. The proposed framework enables to respond automatically to

M. van Sinderen et al. (Eds.): IWEI 2012, LNBIP 122, pp. 146–160, 2012.
© IFIP International Federation for Information Processing 2012

the network dynamics and its sustainability, i.e. changes that occur over the time and impact negatively the interoperable state can be tuned and balanced.

2   Model Driven Engineering

Model-Driven Engineering (MDE), sometimes also referred as Model-Driven Development (MDD), is an emerging practice for developing model driven applications. It represents a promising software engineering approach to address systems complexity, both by simplifying and formalizing the various activities and tasks that comprise an information system life cycle (i.e. from design, to construction, deployment, operation, maintenance and modification). Given today's increase of technology complexity, models are becoming a powerful mechanism to precisely describe problems in a way that avoids delving into technological details, thus allowing developers to focus on more abstract tasks and increasing productivity rather than to computing concepts. MDE is meant to maximize compatibility between systems, simplifying the process of design, and promoting communication between individuals and teams working on the system [1].

MDD/MDE's vision goes even further, invoking the unification principle, which states that *"everything is a model"* (i.e., platforms, components, legacy software, services, etc.), encouraging the support of models at different levels of abstraction, from high-level business models focusing on goals, roles and responsibilities down to detailed use-case and scenario models for business execution [2, 3]. These models are developed through extensive communication among product managers, designers, and members of the development team, and as they approach completion, enable a fast development of product and systems. However, despite obvious potential capabilities for closely matching the EI holistic levels, yielding major productivity and reliability benefits, there is not yet consensus about its technology readiness [4, 5].

2.1   Model-Driven Architecture (MDA)

Among the several realizations of the MDE/MDD principles that exist, such as Agile Model Driven Development [4, 6], Domain-oriented Programming [7], Microsoft's Software Factories [8] and Model Driven Architecture [9, 10], MDA is perhaps the most prevalent at the moment. Since it was launched, in 2001, MDA has been having a major impact on the software development community, and presently, there is a large landscape of tools available for its support.

MDA has as its foundation on three complementary ideas: direct representation, automation and open standards. The first makes use of abstract models to represent ideas and concepts of the problem domain, reducing the semantic gap existing between domain-specific concepts and the technologies used to implement them. The second uses model transformation tools to automate the translation process from high level specifications and formal descriptions of the systems, to the bottom levels and implementation code, therefore increasing speed, code optimization and avoiding human errors in the process. Regarding the last foundation, MDA enforces the usage of open standards to specify the high level models, and the features of the target implementation platforms, promoting interoperability among the entire ecosystem of tool vendors [3, 11].

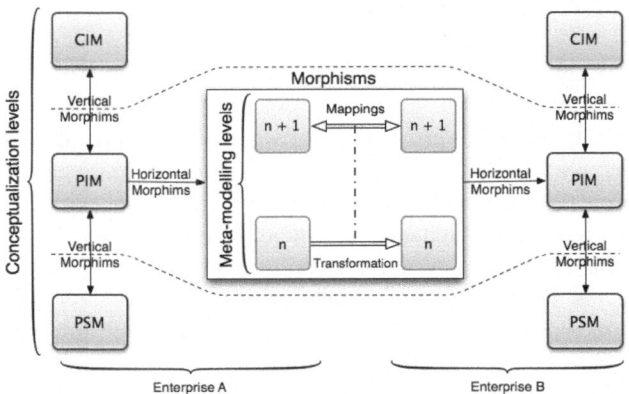

Fig. 1. MDA's Conceptualization Levels and Transformation Types (adopted from [12])

An MDA system can be observed and analyzed from different points of view (see Fig. 1), and in order to support the supra-cited foundations it defines a hierarchy of models at three different levels of information abstraction [13]: (i) Computation Independent Model (CIM), which specifies the requirements for the system and the environment where it will operate. It's also called a domain model since it's meant for the domain practitioners and it's based on the vocabulary of the specific target domain; (ii) Platform Independent Model (PIM), which is the formal specification of the structure and functionality of the system that abstracts away technical details. More concretely, it focuses on the operation details while hiding specific details of any particular platform in order to be suitable for use with several different platforms; (iii) Platform Specific Model (PSM) that combines the specification in the PIM model with details that specify how the system uses a particular type of platform. Thus, a PSM adds to the PIM, technical details and implementation constructs that are available in a specific implementation platform, including middleware, operating systems and programming languages (e.g. Java, C++, EJB, XML, Web Services, etc).

2.2   Model Transformations

Based on model transformations, the MDA unifies every step of the development of an application or integrated suite from its start as a CIM of the application's business requirements through PIM defined functions and behavior, one or more PSMs, to generated code and a deployable application. The PIM remains stable as technology evolves, extending and thereby maximizing software return on investment. Portability and interoperability are built into the MDA architecture, which also introduces the distinction between vertical and horizontal transformations (evidenced in Fig. 1).

Vertical Transformations: Imply a change on the abstraction level of the resulting model, e.g. going from PSM to PIM implies a generalization transformation, and from PIM to PSM implies a specialization transformation. The amount of generated code depends on both the code generator and also the level of detail represented in the PSMs (i.e. how well the PSM captures the details of the physical platform). Ideally, only small portions of missing code should have to be added by the human developer in order to ensure that the generated code and auxiliary files are ready for compilation, linking and deployment.

However, today, MDA vertical transformations are still an open issue. Incomplete applications have been developed from CIM to PIM due to the lack of efficient tools and methods for transformation [14]. For this purpose, new concepts, methods and tools are necessary.

Horizontal Transformations: In this case (e.g. refactoring of individual models, language translation, or even joining different models), the level of abstraction remains unchanged, leading to solutions for interoperability problems at the same enterprise level [15]. Both input and output models must be an instance of a well-defined meta-model, and have to be classifiable according to the meta-modelling level they belong to. Due to that, greater interoperability benefits but also harder complications are expected in horizontal transformations, since at the time of the transformation specification (mapping), one has to be concerned with different language-related specificities [12]. In fact, different languages might enable to describe the same objects with different detail levels (e.g. properties, constraints, etc.).

With horizontal transformations, companies can specify P2P mappings to translate any data from one format to the other, thus allowing an exchange of information. When performing this type of transformation (e.g. converting instances of a model to instances of another model) an explicit or an implicit mapping of the meta-model has to be performed. Thus, as depicted in Fig. 1, the idea is that when performing a transformation at a certain level "n", this transformation has (implicitly or explicitly) to be designed by taking into account mappings at level "n+1". Once the "n+1" level mapping is complete, executable languages can be used to implement the transformation, e.g. ATL[1] and the QVT[2]. This is valid either for CIM, PIM or PSM models.

Horizontal transformations, which are targeted in this paper's research, are traditionally static processes that once defined can be repeated any number of times achieving the same results. The major difficulty is defining them while supporting network dynamicity, joining the efforts of business and technical specialists at reduced costs.

3   Model Morphims (MoMo)

The concept of morphism is described in mathematics as an abstraction of a structure-preserving map between two mathematical structures [16]. Recently, this concept is gaining some meaning in computer science, more exactly in systems interoperability.

---

[1] ATL – Atlas Transformation Language (www.eclipse.org/m2m/atl/)
[2] QVT – Query View Transformation (www.omg.org/spec/QVT/)

This new meaning of Morphism describes the relations (e.g. mapping, merging, transformation, etc.) between two or more information specifications as the ones needed to define MDA horizontal transformations.

In this context, the research community identifies two core classes of MoMo: non-altering and model altering morphisms [15]. In the first, given two models (source *A* and target *B*), a mapping is created relating each element of the source with a correspondent element in the target, leaving both models intact. In model altering morphisms, the source model is transformed using a function that applies a mapping to the source model and outputs the target model. Other relations, such as the merge operation, can also be classified as model altering morphisms, however they are not detailed in this paper.

3.1   MoMo Formalization

The research community has developed many proposals to morphisms formalization [15]. Graph theory has been used in some, although other theories can be considered to achieve the envisaged goals, e.g., set theory [17], model management [18], or semantic matching [19]. However there is not a single perfect solution that can be used to achieve all the morphisms goals at once. Some are ideal for structural issues, others for semantics providing good human traceability, and others are more formal and mathematical based. Agostinho et al. ([20]) proposes a 5-tuple mapping expression, with the objective to consolidate and complement existent approaches:

$$MapT: <ID, MElems, KMType, MatchClass, Exp> \tag{1}$$

- *ID* is the unique identifier of the MapT;
- *MElems* is the pair (a,b) that indicates the mapped elements in the source and destination models;
- *KMType* stands for Knowledge Mapping Type, and is used to identify the morphism as "Conceptual" if mapping concepts or terms; "Structural" if mapping model schemas; or "InstantiableData" if the mapping instantiable properties;
- *MatchClass* stands for Match/Mismatch Classification and is used to classify with reference data, knowledge about the mapping mismatches, i.e., inconsistencies of information that can appear when a mapping between two models is created, derived from the multiple conflicts between the entities;
- *Exp* stands for the mapping expression that translates and further specifies the previous tuple components.

The idea of using a tuple brings many advantages, e.g. being human traceable and readable, adding knowledge concerning mismatch. When used by intelligent systems, the tuple's information enables automatic data transformations and exchange between two organizations working with/on different information models. Therefore, it was decided that the tuple would represent morphism in the framework proposed.

According to the tuple philosophy, all the information about the mappings should be stored in a dedicated knowledge base so that it becomes computer processable, and readjustments can be easier to manage and data exchange re-established automatically in a sustainable environment. To reach these objectives, Sarraipa et al. [19, 20] proposed the Communication Mediator (CM), and also proposed that all the business partners in the same collaboration network it embedded in their local system.

3.2   Graphical Representation of Mapping Morphisms

In addition to the formalization, also models visualization is important. Frequently information modeling languages are associated to very specific and technically driven graphical representations which damage the abstraction purposed behind modeling.

Graphical browsing of standard models and product data visualization, play important roles in the interoperability achievement, and should be considered in MoMo frameworks. When in the development and implementation stages of an information model, it is frequently necessary to have an easy view and graphical understanding of the full scope of the model. The same happen in the mapping establishment. Thus, non-technical visual representation facilitates the understanding of the reference model, and the abstraction levels that a visual object may represent, brings a suitable and attractive mechanism to understand, navigate and manage the contents of the model, and the model structure itself [21].

For example, nowadays, browsing approaches have been used to assist in the development of some product data standards (e.g. STEP [22]). Efforts towards this kind of visualization were first noticed in XML editors with the introduction of grid layouts. Nevertheless, other more promising technologies exist for these purposes, like hyperbolic tree representation and graph representation. In the first (hyperbolic tree), a tree-like three dimensional hierarchical structure visualization of the information is given, providing the possibility to have represented levels of abstraction with expand/collapse functionalities. Sometimes, despite being technology independent, this type of visualization becomes rapidly complex when models are too large. The second, interactive graph-based representations also do not impose any kind of restrictions on the relationships between the nodes and are considerably more widespread with examples available in many commercial and open source solutions (Microsoft Visio ®, Annas[3], JGraph[4], JUNG[5], etc..)

4   MDA-Based Framework for Interoperability Establishment

In order to materialize the vision of being able to put aside the low-level implementation details and have domain experts defining interoperability through the use of language independent information models, a framework based on the four levels of the model-driven architecture, relating meta-models, information models and data is presented in Fig. 2.

---

[3] https://sites.google.com/site/annasproject/Home
[4] http://www.jgraph.com/jgraph.html
[5] http://jung.sourceforge.net/

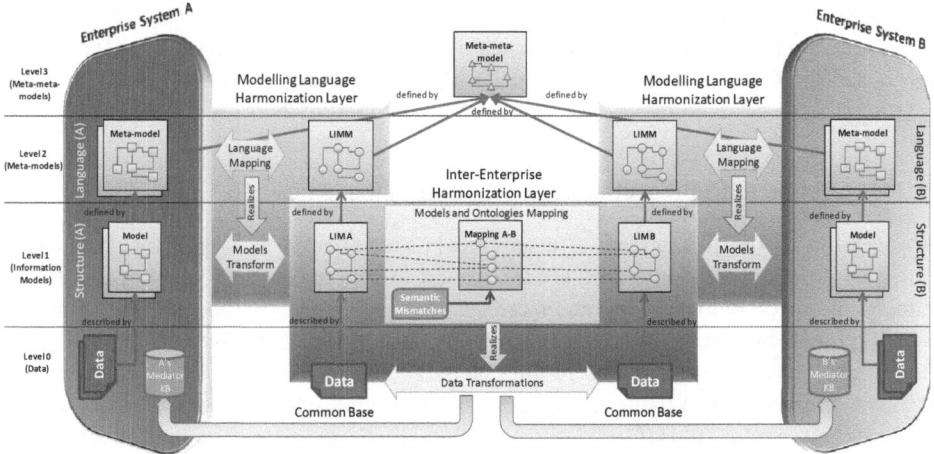

Fig. 2. MDA-based Framework for Interoperability Establishment

The left and right-hand sides of Fig. 2 represent two different organization's information systems with different internal legacy models, where information is presented following the model- language-meta-model. The core of the architecture is focused on the middle part of the figure, enabling two complementary layers, i.e. the modeling language harmonization layer and the inter-enterprise harmonization layer:

- The first (boundaries shared with the enterprises), is focused on the definition of mapping morphisms at the meta-model level, i.e. the modeling language used in each information model. It is therefore the layer realizing the transformation of models from one language to the other, which in our case, is used as an intermediate step for interoperability establishment. Enterprise system models, standards or even reference ontologies are transformed to their abstract interfaces (and vice-versa) using metadata descriptions (the Language Independent Meta-Model - LIMM, presented in next section 4.3) similar to the suggested in ISO/IEC 11179 Metadata Registries (MDR) [23].
- The last (center), works sequentially after the first and is responsible for the model and semantics harmonization, defining mapping morphisms among the different abstract model interfaces (LIMs). The process includes storing this knowledge in a CM knowledge base (as the one of [20]) replicated by the involved organizations, which serving as a standard during the mapping establishment will support the package for sustaining systems interoperability.

The architecture makes use of MDA's horizontal transformations to support the harmonization of modeling languages, models and data levels, within a platform independent context.

4.1   Model Morphisms

Model morphisms are used across the multiple harmonization layers and throughout the MDA levels: Level 2 – language mapping; Level 1 – models and ontologies mapping, as well as the model transformation morphims; Level 0 – data transformation morphisms.

The MoMo's associated with the mappings are model non-altering $"\theta(A,B)"$, which are described by mapping tables for each modelling language linked to the LIMM. These mappings are then implemented using an executable language, realizing the model altering morphisms (transformations $"\tau: A \times \theta \rightarrow B"$) on the respective inferior level. Since there are not so many modeling languages available, level 2 mappings are expected to be pre-defined and transformation scripts relatively static as changes in modeling languages specification is not common. They can be updated, but the mechanism for doing so is not envisaged to be as dynamic as the model and ontology mappings from the intra-enterprise harmonization layer (level 1).

4.2   Modeling Language Harmonization Layer

As specified, this architecture layer is responsible for translating information models. Mappings here defined are accomplished by establishing a correspondence, at the meta-model level (level 2 of the MDA), between any specific language constructs and the language independent metadata, enabling bidirectional transformations at any enterprise information model (level 1).

By being able to transform any given input back and forth to the LIM format (LIM meta-model - LIMM), the architecture accomplishes the objective of modeling language independency, helping enterprises to further abstract from technology. To unleash it, executable rules can be applied to transform any N-1 level, according to the Nth level of the mapping. This way, one can represent multiple models according to LIMM (level 2) and, if there is a mapping defined between each input modeling language and the latter, multiple models from multiple languages can be represented by equal number language independent models (LIM).

The language mapping procedure is a manual process since meta-models must be analyzed and mapped between them by experts, but the language transformations are always automatic and repeatable. Given that each language map is done only once independently of the number of times it is used or executed, it is an acceptable cost.

4.3   Language Independent Meta-Model (LIMM)

LIMM serves as an abstract interface on top of enterprises' information models. Through its usage, becomes possible to abstract the technology and implementation details associated with the different modeling languages, and thus, enlarge the scope of users involved in a traditional mapping definition activity. Having manager and domains experts involved in this process increases the quality of the mappings that will enable interoperable relationships. In comparison to most modeling languages, it is intended to enable as little loss of expressiveness as possible, but at the same time, be simple and generic to support multiple language mappings.

Also, LIMM resemblances with ISO/IEC 11179 [23] standard are not by fortuity. This abstract interface was based on the standard's foundations and concepts in order to give support to mechanisms for enabling global data interchange, particularly across application areas. A bridge between major LIMM concepts and ISO/IEC 11179 can be made, e.g. the standard's "Entity", "Property" and "Representation" concepts correspond to LIMM's "Entity_Concept", "Property" and "Representation" constructs, respectively. The language independent meta-model proposed is described as an UML class diagram in Fig. 3.

Many of the information modeling languages, e.g. EXPRESS [24], UML class infrastructure [25], OWL and XSD specification [26, 27] have been analyzed in detail and they were the focus of the attention to create this comprehensive meta-model and, as far the mappings defined for those languages demonstrate, LIMM is able to support them with little loss of expressiveness. In resemblance to what happens in the OWL language, LIMM is capable of representing both models and data levels of MDA (Level 1 and Level 0, respectively), enabling the combined transformation of both levels at the same time, or each independently if required. With this, not only the meta-model is prepared to deal with harmonization of modeling languages, but is also capable of representing instances of models, meaning that it can be used as an intermediate platform for data harmonization (represented by the "LIMM_Instances" package, on the bottom).

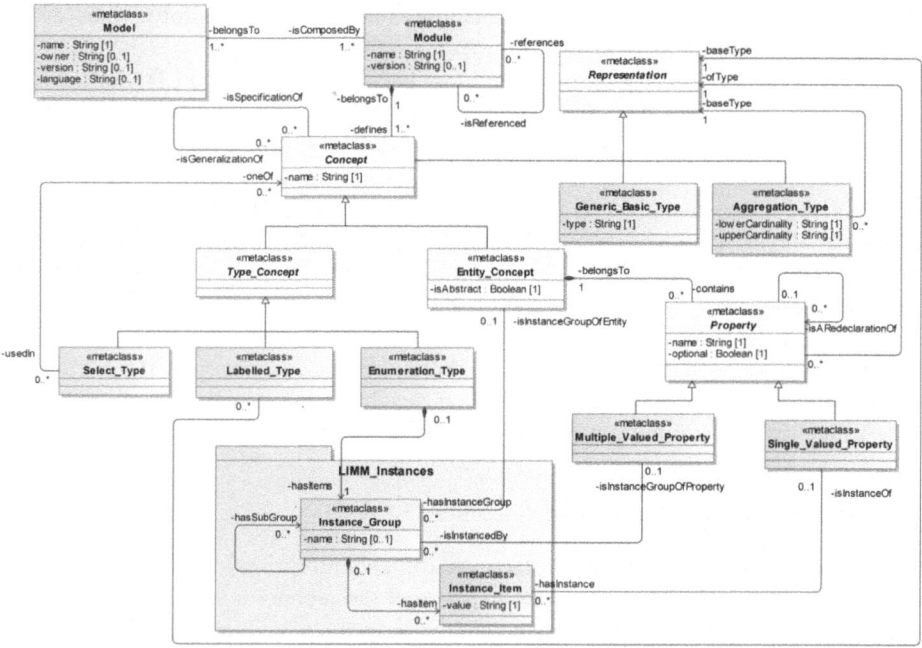

Fig. 3. Language Independent Meta-model (LIMM)

Concerning modeling concepts, the meta-model considers the representation of entities, types, properties, basic types, aggregations, etc. Nevertheless, some languages (e.g. EXPRESS) enable explicit behavioral expressions (instantiation rules) and functions, which are not supported. However, they are considered non-fundamental for the envisaged mapping process which is mainly focused on the information model mapping at the level 1 of the framework.

4.4   Inter-Enterprise Harmonization Layer

Once all modeling languages from the different enterprises involved in the mapping definition are harmonized with the LIMM, and the models made available as LIMs, experts from each company should begin cooperating to define the actual P2P, P2Standard or P2Ontology mapping definition. As specified in the center of Fig. 2, the inter-enterprise harmonization layer is responsible for this activity, following the same MDA horizontal transformation paradigm as before, and enabling automating transformations at the level N-1.

Besides the traditional connectivity, the semantic mismatches, found along the various model elements being mapped, are a very important topic regarding the experts' collaboration. Many of the mapping morphisms will be imperfect due to a number of factors that can go from a simple encoding difference in equivalent properties to a granularity divergence. These can never be solved, but for change management and sustainability this is an important issue and the proposed architecture takes this in consideration, registering the complementarity between the model element correspondence and the semantic mismatch.

The mappings realized at this point do not suffer from the extra complexity of dealing with multi-modeling languages, focusing just on the business related constructs and easing the process of harmonizing the semantic and structure level of models and ontologies. As a result of the entire process, generation of transformation morphisms for data from different enterprise nodes, or even to a reference format, is achieved, thus establishing interoperability.

Each pair of morphims (mappings and transformations) is stored on dedicated Communication Mediators. The objective is that each organization keeps its own CM to track relationships of their inner-elements with its business partner ones, thus maintaining a traceable record of relationships to support monitoring and intelligence activities of the package for sustaining systems interoperability, as well as "on-the-fly" composition of transformations. MoMos defined at the modeling language harmonization layer could also be stored on each CM. However, those transformations are only used to enable the inter-enterprise mapping process, and do not have the same need for dynamicity nor monitoring. The union of the two transformations (for each direction of communication) unleashes the capability of, both automatic and transparently, communicate and collaborate with other organizations, with different modeling languages, models, semantics and ontologies.

The complete automatic data exchange and translation can be accomplished between different model instances at the MDA level 0, thus completing the base for sustainable systems interoperability. Also, since all mappings of level 1 can be stored on a local knowledge base, it enables to gradually add more mappings with other partnering organizations and even to edit or delete past mappings. This provides the required adaptability of the framework to small collaboration networks, and being able to escalate to larger scenarios.

Although the MDA-based framework for interoperability establishment proposes a complete solution to enable the model and language independency in multi-sized business networks, it is more focused in enabling the harmonization of the heterogeneous information models from the multiple organizations involved in the collaboration network. Semantics analysis through terminology mapping is also possible but, the further refinement of semantic interoperability is not in the scope of this paper.

5   Proof-of-Concept Implementation

Given the context of MDA, QVT is the standard transformation language proposed by OMG. However, considering the languages analyzed, ATL has currently the largest user-base and the most extensive information available such as reference guides, tutorials, programmers' forums, etc. As evidenced by [28], it is a largely used language to implement MDA based tools, having a specific development toolkit plug-in available in open source[6]. By all these reasons it was decided to use ATL to implement model and language transformations in the scope of the MDA-based framework for interoperability establishment.

The proof-of concept (POC) here described, is focused on the implementation details as required by an industrial case-study in the frame of the European Project CRESNDENDO [29], which among other modeling languages is concerned with OWL. This way, Fig. 4 is focused on step required to instantiate the framework previously presented with information models described in that language.

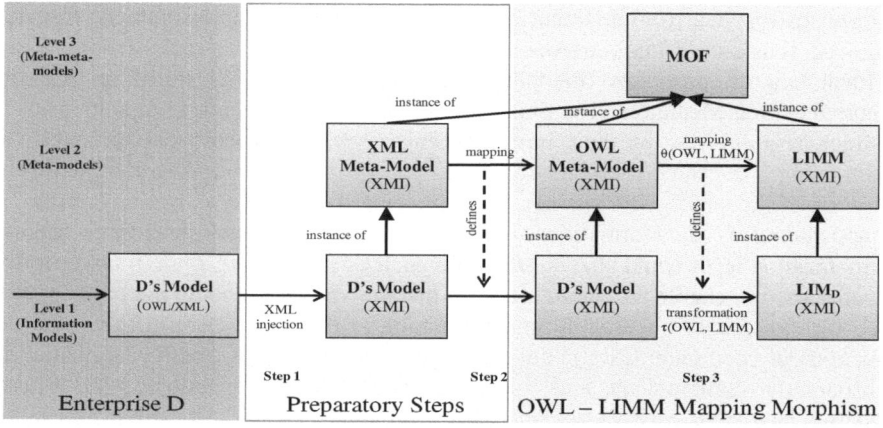

Fig. 4. OWL Instantiation of the Modeling Language Harmonization Layer

5.1   Modeling Language Harmonization Layer

To enable a mapping among the OWL meta-model [30] and the LIMM, one needs firstly to put the OWL data in an XMI serialization following the OWL meta-model specifications. Nevertheless the procedure to do so is not as straightforward as desirable since, in spite of the inputting OWL model is already XML serialized, it cannot be directly processed by the ATL toolkit which needs XMI as an input. The

---

[6] Eclipse Modelling Project - http://www.eclipse.org/modeling/

complete process for accomplishing the language mapping test case is illustrated in Fig. 4, where the first step consists in doing an injection of the original model to an XML MOF meta-model specification. Following that, the second preparatory step consists in mapping that XML format to the reference OWL meta-model which will be the starting point for the actual $\theta(OWL, LIMM)$ language mapping (step 3).

According to the architecture specified in section 4, the language transformation is a direct consequence of the mapping. In fact, by using ATL as the MDA language, one is at the same time specifying the mapping and defining the transformation rules (illustrated under step 3).

5.2   Inter-Enterprise Harmonization Layer

LIMM has the unusual capacity of storing both model and data instances within the same physical file, in resemblance to what happens with OWL. It potentiates the actual data transformation at a language independent form as well, thus avoiding the definition of mapping morphisms at this abstract level, which would have to be reengineered back to the original model languages. This integration of model and data maintains a forward flow of activities from company "X" to the abstract interface, and from there to the company "Y". However, as illustrated in Fig. 5, before the definition of the model mapping (step 5), similar steps as the ones conducted for the modeling language harmonization layer need to be followed to append data into the LIM model (step 4). For this TC, since enterprise "A" was already part of the network, that preparatory step 4 is not required.

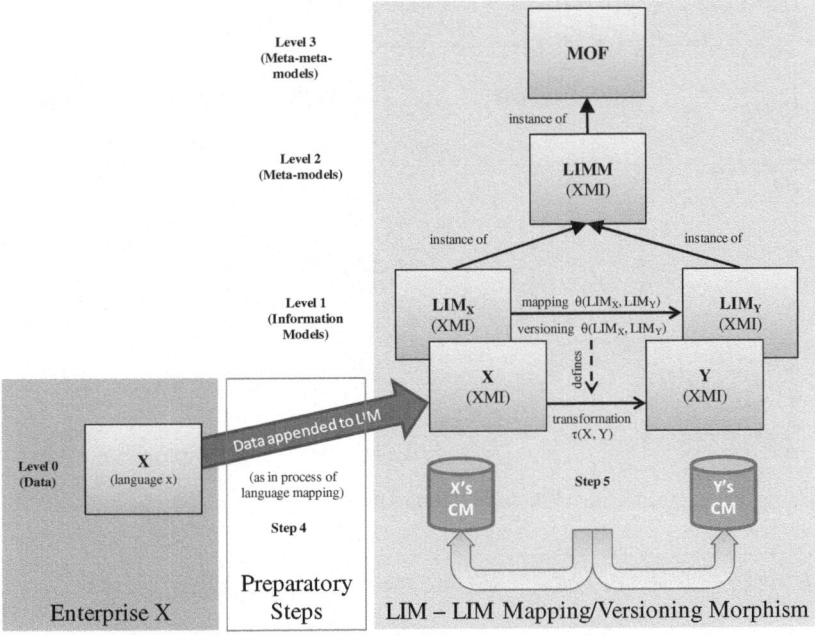

Fig. 5. Instantiation of the Inter-Enterprise Harmonization Layer

It is very important to preserve the user's technology abstraction, envisaged by LIMM, thus the mapping process is supported by a collaborative tool capable of visualizing and interacting with models and concepts in a way that model element' relationships and dependencies are easily understood by domain actors with no knowledge of technical rules. For this purpose, graph-like visualization tools have been analyzed, not being associated with other types of technical diagrams (e.g. UML, etc.). As in the language transformation, data transformation is a direct consequence of the mapping.

5.3   Mapping Tool

JGraph has been elected and modified to read LIM model files and store morphisms at the CM. It is a widely used open source project for graph visualization and manipulation, similar to Microsoft Visio®, with good documentation and several examples. Features include a complete selection of layouts to automatically position the graph, many styles of shapes and edges, validation of connections, as well as an undo and redo manager. Naturally, some adjustments had to be made to enable the interaction (mapping definition) among two different graphs, and to become integrated with LIMM's *Entity_types*, *Type_Concepts*, and *Instance_Groups*. A JAVA binder (JAXB[7]) was included to allow the unmarshalling (interpretation) of LIM files, and JENA[8] - a Java API for OWL providing services for model representation, parsing, database persistence, querying - was used for the integration with the communication mediator.

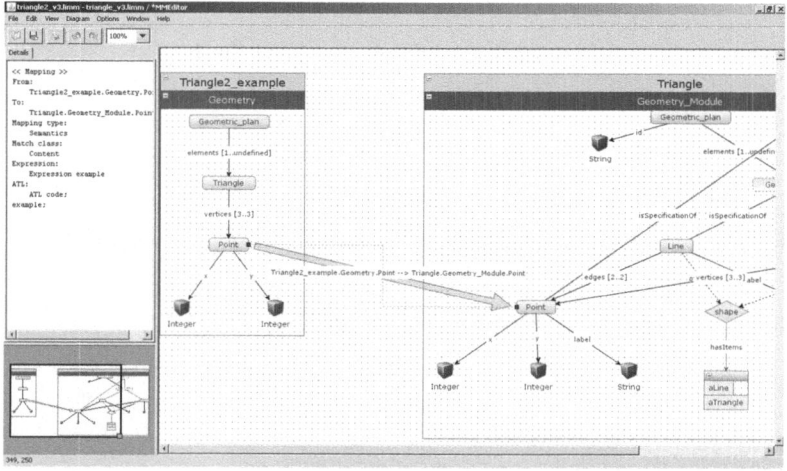

Fig. 6. Mapping Tool Snapshot

---

[7] JAXB: http://www.oracle.com/technetwork/articles/javase/index-140168.html

[8] Available at: http://protege.stanford.edu/plugins/owl/jena-integration.html

A snapshot of the tools in included in Fig. 6 where is possible to see two information models represented using very simple shapes, metadata of the selected object on the left, and the mapping linking both model objects. The complete that can be defined between both models is represented not only graphically. It can be edited according to the formalization tuple described in section 3.1 – equation 1, and complemented with the required ATL code.

6   Conclusions and Future Work

The proposed conceptual framework envisages that enterprises willing to join a collaboration network do not have to change their legacy software. The choice of MDA/MDI as the enabling technology for the interoperability establishment is motivated by morphisms modularity and repeatability through the existing landscape of tools available to support horizontal and vertical transformations. Depending on the initial situation (i.e. already having a legacy system, or wanting to develop a new one), either of these methods can prove to be the more efficient to establish interoperability, thus allowing a seamless exchange of information among partners.

This branch of applied research could be explored in the future, checking the feasibility of creating smaller, more parameterized software or services developed specifically for managing networked business relationships. Nevertheless, since there are scarce implementations of transformations from context independent models (CIM), where the business requirements are specified, to platform independent models (PIM), where the information structure is detailed, new concepts, methods and tools are demanded to cover this gap.

Acknowledgments. Authors would like to acknowledge the European funded Project UNITE (FP7 248583), namely its secondment programme coordinated by UNINOVA-GRIS, that supported the development of various ideas and concepts presented in this. Also, recognition goes to all the involved in CRESCENDO FP7-234344 and MSEE FP7-284860 that in somehow have contributed to this work.

References

1. Selic, B.: The pragmatics of model-driven development (2003)
2. Bézivin, J.: Model Driven Engineering: An Emerging Technical Space. In: Lämmel, R., Saraiva, J., Visser, J. (eds.) GTTSE 2005. LNCS, vol. 4143, pp. 36–64. Springer, Heidelberg (2006)
3. Frankel, D.: Model Driven Architecture – Applying MDA to Enterprise Computing. OMG Press (2003)
4. Ambler, S.W.: Agile Model Driven Development Is Good Enough. IEEE Software 20, 71–73 (2003)
5. Czarnecki, K., Helsen, S.: Feature-based survey of model transformation approaches. IBM Systems Journal 45, 621–645 (2006)
6. Ambler, S.W.: Effective Practices for Modeling and Documentation, http://www.agilemodeling.com/

7. Thomas, D., Barry, B.M.: Model Driven Development: The Case for Domain Oriented Programming. In: OOPSLA 2003. ACM Press (2003)
8. Greenfield, J., Short, K., Cook, S., Kent, S.: Software Factories: Assembling Applications with Patterns, Models, Frameworks, and Tools. Wiley (2004)
9. MDA Guide Version 1.0.1 (omg/2003-06-01). Object Management Group (2003)
10. OMG: Model Driven Architecture, http://www.omg.org/mda/
11. Delgado, M.: Harmonisation of STEP and MDA conceptual models using Model Morphisms, MSc Thesis (2008)
12. Agostinho, C., Correia, F., Jardim-Goncalves, R.: Interoperability of Complex Business Networks by Language Independent Information Models. In: CE 2010. Springer, Cracow (2010)
13. Berre, A.-J., Liu, F., Xu, J., Elvesæter, B.: Model Driven Service Interoperability through Use of Semantic Annotations. In: I-ESA 2009. IEEE, Beijing (2009)
14. MSEE: Deliverable D1.1.1: Service concepts, models and method at CIM-PIM-PSM level. MSEE IP (FP7 284860) (2012)
15. INTEROP: Deliverable DTG3.1 (MoMo.2): MoMo Roadmap. INTEROP NoE Project (FP6 IST-1-508011) (2005)
16. Ogren, I.: On Principles for Model-Based Systems Engineering. Systems Engineering Journal 3, 38–49 (2000)
17. Dauben, J.W.: Georg Cantor: His Mathematics and Philosophy of the Infinite. Harvard University Press (1979)
18. Bernstein, P.A.: Applying Model Management to Classical Meta Data Problems. In: First Biennial Conference on Innovative Data Systems Research (2003)
19. Sarraipa, J., Jardim-Goncalves, R., Steiger-Garcao, A.: MENTOR: an enabler for interoperable intelligent systems. International Journal of General Systems 39, 557–573 (2010)
20. Agostinho, C., Sarraipa, J., Goncalves, D., Jardim-Goncalves, R.: Tuple-Based Semantic and Structural Mapping for a Sustainable Interoperability. In: Camarinha-Matos, L.M. (ed.) DoCEIS 2011. IFIP AICT, vol. 349, pp. 45–56. Springer, Heidelberg (2011)
21. Delgado, M., Agostinho, C., Malo, P., Jardim-Goncalves, R.: A framework for STEP-based harmonization of conceptual models. In: IEEE IS 2006, London UK (2006)
22. ISO TC184/SC4: Standard for the Exchange of Product Data - ISO 10303 (STEP) (1994), http://www.tc184-sc4.org
23. ISO/IEC: Information Technology - Metadata registries (MDR) - Part 1: Framework (ISO/IEC 11179-1:2004) (2004)
24. ISO TC184/SC4: Industrial automation systems and integration – Product data representation and exchange – Part 11: Description methods: The EXPRESS language reference manual (ISO 10303-11:2004) (2004)
25. OMG: OMG Unified Modeling LanguageTM (OMG UML), Infrastructure - version 2.4.1 (2011), http://www.omg.org/spec/UML/2.4.1/Infrastructure/PDF/
26. W3C: OWL 2 Web Ontology Language Structural Specification and Functional-Style Syntax (2009), http://www.w3.org/TR/owl2-syntax/
27. W3C: XML Schema (XSD) (2001), http://www.w3.org/XML/Schema
28. Jouault, F., Kurtev, I.: On the interoperability of model-to-model transformation languages. Science of Computer Programming 68, 114–137 (2007)
29. CRESCENDO IP: Collaborative and Robust Engineering using Simulation Capability Enabling Next Design Optimisation, FP7-234344 (2012)
30. W3C: OWL 2 Web Ontology Language MOF-Based Metamodel (2008), http://www.w3.org/2007/OWL/wiki/MOF-Based_Metamodel

An Approach for Validating Semantic Consistency of Model Transformation Based on Pattern

Jin Li[1,2], Dechen Zhan[1], Lanshun Nie[1], and Xiaofei Xu[1]

[1] School of Computer Science and Technology, Harbin Institute of Technology,
92 West Dazhi Street, Harbin 150001, China
[2] School of Computer Science and Technology, Harbin Engineering University,
145 Nan Tong Street, Harbin 150001, China
miaookok@163.com, {dechen,nls,xiaofei}@hit.edu.cn

Abstract. The correctness of model transformation is an import research field in model-driven architecture. Syntactic correctness and semantic consistency are hot topics in the field of model transformation. Syntactic correctness has many mature solutions. However the validation of semantic consistency has some problems. Therefore, how to validate semantic consistency of model transformation is a major problem in model-driven development. In this paper, we propose a validation approach for semantic consistency of model transformation, which is based on pattern. We analyze some patterns in models and make these patterns as transformation pattern. We define transformation rule with transformation pattern and analyze three parts of semantic transformation. We present two theorems to validate semantic consistency of model transformation. Finally, we give a case to illustrate the effectiveness of our approach.

Keywords: Model transformation, Transformation rule, Transformation pattern.

1 Introduction

The correctness of model transformation is an important research field in model-driven architecture (MDA) [1-2]. The research mainly focuses on syntactic correctness and semantic consistency [3]. Syntactic correctness has some mature solutions [4], e.g. planning algorithm [5]. However the validation of semantic consistency has some problems, e.g. effective theory. Therefore, how to validate semantic consistency of model transformation is a major problem in model-driven development of software systems.

Model transformation consists of transformation rules which describe how a set of elements of the source model are transformed into a set of elements of the target model through transformation relationships [6]. Semantic consistency of model transformation is for maintaining consistency between source model and target model in the semantics. So, the validation problem for semantic consistency of model transformation is equivalent to the formulization proof of semantic consistency in the process of model transformation.

The original version of this chapter was revised: The copyright line was incorrect. This has been corrected. The Erratum to this chapter is available at DOI: 10.1007/978-3-642-33068-1_20

M. van Sinderen et al. (Eds.): IWEI 2012, LNBIP 122, pp. 161–171, 2012.
© IFIP International Federation for Information Processing 2012

Many methods to solve semantic consistency of model transformation have emerged from industrial and academic research. Varró [7] defined and validated the model constraints to preserve semantic consistency of model transformation. Jinkui Hou [8] proposed a semantic description framework, and promoted category theory to describe and validate semantics of model transformation. Caplat [9] extended formal language to describe and validate model semantics. Engles [10] provided the relationships of semantic objects of UML-RT to describe the consistency required among models, and proved these relationships through static analysis. XiaoHe [11] extended QVT Relations with three new concepts and discussed the semantics of the mapping pattern and creating model.

Different model transformation methods may need different methods to preserve semantic consistency of model transformation. The paper proposes a validation approach for semantic consistency of model transformation based on pattern. We make some patterns, e.g. sequence pattern, branching pattern and loop pattern, in models as transformation patterns and use these transformation patterns to define transformation rule. There are three parts of the validation process of semantic consistency: (1) the semantic mapping from source model to source transformation pattern; (2) the semantic mapping from source transformation pattern to target transformation pattern; (3) the semantic mapping from target transformation pattern to target model. Then, the validation problem for semantic consistency of model transformation is equivalent to the problem about the three semantic mappings.

The rest of this paper is structured as follows. In Sect. 2, we propose the motivating example which will be used throughout the paper. Section 3 provides the core concepts. Section 4 presents the validation theory of semantic consistency of model transformation. Section 5 illustrates the validation theory. Sect. 6 concludes the paper and further work.

2   Motivation Example

There are some basic patterns in models, e.g. sequence pattern, branching pattern, and loop pattern, which belong to business process model. The three patterns are shown in Fig.1 (a). We use the model transformation from UML Activity Diagram Model (UADM) to Java Business Process Model (JBPM) to describe how to preserve model semantics during model transformation. The UADM and JBPM are shown in Fig.1(b). The UADM describes a business process of submitting sale order. The process is: firstly query sale data, secondly fill these data into a sale order, thirdly audit the sale order, and finally submit the sale order. The activity about auditing the sale order has a judging condition, i.e. if the sale data is less than 1000, the sale order should be submitted directly. Otherwise the manager should audit the sale order. If the manager agrees the sale order, he submits the sale order. Otherwise the sale data will be queried again.

The UADM contains these three patterns above. For example, the operations of querying sale data and filling the sale order correspond to the sequence pattern; the operation of checking the sale data corresponds to the branching pattern; the operation of auditing the sale order corresponds to the loop pattern, and the auditing loop pattern contains the sequence patter.

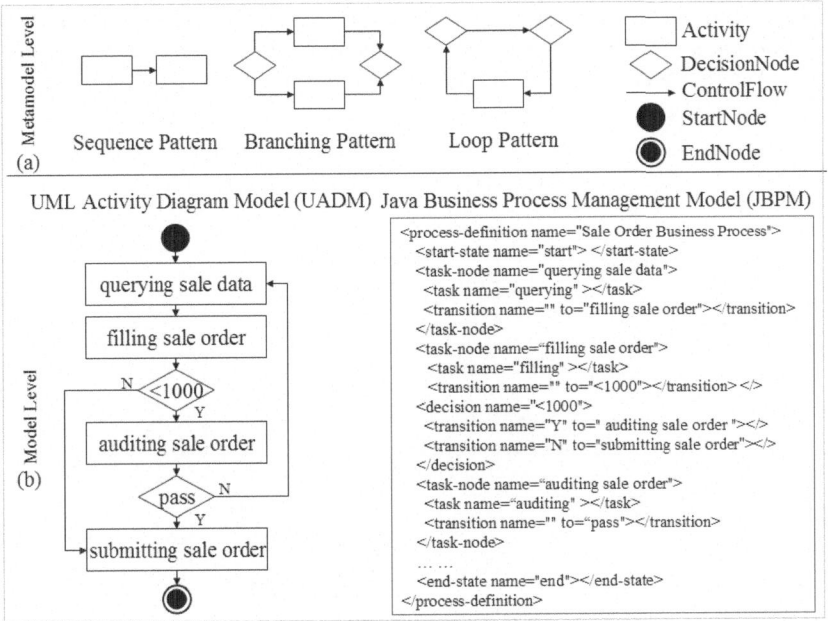

Fig. 1. Motivation example

The approaches of model transformation define transformation rules with the patterns. A pattern is either basic pattern or user-defined pattern. The user-defined pattern is generally defined according to domain business requirements. The patterns are called transformation patterns in transformation rules. These transformation patterns can simplify transformation definition, raise transformation efficiency, and improve transformation quality.

3   Transformation Pattern and Transformation Rule

Transformation rule, which is defined in model transformation based on pattern, contains two patterns: left pattern and right pattern. The two patterns also consist of some basic patterns and user-defined patterns. These basic patterns and user-defined patterns are called transformation pattern in the paper. Transformation patterns must be formed in pairs transformation rule, namely if left pattern contains a transformation pattern TP_s, right pattern should contain another transformation pattern TP_t. The semantics of TP_s and TP_t must be equivalence. The metamodel of transformation rule is shown in Fig.2.

The class *TransformationRule* consists of *LeftPattern*, *RightPattern* and *Constraint*. *LeftPattern* and *RightPattern* are composed of *Element* and *TransformationPattern*. *Element* has three subclasses, and they are *TransformationPattern*, *NodeElement*, and *RelationElement*. *TransformationPattern* is composed of *NodeElement*, *RelationElement*, and *Constraint*. *Constraint* has two subclasses: *interConstraint* and *exterConstraint*. *interConstraint* describes the internal relationships of *LeftPattern* and *RightPattern*, and *exterConstraint* describes the external relationships of *LeftPattern* and *RightPattern*. *interConstraint* can be described by OCL, while *exterConstraint* is described according to the constraint relationships of *NodeElement*, *RelationElement* and *TransformationPattern*. We focus on the semantic information of *exterConstraint* in the paper. We firstly analyze the external relationships of transformation pattern, which are illustrated in Fig. 3.

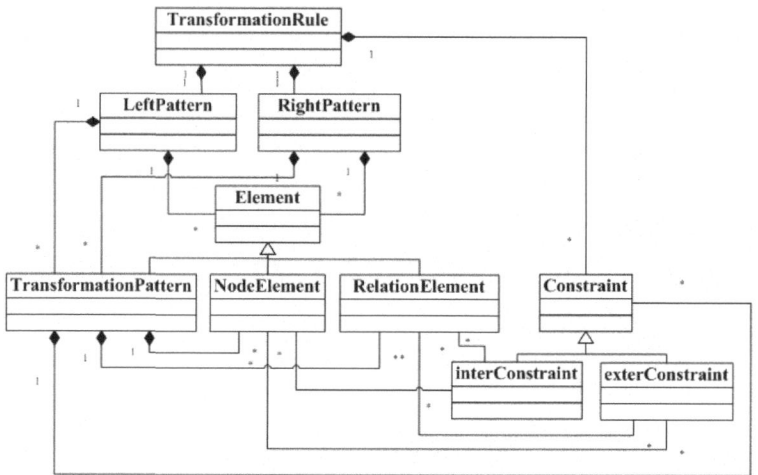

Fig. 2. Metamodel of transformation rule

In Fig. 3, there are two kinds of constraint relationships: Element-Pattern and Pattern-Pattern. In the first constraint relationship, there is a relationship r_1 between the element n_1 and the transformation pattern TP_1. The end element of r_1 is one of elements of TP_1. Because TP_1 contains two elements (n_2 and n_3), there are three conditions of the mapping between n_1 and TP_1: (1) from n_1 to n_2; (2) from n_1 to n_3; (3) from n_1 to n_2 and n_3. There needs an external constraint relationship to accurately describe the mapping condition between n_1 and TP_1. In the second constraint relationship, the identifier r_2 is a relationship between the transformation patterns TP_1 and TP_2. Because the start element of r_2 comes from TP_3 and the end element of r_2 comes from TP_2, we divide the constraint relationship (Pattern-Pattern) into two constraint relationships (Element-Pattern): the relationship between r_2 and TP_2, and the relationship between r_2 and TP_3. The two relationships are similar to the relationship between r_1 and TP_1.

We firstly propose the model definition, the definition of transformation pattern with the external constraint relationship, and the definition of transformation rule.

Definition 3.1 (Model): A model is defined as

$$M=<E, L, rel, meta> \tag{1}$$

Where

- $E=\{e_1,e_2,...,e_s\}$ denotes a finite set of model elements,
- $L=\{l_1,l_2,...,l_t\}$ denotes a finite set of the relationships among model elements,

- $rel(l_k)=[e_i,e_j]$ denotes a relational function between model elements, and describes that e_i is a start element of l_k and e_j is an end element of l_k, $e_i, e_j \in E$, $1 \leq i, j \leq s$, $l_k \in L$, $1 \leq k \leq t$,
- $meta(e_u)$ denotes an instance function, and it describes the metamodel of e_u, $1 \leq u \leq s$.

Note that we use "." to describe the element of model, e.g. $M.E$ describes the element set of M, and $M.L$ denotes the relationship set of M.

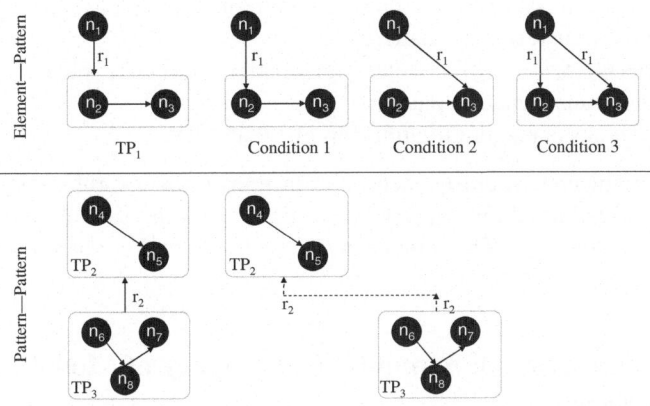

Fig. 3. The external relationship of transformation pattern

Definition 3.2 (Transformation Pattern): A transformation pattern is defined as

$$TP=<N, R, rel, interC, exterC> \qquad (2)$$

Where

- $N=\{n_1,n_2,...,n_p\}$ denotes a finite set of nodes, and its instance element set is $M.E$;
- $R=\{r_1,r_2,...,r_q\}$ denotes a finite set of relationships, and its instance element set is $M.L$;
- $rel(r_k)=[n_i,n_j]$ denotes an element-relationship function, and describes that n_i is a start element of r_k and n_j is an end element of r_k, n_i, $n_j \in N$, $1 \leq i, j \leq p$, $r_k \in R$, $1 \leq k \leq q$,
- $interC=\{iC_1,iC_2,...,iC_m\}$ denotes a finite set of the internal constraint relationships;
- $exterC=\{eC_1,eC_2,...,eC_n\}$ denotes a finite set of the external constraint relationships, $eC_x=<r,TP, \{n_x,n_{x+1},...,n_l\}>$ denotes the constraint relationship between r and TP, $r \notin R$, $1 \leq x, l \leq p$. Every element n_k is either a start element or an end element of r, $n_k \in N$, $1 \leq k \leq p$.

In Fig. 3, the three mapping condition of the constraint relationship between n_1 and TP_1 can be defined as the following:

$$eC_1=<r,TP,\{n_2\}>, \; eC_2=<r,TP,\{n_3\}>, \; eC_3=<r,TP,\{n_2,n_3\}>.$$

When a transformation rule contains an element, we make the element as a transformation pattern. Therefore, the left and right pattern of transformation rule can contain one or more transformation patterns.

Definition 3.3 (Transformation Rule): A transformation rule is defined as

$$TR=<LP, RP, C> \tag{3}$$

Where

-   $LP=\{tp_{s1},tp_{s2},...,tp_{su}\}$ denotes left pattern, and it contains a finite set of source transformation patterns,
-   $RP=\{tp_{t1},tp_{t2},...,tp_{tv}\}$ denotes right pattern, and it contains a finite set of target transformation patterns;
-   C denotes constraint relationship of LP and RP.

The left and right pattern are formed pairs in transformation rule, i.e. if left pattern contain the transformation pattern tp_{si}, right pattern should contain another transformation pattern tp_{tj}. The semantics tp_{si}, is similar to the semantics of tp_{tj}, $1 \leq i \leq u$, $1 \leq j \leq v$.

4   The Validating of Semantic Consistency of Model Transformation

The goal of preserving semantic consistency of model transformation is that the semantics of source and target model is equivalence. During a process of model transformation based on pattern, the semantic transformation process from source model to target model is an implementation process of transformation rules. The processes contain three parts of model semantic mappings: the semantic mapping from left pattern to source model, the semantic mapping from left pattern to right pattern, and the semantic mapping from right pattern to target model. Because the left and right patterns have the equivalent semantics, the problem of preserving model semantic consistency is similar to two the semantic mapping problem: the mapping from left pattern to source model, and the mapping from right pattern to target model. We will propose the theorems to solve the problem.

4.1   Semantic Mapping from Source Transformation Pattern to Source Model

According to the definition 3.3, the left pattern of transformation rule is a set of source transformation patterns. Every element of source transformation pattern is either automatic element or another transformation pattern. So we describe the semantic mapping from left pattern to source model according to two mapping conditions. The identifiers M and TP denote a model and a transformation. If the semantics of M and TP is equivalence, we called the equivalence relationship as $TP \cong M$. We provide a theorem to validate the semantic consistency of the mapping between transformation pattern and model.

Theorem 4.1. Let M be a Model, the node set of M is $M.E=\{\ e_1,e_2,...,e_s\}$, TP is a transformation pattern, the node set of TP is $TP.N=\{n_1,n_2,...,n_p\}$. $TP\cong M$ if and only if Satisfying the following three conditions:

(1) every node $n_i\in TP.N$, then $n_i\in\ \cup\operatorname{meta}(M.E)$;
(2) every relationship $r_j\in TP.R$, then $r_j\in\ \cup\operatorname{meta}(M.L)$;
(3) every external constraint relationship $eC\in TP.exterC$ preserves the semantics.

Proof
(1) Every node of transformation pattern is a certain metamodel element of model element. n_i is an element of TP, $1\leq i\leq p$,
  <i> if n_i is an automatic element, there exists a node $e_k\in M.E$ which satisfies $n_i=\operatorname{meta}(e_k)$. So $n_i\in\ \cup\operatorname{meta}(M.E)$; ①
  <ii> if n_i is a transformation pattern, it should semantic map with a submodel M_i' of M. The node set of M_i' is a sub set of M nodes, i.e. $M_i'.E\subseteq M.E$. Every element n_l of n_i, there exists a node $e_o\in M_i'.E$ and it satisfies $n_l=\operatorname{meta}(e_o)$. So $n_i\in\ \cup\operatorname{meta}(M.E)$; ②
(2) Every relationship of transformation pattern is a certain metamodel relationship of model element. r_j is a relationship of TP, $1\leq j\leq q$. According to the definition 3.2, $rel(r_j)=[n_{j1},n_{j2}]$, n_{j1} and n_{j2} are the elements of TP, i.e. $n_{j1},n_{j2}\in TP.N$. And according to ①②, because $n_{j1},n_{j2}\in\ \cup\operatorname{meta}(M.E)$, there exists two elements $e_u,e_v\in M.E$. They satisfy $n_{j1}=\operatorname{meta}(e_u)$ and $n_{j2}=\operatorname{meta}(e_v)$. To the relationship l_w between e_u and e_v, there exists $rel(l_w)=[e_u,\ e_v]$. So $r_j\in\ \cup\operatorname{meta}(M.L)$; ③
(3) The constraint relationship of transformation pattern satisfies semantic consistency. There are two parts of the constraint relationship: the internal constraint relationship and the external constraint relationship. Preserving the internal constraint relationship can be validated by OCL, while preserving the external constraint relationship is validated according to the definition of the external constraint relationship. There is an external relationship r between the element n_i and the transformation patter TP:
  <i> if n_i is an automatic element, there exists an instance element $l_k(l_k\in M.L)$ of r and $rel(l_k)=[e_i,e_j]$ $(e_i,e_j\in M.E)$. According to ①②, n_i satisfies either $n_i=\operatorname{meta}(e_i)$ or $n_i=\operatorname{meta}(e_j)$, then the external constraint relationship $eC=<r,TP,\{n_i\}>$ preserves the semantics of r and TP; ④
  <ii> if n_i is a transformation pattern TP_i, according to ②, there exists a sub model M_j' of M, and $n_i\cong M_j'$, then a certain element n_k of TP_i may be the start or end element of r, $n_k\in TP_i.N$. According to ④, the external constraint relationship $eC=<r,TP_i,\{n_k\}>$ preserves the semantics of r and TP. ⑤

4.2 Semantic Mapping from Target Transformation Pattern to Target Model

In the session, we will propose the construction process from target transformation pattern to target model, and provide a theorem to validate whether the process preserve the semantics.

TP_s and TP_t are the source and target transformation patterns, and their corresponding mapping models are M_s and M_t. The construction process from TP_t to M_t is the following:

(1) Constructing element. n_t is an element of TP_t, $n_t \in TP_t.N$,

   <i> if n_t is an automatic element, according to the instance relationship of the metamodel and model, constructing a new model element e_i and make n_t=meta(e_i); ⑥

   <ii> if n_t is a transformation pattern, according to the corresponding element n_s of TP_s:

   a) if n_s is an automatic element, constructing a new element e_i, and make n_t=meta(e_i) ; ⑦

   b) if n_s is a transformation pattern, constructing a sub model M_t', and make $n_t.N$=meta($M_t'.E$) ; ⑧

(2) Constructing relationship. r_k is a relationship of TP_t, $r_k \in TP_t.R$. There exists two elements (n_i,n_j) and they satisfy rel(r_k)=[n_i,n_j], n_i,$n_j \in TP_t.N$,

   <i> if n_i and n_j are two automatic elements, according to ①, their instance elements (e_{ti}, e_{tj}) are the automatic elements of M_t. n_i and n_j satisfy n_i=meta(e_{ti}) and n_j=meta(e_{tj}). Then, constructing a relationship l_{tk} from e_{ti} to e_{tj}, and make rel(l_{tk})=[e_{ti},e_{tj}], $l_{tk} \in M_t.L$; ⑨

   <ii> if n_i is a transformation pattern and n_j is an automatic element. According to ②,n_i corresponds to a sub model M_{ti}' of M_t, $M_{ti}'.E$={e_{ti1},e_{ti2},...,e_{tim}}. If there exists an external constraint relationship eC=<r,n_i,{e_{tj}}>, the model element e_{tk} will be found in $M_{ti}'.E$ Then constructing a relationship l_k from e_{tk} to e_{tj}, and make rel(l_k)=[e_{tk},e_{tj}]. In the same way, if n_i is an automatic element and n_j is a transformation pattern, there exists $M_{tj}'.E$={e_{tj1},e_{tj2},...,e_{tjn}}. According to the external constraints relationship eC=<r,n_j,{n_i}>, there exists an element e_{tk}' in $M_{tj}'.E$, constructing a relationship l_k' from e_{ti} to e_{tk}', make rel(l_k')=[e_{ti}, e_{tk}']; ⑩

   <iii> if n_i and n_j are two transformation patterns, according to ②, n_i and n_j are corresponds to the sub model M_{ti}' and M_{tj}', and these sub models satisfy $M_{ti}'.E$={e_{ti1},e_{ti2},...,e_{tim}} and $M_{tj}'.E$={e_{tj1},e_{tj2},...,e_{tjn}}.According to the external relationships eC_1=<r,n_i,{e_{tj1},e_{tj2},...,e_{tjn}}> and eC_2=<r,n_j,{e_{ti1},e_{ti2},...,e_{tim}}>, if there exists two elements e_{tk} and e_{tk}' in $M_{ti}'.E$ and $M_{tj}'.E$, constructing a relationship l_k from e_{tk} to e_{tk}', and make rel(l_k)=[e_{tk}, e_{tk}']. ⑪

Theorem 4.2. Let TP_s and TP_t be two transformation patterns, if they correspond to the source M_s and target model M_t, the semantics of M_s and M_t is equivalence.

Proof

There are three parts of the semantic transformation of source model: the semantic mapping from M_s to TP_s, the semantic mapping from TP_s to TP_t, and the semantic mapping from TP_t to M_t. According to definition 3.3, the semantics of TP_s and TP_t is equivalence. According to the theorem 4.1, the semantics of M_s and TP_s is equivalence. So the preserving semantic problem of M_s and M_t is equivalent to the preserving semantic problem of TP_t and M_t. Because M_t is constructed by TP_t, the preserving semantic problem only validates the semantic equivalence of element and relationship of M_t. The validation of preserving the semantic equivalence of element and relationship are the following:

(1) Element equivalence. n_t is an element of TP_t, $n_t \in TP_t.N$,

    <i> if n_t is an automatic element, according to ⑦, the instance element e_i of n_t satisfies n_t=meta(e_i), then $TP_t.N \cong M_t.E$;

    <ii> if n_t is a transformation pattern, according to ⑧, the instance sub model M_t' of n_t satisfies $n_t.N$=meta($M_t'.E$), then $TP_t.N \cong M_t.E$;

(2) Relationship equivalence. r_k is a relationship of TP_t, $r_k \in TP_t.R$. There exists two elements (n_i, n_j) and they satisfy $rel(r_k)$=[n_i,n_j], $n_i,n_j \in TP_t.N$,

    <i> if n_i and n_j are two automatic elements, according to ③⑥, their instance elements are e_{ti} and e_{tj} which are two elements of M_t. According to ⑨,there exists the instance relationship l_{tk} of l_k, and $rel(l_{tk})$=[e_{ti},e_{tj}], So $TP_t.R \cong M_t.L$;

    <ii> if n_i is a transformation pattern and n_j is an automatic element. According to ③⑩, there exists an element e_{tk} in the instance model M_{ti}' of n_i, and a relationship l_k from e_{tk} to e_{tj}. The relationship satisfies $rel(l_k)$=[e_{tk},e_{tj}], so $r_k \cong M_{ti}'$; In the same way, if n_i is an automatic element and n_j is a transformation pattern, there exists a relationship l_k', so $TP_t.R \cong M_t.L$;

    <iii> if n_i and n_j are two transformation patterns, according to③⑪, if there exists e_{tk} and e_{tk}', the relationship l_k between e_{tk} and e_{tk}', and $rel(l_k)$=[e_{tk}, e_{tk}'], so $TP_t.R \cong M_t.L$.

5　Experiment

We validate the semantic equivalence of UADM and JBPM. There are three parts of the validation process: (1) preserving semantic equivalence of UADM and TP_s; (2) preserving semantic equivalence of TP_s and TP_t; (3) preserving semantic equivalence of TP_t and JBPM. The validation process is the following:

(1) Preserving semantic equivalence of UADM and TP_s

The metamodel of UADM contains *Activity*, *Decision*, *ConstrolFlow*, *Start* and *End*. There are three basic patterns in UADM: sequence pattern, branching pattern and loop pattern. We firstly define three transformation patterns according to these basic patterns.

    (a) A source sequence pattern is composed of *querying sale data, filling sale order* and their relationship in UADM. It is defined as TP_{SS}=<N_{SS}, R_{SS}, rel_{SS}, $interC_{SS}$, $exterC_{SS}$>, where N_{SS}={*Activity*, *ControlFlow*}, R_{SS}={r_1,r_2}, $rel_{SS}(r_1)$=[*Activity*, *ControlFlow*], $rel_{SS}(r_2)$ =[*ControlFlow*, *Activity*], $exterC_{SS}$={eC_1}, eC_1=<r_{s1}, TP_{SS},{*Activity*}>.

    Note that r_{s1} is an external relationship, $r_{s1} \notin rel_{SS}$.

    (b) A source branching pattern is composed of *auditing sale order*, *pass*, and TP_{SS}. It is defined as TP_{SB}=<N_{SB}, R_{SB}, rel_{SB}, $interC_{SB}$, $exterC_{SB}$>, where N_{SB}={*Activity*, *Decision*, *ControlFlow*, TP_{SS}}, R_{SB}={r_3,r_4,r_5,r_6}, $rel_{SB}(r_3)$=[*Decision*, *ControlFlow*], $rel_{SB}(r_4)$=[*ControlFlow*, *Activity*], $rel_{SB}(r_5)$=[*Activity*, *ControlFlow*], $rell_{SB}(r_6)$= [*ControlFlow*, *Decision*], $exterC_{SB}$={eC_2}, eC_2=<r_{s2}, TP_{SB},{ *Decision*}>

    Note that r_{s2} is an external relationship, $r_{s2} \notin rel_{SB}$.

(c) A source loop pattern is composed of less 1000, *auditing sale order*, *pass*, and TP_{SS}. It is defined as $TP_{SL}=<N_{SL}, R_{SL}, rel_{SL}, interC_{SL}, exterC_{SL}>$, where $N_{SL}=\{Activity, Decision, ControlFlow, TP_{SS}\}$, $R_{SL}=\{r_7,r_8,r_9,r_{s1}\}$, $rel_{SL}(r_7)=[Decision, ControlFlow]$, $rel_{SL}(r_8)=[ControlFlow,TP_{SS}]$, $rel_{SL}(r_{s1})=[TP_{SS}, ControlFlow]$, $rel_{SL}(r_9) =[ControlFlow, Decision]$, $exterC_{SL}=\{eC_3\}$, $eC_3=<r_6, TP_{SL},\{Activity\}>$.

According to the theorem 4.1, we validate the semantic equivalence of source transformation patterns and UADM. The instance model of TP_{SS} contains the elements *querying sale data* and *filling sale order*. When the auditing order is error, the sale data should be queried again. So there is a relationship between TP_{SS} and r_{s1}. TP_{SS} contains an external relationship $eC_1=<r_{s1}, TP_{SS},\{Activity\}>$ to describe the relationship. When the auditing order is ok, there exists a relationship between TP_{SL} and TP_{SB}. Then there is a relationship r_6 between TP_{SL} and TP_{SB}. TP_{SL} contains an external relationship $eC_3=<r_6, TP_{SL},\{Activity\}>$ to describe the relationship. So the transformation patterns (TP_{SS}, TP_{SB}, TP_{SL}) preserve the semantic equivalence of M_s.

(2) Preserving semantic equivalence of TP_s and TP_t

We firstly define three target transformation patterns. JBPM contains *TaskNode*, *DecisionNode*, and *Transition*.

(d) Target sequence pattern contain two *TaskNodes* and a *Transition*. Target sequence pattern $TP_{TS}=<N_{TS}, R_{TS}, rel_{TS}, interC_{TS}, exterC_{TS}>$, where $N_{TS}=\{TaskNode, Transition\}$, $R_{TS}=\{r_{10},r_{11}\}$, $rel_{TS}(r_{10})=[TaskNode, Transition]$, $rel_{TS}(r_{11})=[Transition, TaskNode]$, $exterC_{TS}=\{eC_4\}$, $eC_4=<r_{t1}, TP_{TS},\{TaskNode\}>$

(e) Target branching pattern contain a *TaskNode*, a *DecisionNode*, a *Transition* and a TP_{TS}. It is defined as $TP_{TB}=<N_{TB}, R_{TB}, rel_{TB}, interC_{TB}, exterC_{TB}>$, where $N_{TB}=\{TaskNode, DecisionNode, Transition, TP_{TS}\}$, $R_{TB}=\{r_{12},r_{13},r_{14},r_{t1}\}$, $rel_{TB}(r_{12})=[DecisionNode, Transition]$, $rel_{TB}(r_{13})=[TaskNode, Transition]$, $rel_{TB}(r_{14})=[TaskNode, DecisionNode]$, $rel_{SB}(r_{t1})=[DecisionNode, TP_{TS}]$, $exterC_{TB}=\{eC_5\}$, $eC_5=<r_{t2}, TP_{TS}, \{TaskNode\}>$

(f) Target loop pattern contain two *DecisionNodes*, a TP_{TS}, and a *TaskNode*. It is defined as $TP_{TL}=<N_{TL}, R_{TL}, rel_{TL}, interC_{TL}, exterC_{TL}>$, where $N_{TL}=\{TaskNode, DecisionNode, Transition, TP_{TS}\}$, $R_{TL}=\{r_{15},r_{16},r_{17},r_{18},r_{t1}\}$, $rel_{TL}(r_{15})= [DecisionNode, TP_{TS}]$, $rel_{TL}(r_{16})=[TP_{TS}, TaskNode]$, $relT_L(r_{17})= [DecisionNode, TaskNode]$, $rel_{TL}(r_{18})=[TaskNode, DecisionNode]$, $exterC_{TL}=\{eC_6\}$, $eC_6=<r_{t3}, TP_{TL}, \{TaskNode\}>$

The semantics of TP_s and TP_t is equivalence. This is not the focus of this paper, and therefore, we will not describe it here.

(3) Preserving semantic equivalence of TP_t and JBPM

M_t is constructed by TP_t. According to the theorem 4.2, the semantics of the constructed elements and relationships is equivalence is equivalent to the semantics of M_s. So the mapping between TP_t and M_t preserves the semantic equivalence.

As noted above, the semantics of UADM to JBPM is equivalence.

6   Conclusions and Future Work

In this paper we propose an approach for validating semantic consistency of model transformation. We analyze some basic patterns in models, e.g. sequence pattern, branching pattern, and loop pattern, and use these basic patterns to define transformation rules. Therefore, the semantic transformation of source model has been divided three parts: (1) the semantic mapping from source transformation pattern to source model; (2) the semantic mapping from source transformation pattern to target transformation pattern; (3) the semantic mapping from target transformation pattern to target model. The validation problem for semantic consistency of model transformation is equivalent to the problem about the three semantic mappings. The motivation example illustrates the effectiveness of our approach.

Future work is to optimize transformation rules constructed through our approach transformation. For this reason, we plan to analyze the typical business patterns in models and compose some transformation rules using these patterns to improve the efficiency of model transformation.

Acknowledgments. Research works in this paper are supported by the National Natural Science Foundation of China (60773064, 60904080), the National High-Tech Research and Development Program of China (2009AA04Z153, 2008GG1000401028).

References

1. Miller, J., Mukerji, J.: MDA Guide Version 1.0.1 [EB/OL]. OMG Document number omg/2003-06-01 (2003), http://www.omg.org/docs/omg/03-06-01.pdf
2. Hailpern, B., Tarr, P.: Model-driven development: The good, the bad, and the ugly. IBM System Journal 45(3), 451–461 (2006)
3. Beydeda, S., Book, M., Gruhn, V.: Model-Driven Software Development-Volume of Research and Practice in Software Engineering. Springer, Berlin (2005)
4. Hausmann, J.H., Heckel, R., Sauer, S.: Extended model relations with graphical consistency conditions. In: UML, Workshop on Consistency Problems in UML-based Software Development, pp. 61–74 (2002)
5. Varró, D., Varró, G., Pataricza, A.: Designing the automatic transformation of visual languages. Science of Computer Programming 44(2), 205–227 (2002)
6. Kleppe, A., Warmer, J., Bast, W.: MDA Explained: The Model Driven Architecture: Practice and Promise. Addison-Wesley, Boston (2003)
7. Varró, D., Pataricza, A.: Automated Formal Verification of Model Transformation. In: Proceedings of Workshop on Critical Systems Development with UML (CSDUML), Technische Unviersitat Munchen, pp. 63–78 (2003)
8. Hou, J., Wang, H., Ma, J., et al.: Semantic Description Framework for Architecture-Centric Model Transformation. Journal of Software 20(8), 2113–2123 (2009)
9. Caplat, G., Sourrouille, J.L.: Model Mapping Using Formalism Extensions. IEEE Software 2(22), 44–51 (2005)
10. Engels, G., Heckel, R., Küster, J.M., Groenewegen, L.: Consistency-Preserving Model Evolution through Transformations. In: Jézéquel, J.-M., Hussmann, H., Cook, S. (eds.) UML 2002. LNCS, vol. 2460, pp. 212–227. Springer, Heidelberg (2002)
11. He, X., Ma, Z., Zhang, Y., Zhang, W.: Extending QVT Relations for business process model transformation. Journal of Software 22(2), 195–210 (2011)

Negotiations Framework for Monitoring the Sustainability of Interoperability Solutions

Carlos Coutinho[1], Adina Cretan[2], and Ricardo Jardim-Goncalves[1]

[1] CTS, Departamento de Engenharia Electrotecnica, Faculdade de Ciencias e Tecnologia,
Universidade Nova de Lisboa, Portugal
c.coutinho@campus.fct.unl.pt, rg@uninova.pt
[2] Computer Science Department, "Nicolae Titulescu" University of Bucharest, Romania
badina20@yahoo.com

Abstract. The competition inherent to globalisation has led enterprises to gather in nests of specialised business providers with the purpose of building better applications and provide more complete solutions. This, added to the improvements on the Information and Communications Technologies (ICT), led to a paradigm shift from product-centrism to service-centrism and to the need to communicate and interoperate. Traditional segments like banking, insurance and aerospace subcontract a large number of Small and Medium Enterprises (SMEs) that are undergoing this change, and must ensure the criticality and accuracy of their business is not affected or impacted in any way. This paper proposes a methodology and a framework that provide critical businesses a control mechanism over the interoperability solutions in place on their subcontracted enterprises, imposing negotiations which formalise the solutions applied. It then focuses on its application on the business case of the Concurrent Design Facility of the European Space Agency (ESA-CDF).

Keywords: Sustainable Enterprise Interoperability, Negotiations, Control, Aerospace.

1 Introduction

The service globalisation perpetrated by the Internet has led to a need for change in the traditional businesses. Market terms and conditions dictate a constant need to change and adapt to new environment conditions, new paradigms and solutions, platforms and technology solutions, trends and fashions. Thus, being the best-of-breed no longer means being the most efficient or having the highest performance, it means keeping up with the look & feel trends, being available in many platforms and heterogeneous environments, i.e. implicates a continuous change. Many manufacturing enterprises currently have a very clear update and delivery schedule plan, e.g. when deploying a new car model, it is possible to know what the next version(s) of that car will look like and what it shall feature.

This heterogeneity, constant change and subsequent need for interoperability are worrying traditional business areas like finances (banking, insurance), aeronautics and aerospace, which usually tend to be very conservative towards change on account to

---

The original version of this chapter was revised: The copyright line was incorrect. This has been corrected. The Erratum to this chapter is available at DOI: 10.1007/978-3-642-33068-1_20

M. van Sinderen et al. (Eds.): IWEI 2012, LNBIP 122, pp. 172–184, 2012.
© IFIP International Federation for Information Processing 2012

accuracy and stability. As an example, the aerospace industry is served by a small set of large enterprises that implement projects and missions, and which then subcontract several Small and Medium Enterprises (SMEs) for supporting their development, thus creating a network of dependencies. The need for interoperability with the other players in these networks is as crucial for staying in business, as the ability to do so while maintaining the proprietary business assets protected from the competition.

The evolution of ICT permitted faster, more secure and robust data exchanges, promoting the development of solutions as result of the contributions of the several enterprises working in a network, thus allowing the gathering of multiple competences and expertise into higher-valued products and solutions. Emerging paradigms like the Internet of Things [1] (IoT, which is reshaping the world in the form of categorized discoverable items) and the Internet of Services [2], [3] (IoS), together with the evolving cloud computing's concepts [4] of Infrastructure as a Service (IaaS), Platform as a Service (PaaS) and Software as a Service (SaaS) are gradually transforming the existing reality into a set of available commoditised virtual objects, services, enterprises and networks.

This increase of availability and demand of combined solutions removed all traditional boundaries and allowed the specialisation of enterprises (particularly SMEs) and the building of complex and heterogeneous provider networks. This move from product-concentric to service-dispersed strategies is leading to concerns about reaching and maintaining the interoperability.

To large contractors or even final customers like banks and space agencies, which depend on the performance of this network of SMEs to conduct their business, the improvement coming from the specialisation needs to be balanced with the increase on control of the outcomes that result of multiple sources. The misunderstanding of a concept, a change in a data unit, a mistaken method on a single enterprise in the network can lead to chained mistakes on its counterparts and consequently to errors in the final result that are very difficult to detect and even more difficult to trace and resolve.

It is then essential that more than describing data and interface contracts, the interacting enterprises publish their models, ontologies and methods so that their partners can understand and cooperate with them easier. Moreover, it is important that a controlling entity (e.g. the prime contractor or the customer) is able to control if these models and concepts are aligned with the desired outcome.

Section 2 proposes research questions and hypotheses. Section 3 presents a proposed solution. Section 4 describes the application of this solution to the actual business case of the ESA-CDF. Section 5 presents final statements and future work.

2   Research Questions and Hypotheses

As result of the needs focused on section 1, some research questions are proposed:

- How can businesses monitor and control the interoperability stability and solutions provided by their subcontracted enterprises?
- How can SMEs provide extended information about their operations without periling proprietary knowledge to their competition?

The research conducted proposes the following hypotheses:

- If the interoperability solutions required between the partners in the network are formalised then it will be easier for a contracting enterprise to monitor it and ensure it is aligned with the required purposes;
- To allow the proper control from the contracting enterprise, as well as to allow settling of divergences towards a faster achievement of interoperability with a smaller effort, this formalisation should be shaped in the form of negotiations between the interested parties and also with the influence of the controlling party;
- If the formalisation of the negotiations towards interoperability solutions includes proper encapsulation and access restrictions, then besides handing the important information to the right partners, it will prevent unsolicited data from being exposed.

3   Proposed Solution

Each enterprise works on its own premises, developing its own business concepts, trades, skills, functionalities and methods. Although the establishment and embracement of standards is becoming more frequent, most of the business knowledge is based on past experiences, other partners' knowledge and new ideas. When two or more enterprises settle in the establishment of a partnership, several of these ideas may collide, which means they need time to harmonise. The relation between the complexities in the interoperation between them and the time and effort that is necessary to solve them is not linear, which means they need to develop a way to optimise this time and effort, thus reducing the time where there is no operation.

The proposed solution combines a methodology and framework that have at its core the need for negotiations in the development of interoperability solutions. These negotiations can have multiple participants (e.g. the partners and the supervision of their prime contractor or customer).

Enterprise Interoperability (EI) concerns the seamless exchange of information that allows an enterprise to perform globally, independently if the exchange of information is internal (between the various departments and parties that compose the enterprise), external (between the enterprise or part of it and an external party), or both [5]. Additionally, EI denotes that the exchanged information is understood in the same way by all of them. While the large prime contractors can determine the interoperability rules towards its network of dependencies, by setting the market standards and compelling the surrounding environment to comply with these standards, SMEs are much more sensible to the variations on their environment.

Achieving a sustainable EI is then [6] an integrated and interactive process of adaptation in a constant and iterative effort to recheck the existing interoperable status, while maintaining the existing interoperability towards the surrounding environment. Knowledge, adaptation and flexibility are therefore the pillars for undertaking a Sustainable EI (SEI).

3.1 Framework Methodology

One of the first problems that face interoperability is the detection of the problem itself. For that purpose, the first step of this methodology is to gather knowledge from the interacting parties. To do so, the proposed framework provides a set of questionnaires and interviews with appropriate stakeholders to allow the capturing of the enterprise information. Traditionally, this capture focused only the technological issues regarding interfaces and data formats, tools and ontologies. The authors propose that besides the technology capture, and based on the work of the MSEE project [7], that it is as well important to capture the intangible business needs, the human interactions and behaviours, and the operational use of the technology ("business and people").

The result of the knowledge capture phase is then applied to reference models [8], formalising it into Model-Driven Architectures (MDA [9]) and Model-Driven Interoperability (MDI [10], [11]). Actually, to set the difference to the current MDA and MDI, which the SSME research [12] considers as being essentially focused on the technological assets, the authors propose complementing the MDA and MDI (for the technological items) with a "Business" B-MDA and a "Business" B-MDI to deal with the "business and people" aspects, as can be seen on Fig. 1.

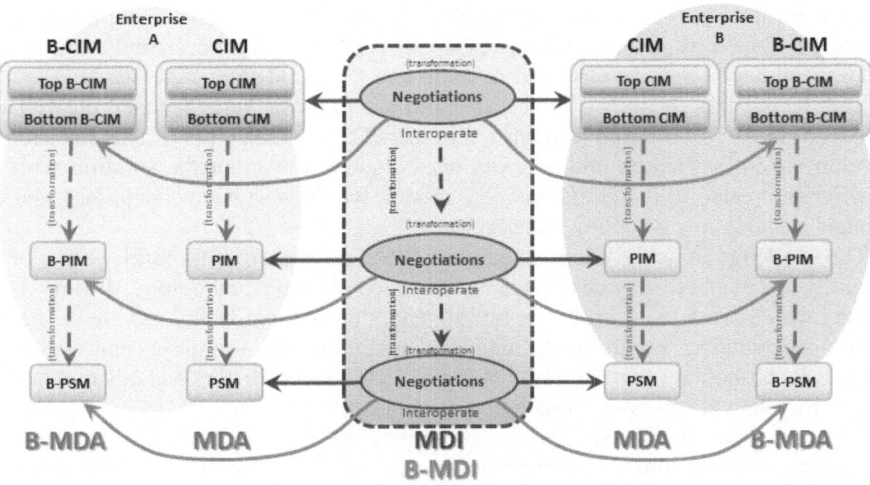

Fig. 1. MDA, B-MDA, MDI and B-MDI negotiating the interoperability solutions

The captured knowledge is then shaped in the form of a Computation-Independent Model (CIM) that describes the foundations for the design and interoperability, e.g. methodologies, functionalities, high-level objectives and visions. A complementing Business-CIM (B-CIM) shall describe e.g. strategies, organisation responsibilities, balance scorecards, HR hierarchies and roles, authorisations, objectives, behaviours and targets for each role. These models are independent of any algorithm or code. They are developed in UML, UEML and OCL to describe the foundations for the design and for the interoperability [13].

The CIM layer can be split into two layers [14]:

- Top CIM (and B-CIM) layers handle the strategic business functionalities, that are stable and conformant to requirements and needs ("as-is"), which include the interoperability needs towards other existing partners;
- Bottom CIM (and B-CIM) layers handle the operational transients and the proposed changes towards new partners, additional self-improvements (due to e.g. adoption of new technologies, supported platforms, lessons learned and best practices) and new interoperability challenges [15].

Then, the CIM is transformed into a Platform-Independent Model (PIM) which handles e.g. terminologies, ontologies, and algorithms, while still independently of any code or underlying platform, and the B-CIM is transformed into a Business-PIM (B-PIM), which handles e.g. operational workflows, management plans, and how each HR role shall fit and contribute in the system. These models shall be specified in the shape of ontologies, knowledge bases and rules.

Finally, the PIM is transformed into a Platform-Specific Model (PSM), producing pseudo-code and code that implements the rules and algorithms, and the B-PIM is transformed into a Business-PSM (B-PSM), resulting in e.g. rule and workflow engines, operational and deployment manuals, work permits, training and schedules.

The framework implements the PSM and B-PSM models in the shape of a set of services [16], as services (and web-services in particular) are considered very flexible, adaptable, reusable [17] and hence, suitable for the purpose of enhancing EI. Services can be developed by several parties, reshaped, versioned, composed and orchestrated, and governed by a Service Oriented Architecture (SOA) [18].

Still facing the flexibility target, the authors propose that the resulting SOA is deployed in a cloud-based infrastructure (IaaS and SaaS) [19]. The decision to develop the infrastructure and services over clouds is to grant the solution with the benefits associated to the cloud business model, which is to have cheap, fast, and on-demand scalable infrastructure and services.

The challenge to achieve a Sustainable EI (SEI) is therefore to build, on top of the currently established services, other services concerning technology, business and people, which provide the ability to rapidly adapt to innovation and imminent changes in the surrounding environment and yet maintain the seamless interoperability towards its ad-hoc network of partners, providers, subcontractors and customers. This pushes EI a step ahead towards its complete life cycle.

Each of the MDI/B-MDI layers presented on Fig. 1 is defined and shaped accounting negotiations. Negotiations in the CIM/B-CIM layer shall comprise business alignment, understanding of roles and strategies. In the PIM/B-PIM layer, negotiations shall deal with understanding the workflows, work packages, harmonising ontologies into a reference ontology [20] and specifying black-box tests. Finally, negotiations in the PSM/B-PSM layer mean dealing with middleware and platform issues, implementing specific policies and rules, interfaces, operational manuals, communication channels, deployment procedures and so on.

On each negotiation, in any of these layers, the problems are exposed and formalised, the benefits are presented and the interoperability solution alternatives are enumerated. The negotiations can then reach several conclusions:

- One of the partners agrees in changing to the other's definition;
- Both partners agree in a compromise solution;

- The partners agree in a solution imposed by the supervisor;
- The partners agree that interoperability can only be achieved via the use of translators and mediators;
- The partners agree that interoperability can only be achieved partially and thus need to redefine the scope;
- The partners agree that interoperability is not possible, not desired or not worth the changes/effort/time needed to achieve it.

This means that interoperability negotiations may start from the very enterprises' foundations, where it is easier to discuss business-related concepts and ideas, and then the progressive steps of transformation into lower-level models may also be synchronised to refine this interoperability, so that the overhead of transforming the concepts into code is performed by automation tools.

3.2   Framework Architecture

The resulting framework (Fig. 2) is then composed by a multi-levelled set of services defined over a Cloud SaaS platform adopting the MDA, MDI, B-MDA and B-MDI paradigms, and split into three negotiation levels:

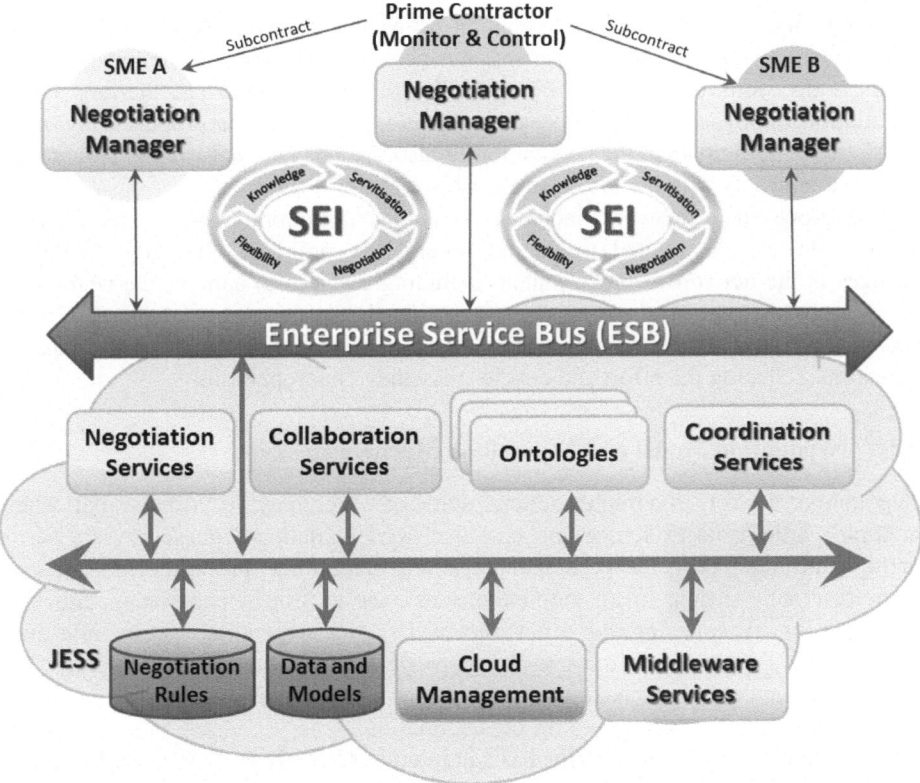

Fig. 2. Architecture of the framework for Sustainable Enterprise Interoperability (SEI)

Negotiation level 1 (Bottom – Middleware Services): Technical level, deals with middleware provision, supporting the aspects related with the basic infrastructures, handling the heterogeneity related with multiple negotiation players, which shall interact using an Enterprise Service Bus (ESB) for dealing with technical interoperability issues. It includes services that handle heterogeneity issues on the basic interoperability level (e.g. authentication, permissions, communications, syntax, session, and data), infrastructure and ICT.

Negotiation level 2 (Intermediate – Coordination Services): Intermediate conceptual level with the purpose to assist the negotiations at a global level (negotiations with different participants on different jobs) and at a specific level (negotiation on the same job with different participants). It handles the issues regarding communication at this level (synchronisation between the CSs of the several parties that are taking place in the negotiation), and manages the on-going transactions and negotiation data persistence, controlling the semantic discrepancies between the negotiating parties. It includes services that perform management of data transactions, semantic interpretation, dynamic discovery of services, and implementation of the business model rules, persisting its data (e.g. business-specific data, semantic ontologies, rules) on a IaaS infrastructure modelled using standard reference models and data access [21];

Negotiation level 3 (Top – Negotiation Manager): Strategic level, enables high-level operations close to the enterprises' business decision centres, implementing the business decisions that need to be taken for the negotiation, e.g. Starting a new negotiation, submission of a proposal, acceptation/rejection of a proposal, inviting a new party to participate in the negotiation. It also manages the negotiation parameters, and communicates with the lower levels using web-services.

The proposed framework includes mechanisms (autonomous agents [22]) to identify the aspects related to the interoperability problems that are sensible to changes in the networked environment, including services to support the negotiating of solutions that act on these changes, enabling the sustainability of the enterprise-networked interoperable environment along its life cycle with less transient downtime, reducing the effort and cost to (re)achieve interoperability.

3.3   Negotiation Model and Negotiation Mechanism

Negotiations are sets of complex actions, some of which may occur in parallel, where multiple participants exchange and take decisions in multiple phases over a set of multiple attributes [23]. The participants to a negotiation may propose offers and each participant may decide in an autonomous manner to stop a negotiation either by accepting or by rejecting the offer received. Also, depending on its role in a negotiation, a participant may invite new participants to the negotiation. The negotiation services shall make use of negotiation techniques and negotiation model to determine the best alternatives for the negotiation.

The Negotiation Model is defined as a quintuplet $M = <T, P, N, R, O>$ where:

- T denotes the time of the system, assumed to be discrete, linear, and uniform;

- P denotes the set of participants in the negotiation framework. The participants may be involved in one or many negotiations;
- N denotes the set of negotiations that take place within the negotiation framework;
- R denotes the set of coordination rules among negotiations that take place within the negotiation framework;
- O denotes the common ontology that consists of the set of definitions of the attributes that are used in a negotiation.

A negotiation is thus described at a time instance through a set of negotiation sequences:

Let $Sq = \{si \mid i \in \mathbb{N}\}$ denote the set of negotiation sequences, such that

$\forall si, sj \in Sq, \; i \neq j$ implies $si \neq sj$.

A negotiation sequence $si \in Sq$ such that $si \in N(t)$ is a succession of negotiation graphs that describe the negotiation N from the moment of its initiation and up to the time instance t. The negotiation graph created at a given time instance is an oriented graph in which the nodes describe the negotiation phases that are present at that time instance (i.e., the negotiation proposals sent up to that moment in terms of status and of attributes negotiated) and the edges express the precedence relationship between the negotiation phases.

According to the defined approach regarding the negotiation, the participants to a negotiation may propose offers and each participant may decide in an autonomous manner to stop a negotiation either by accepting or by rejecting the offer received. Also, depending on its role in a negotiation, a participant may invite new participants to the negotiation.

The metaphor Interaction Abstract Machines (IAMs) will be used to facilitate modelling of the evolution of a multi-attribute, multi-participant, multi-phase negotiation. In IAMs, a system consists of different entities and each entity is characterized by a state that is represented as a set of resources.

The evolution of all negotiation phases takes place in parallel. By modelling this parallel evolution in a dynamic environment, the proposed model allows us to describe and manage negotiations on multi-attribute negotiation objects and involving multiple participants. It also allows us to model different negotiation scenarios from single linear negotiation to concurrent and dependent multi-proposal negotiations.

The negotiation mechanism (Negotiation Services) that was built to implement this negotiation model shall comprise a set of rules defined in the Java Expert System Shell (JESS [24]), using the Web Ontology Language (OWL [25], [26]) and the Semantic Web Rule Language (SWRL [27], [28]) and inferred by the framework's Inference Engine.

4   Application to a Real Business Case in the Aerospace Field

The European Space Agency – Concurrent Design Facility (ESA-CDF) performs design studies to determine the viability of space missions. Each study encompasses a set of design sessions carefully planned and scheduled, as each session comprises the gathering of several of their highest-skilled engineers, hence convey an expensive effort. This expertise is required as the study outcomes are providing decision support evidences for large-scale investments.

The complex process associated with each study involves multiple domains (e.g. Mission analysis, Thermal, Propulsion), which match the different views and interests of the mission. Each of these domains is a complex field where state-of-the-art design techniques combine with the expertise of the field engineers towards developing a model, responsible for providing a set of parameters that support mission decisions.

The difficulty about this process, besides the inherent complexity of the referred subjects, is the adoption of the concept of Concurrent Engineering methods [29], which fast-track the design into a scenario where multi-disciplinary teams perform their activities in parallel.

Despite each domain design team models its own view of the mission, the teams need to define and exchange a large set of mission parameters, required to satisfy the mission and to ensure that all views are fully integrated and fit perfectly.

With the heterogeneity related to the various systems and applications used by each design team and mission, problems of misunderstandings regarding the exchanged data and its dependences are frequent, leading to additional rework.

Each domain engineering team performs its design using different tools (e.g. CATIA, STK, Matlab) and is provided and supported by a network of partners and suppliers (its collaborative environment).

Interoperability in this case is defined in two levels:

- The one between each domain and its tools, partners and suppliers in the supply chain, towards the target of defining the domain design or vision of the mission;
- The one between the various domains of a mission-related study, where all the domains present their view and compete for their interests into setting the values for mission-related parameters (e.g. Spacecraft dry mass, Electrical power, Launch mass).

The main issues detected in this scenario are precisely when dealing with the execution of the study, where all different visions, concepts, definitions, methods and relationships need to be harmonised and coordinated towards the evolution of the parameters that define the mission.

These mission parameters are inter-related (e.g. changes in the structure or in the number of instruments naturally affect the total dry mass) and their values are kept under control by the mission requirements. The interactions between design domains are performed in a set of closed-room sessions [30] where all involved domains and stakeholders are represented in a single room (the CDF room, with its special configuration [31]) and each domain presents its design solutions and the corresponding impact on the mission design.

The design of each study domain is executed and reported in a domain specific spreadsheet, where the exchanged data is carefully specified in specific rows and cells, and the data exchange between the domains is accomplished by linking all the domain spreadsheets in a moderated environment. Data dissemination and decisions are taken via the sharing of presentations planned, controlled, moderated and performed orderly by each domain.

This interoperable environment is very unstable, as it depends on the synchronisation of the different methodologies used by each domain to perform the design, as well as the perfect synchronisation of the data in the linked spreadsheets. A simple mistake in an inserted value, a misunderstanding about a parameter's unit, a network communication failure, an error in a design macro or a spreadsheet cell name with a typo is enough to break the interoperability [32].

Interoperability in this unstable scenario is the responsibility of the study Team Leader which moderates the discussions, and of the Systems Engineer and related Assistants which provide local support to the domain engineers. The seniority of the domain experts, which are especially recruited to participate in the study, is actually a crucial factor to improve interoperability.

The application of the proposed framework to the ESA-CDF environment was performed, firstly by submitting questionnaires that qualify the space environment in terms of requirements, needs and achievements, and major interoperability problems found. The consequent knowledge was then shaped into MDA and MDI.

The ESA-CDF design process is clearly human-oriented; hence, it was very important to split the modelling into MDA and B-MDA, MDI and B-MDI. This top-down analysis performed to model the CDF operation, started by defining the CIM and B-CIM layers. These include the modelling of the CDF study definitions, objectives, each domain, hierarchies and roles associated with a study, the concepts and stakeholders of CDF study, the expected behaviour of the system as a whole, the organisation hierarchy, and major functionalities. These models also captured methodologies, best-practices and operational knowledge, along with the needed functionality and dependencies.

These models were then transformed to PIM and B-PIM layers that allowed the CDF processes, structures and operations to be defined independently of the technology that will support them (e.g. the split of the mission into domains, what each will do, when will each interact towards the others, the definition of lessons-learned and capture of domain knowledge and practices, the relationship towards external parties, the configuration items). This also included the setting of a space-related ontology that describes, relates, and models the common space mission definitions, i.e. ESA-SERDL (Space Engineering Reference Data Library [33]) and the creation of the central data model defined by the standard ISO10303 STEP and EXPRESS statements, i.e. ESA-SEIM (Space Engineering Information Model [34]), as well as study workflows (e.g. the flow in which each domain presents their outcomes, policies about exchanging the data parameters).

Finally the models were transformed to PSM and B-PSM layers, which defined a set of web-services interconnecting the various domains, all connected via a central Enterprise Service Bus, and human and operational policies including rules, manuals and wizards.

On each of the MDA/B-MDA layers defined for the CDF environment and for its network of dependences (prime contractors and subcontracted SMEs), negotiations were modelled to handle the harmonisation of CIM/B-CIM objectives and understandings, the harmonisation of the PIM/B-PIM ontologies and flow outcomes, and the PSM/B-PSM middleware heterogeneities, formats, units and operations.

Whenever a new partner enters or shows changes in the interoperable space, the negotiation services, powered by the JESS negotiation rules, will be used to inquire the parties for the motivations, strengths, benefits, threats, prejudices, opportunities and impacts (e.g. time, effort, cost, dependences) due to the changes. Then, the negotiations take place in order to reach the most suitable solution in terms of impact and stability of the networking peers, along its life cycle. These negotiations are performed by the interested parties (e.g. SMEs) and the prime contractors and ESA-CDF domain supervisors can also participate for controlling the decisions that are taken and making sure they are aligned with the domain specifications. Regardless of the outcome of the negotiation, knowledgeable and mature decisions can be taken centred on accurate information about the other parties, based on facts and with decision support, able to be tracked and documented, hence providing lessons-learned and knowledge for future negotiations.

5   Final Considerations and Future Work

This paper described common problems found in the EI domain, particularly on the proposed business case of feasibility studies for aerospace missions, and proposed a collaborative framework to enhance business knowledge, to allow the adaptation of enterprises, and to allow the negotiation of solutions for the detected interoperability changes.

Driven by the formulated research question, the authors foresee that by adopting the proposed framework, major contractors and final customers have a mechanism that allows them to follow and influence (monitor and control) the interoperability solutions that are taken in subcontracted enterprises, aligning them with their objectives.

The formalisation of the negotiations into the defined negotiation model allows SMEs to perform the negotiation keeping their knowledge assets encapsulated in the negotiation model's entities, thus allowing them to negotiate without exposing them to the competition. Through the negotiation mechanism, the sustainability of the interoperable environment will be robust and easy to maintain.

This paper concludes that interoperability typically breaks because it is often developed over a poorly described (and rarely modelled) tacit knowledge. The integration of formal procedures for modelling, storing and documenting the business activities into MDA, MDI, B-MDA and B-MDI models allows a comprehensive analysis of the processes and of the possible alternatives. Adding the ability to negotiate the interoperability solutions leads to maximised results, stronger capabilities and relationships, thus contributing to reduce the risk of losing interoperability. The use of an adaptive framework that allows flexibility in terms of rearrangement, composition, reuse and scalability will result in a seamless, sustainable interoperability which favours its maintenance across time. The ability to reach and interoperate with more enterprises stimulates more business opportunities and stronger and healthier interactions.

Future research shall include the improvement of the framework's supporting tools: ontologies, questionnaires, tools, guidelines and processes (e.g. contract management, negotiation and renegotiation, development methodologies).

Acknowledgments. The authors wish to acknowledge the support of the European Commission through the funding of the UNITE, MSEE and ENSEMBLE FP7 projects, and the European Space Agency - Concurrent Design Facility (ESA-CDF) for their support, interaction and contribution in the development of the business case that is presented on this paper.

References

[1] Internet of Things - An action plan for Europe. In: CORDIS, p. 13 (2009)

[2] Cardoso, J., Voigt, K., Winkler, M.: Service Engineering for the Internet of Services. In: Filipe, J., Cordeiro, J. (eds.) ICEIS 2008. LNBIP, vol. 19, pp. 15–27. Springer, Heidelberg (2009)

[3] Internet of Services (2012), http://www.internet-of-services.com

[4] Jeffery, K., Neidecker-Lutz, B.: The Future of Cloud Computing: Opportunities for European Cloud Computing Beyond 2010. In: Analysis, p. 71 (2010)

[5] Li, M.-S., Cabral, R., Doumeingts, G., Popplewell, K.: Enterprise Interoperability Research Roadmap. In: European Commision - CORDIS, p. 45 (July 2006)

[6] Jardim-Goncalves, R., Agostinho, C., Steiger-Garcao, A.: Sustainable Systems ' Interoperability: A reference model for seamless networked business. In: 2010 IEEE International Conference on Systems, Man, and Cybernetics (SMC 2010), pp. 1785–1792 (2010)

[7] MSEE Project (2012), http://www.msee-ip.eu/project-overview (accessed: April 10, 2012)

[8] Doumeingts, G., Vallespir, B., Chen, D.: GRAI GridDecisional Modelling. In: Handbook on Architectures of Information Systems, pp. 321–346. Springer (2006)

[9] OMG, Model Driven Architecture (2011), http://www.omg.org/mda (accessed: December 20, 2011)

[10] Lemrabet, Y., Bigand, M., Clin, D., Benkeltoum, N., Bourey, J.-P.: Model Driven Interoperability in practice: preliminary evidences and issues from an industrial project. In: First International Workshop on Model-Driven Interoperability (MDI 2010), pp. 3–9 (2010)

[11] Athena Consortium, Athena Interoperability Framework (2011), http://www.modelbased.net/aif (accessed: December 20, 2011)

[12] Xiong, G., Liu, Z., Liu, X.-W., Zhu, F., Shen, D.: Service Science, Management, and Engineering: Theory and Applications. Academic Press (2012)

[13] Ullberg, J., Lagerstrom, R., van Sinderen, M., Johnson, P.: Architecture Modeling for Interoperability Analysis on the Future Internet. In: 6th International Conference on Interoperability for Enterprise Systems and Applications, I-ESA 2012 (2012)

[14] Lemrabet, Y., Liu, H., Bourey, J.-P., Bigand, M.: Proposition of Business Process Modelling in Model Driven Interoperability Approach at CIM and PIM Levels. In: Enterprise Interoperability V, pp. 203–215. Springer (2012)

[15] Nie, L., Xu, X., Chen, D., Zacharewicz, G., Zhan, D.: GRAI-ICE Model Driven Interoperability Architecture for Developing Interoperable ESA. In: Enterprise Interoperability IV, pp. 111–121. Springer (2010)

[16] Zdun, U., Dustdar, S.: Model-driven and pattern-based integration of process-driven SOA models. International Journal of Business Process Integration and Management 2(2), 109–119 (2007)

[17] Papazoglou, M.P., Traverso, P., Dustdar, S., Leymann, F.: Service-Oriented Computing: a Research Roadmap. International Journal of Cooperative Information Systems 17(02), 223 (2008)

[18] Jardim-Goncalves, R., Grilo, A.: SOA4BIM: Putting the building and construction industry in the Single European Information Space. Automation in Construction 19(4), 388–397 (2010)

[19] Sharma, R., Sood, M.: Cloud SaaS and Model Driven Architecture. In: International Conference on Advanced Computing and Communication Technologies (ACCT 2011), no. Acct, pp. 978–981 (2011)

[20] Sarraipa, J., Jardim-Goncalves, R., Steiger-Garcao, A.: MENTOR: an enabler for interoperable intelligent systems. International Journal of General Systems 39(5), 557–573 (2010)

[21] Jardim-Goncalves, R., Agostinho, C., Malo, P., Steiger-garcao, A.: Harmonising technologies in conceptual models representation. International Journal Of Product Lifecycle Management 2(2), 187–205 (2007)

[22] Coutinho, C., Cretan, A., Jardim-Goncalves, R.: Sustainable Interoperability Framework for supporting Negotiation Processes. In: 6th International Conference on Interoperability for Enterprise Systems and Applications, I-ESA 2012 (2011)

[23] Jardim-Goncalves, R., Sarraipa, J., Agostinho, C., Panetto, H.: Knowledge Framework for Intelligent Manufacturing Systems. Journal of Intelligent Manufacturing 22(5), 725–735 (2009)

[24] JESS Rule Engine (2012), http://www.jessrules.com/jess/index.shtml (accessed: February 15, 2011)

[25] OWL - Web Ontology Language (2012), http://www.w3.org/2004/OWL (accessed: November 14, 2011)

[26] Protégé-OWL editor (2012), http://protege.stanford.edu/overview/protege-owl.html (accessed: March 14, 2012)

[27] O'Connor, M.F., Knublauch, H., Tu, S., Grosof, B.N., Dean, M., Grosso, W., Musen, M.A.: Supporting Rule System Interoperability on the Semantic Web with SWRL. In: Gil, Y., Motta, E., Benjamins, V.R., Musen, M.A. (eds.) ISWC 2005. LNCS, vol. 3729, pp. 974–986. Springer, Heidelberg (2005)

[28] SWRLJessTab (2012), http://protege.cim3.net/cgi-bin/wiki.pl?SWRLJessTab (accessed: March 20, 2012)

[29] Bandecchi, M.: The ESA Concurrent Design Facility (CDF): concurrent engineering applied to space mission assessments. In: 2nd Nordic Systems Engineering Boat Seminar (FinSE 2001), pp. 1–36 (2001)

[30] Kolfschoten, G., Matthyssen, A., Fijneman, M.: Theoretical foundations for Concurrent Design. In: 4th International Workshop on System & Concurrent Engineering for Space Applications (SECESA 2010), vol. (1) (2010)

[31] ESA-CDF, ESA-CDF (2012), http://www.esa.int/esaMI/CDF/ (accessed:January 10, 2012)

[32] Koning, H.P.D., Eisenmann, H., Bandecchi, M.: Evolving Standardization Supporting Model Based Systems Engineering. In: 4th International Workshop on System & Concurrent Engineering for Space Applications (SECESA 2010), vol. (1) (2010)

[33] ESA-SERDL (2012), http://atlas.estec.esa.int/uci_wiki/SERDL (accessed: January 10, 2012)

[34] ESA-SEIM (2012), http://atlas.estec.esa.int/uci_wiki/SEIM (accessed: January 10, 2012)

A Hypergraph Partition Based Approach to Dynamic Deployment for Service-Oriented Multi-tenant SaaS Applications

Ying Pan, Lei Wu*, Shijun Liu, and Xiangxu Meng

School of Computer Science and Technology, Shandong University
250101, Jinan, P.R.China
panying0501@mail.sdu.edu.cn, {i_lily,lsj,mxx}@sdu.edu.cn

Abstract. In a service-oriented multi-tenant SaaS application, all tenants share services and user requests of the service change dynamically. In order to provide high-quality web services, we must solve the problem of the load unbalance caused by dynamic user requests' change. This paper proposes an approach based on hypergraph partition to keep load balance for service-oriented multi-tenant SaaS application. A hypergraph-based service model is used to present hierarchical services and multi-tenant applications. This approach adjusts service distribution on the servers based on hypergraph partition to keep load balance. According to the experiments, this approach effectively solves the problem of load unbalance caused by the change of user requests.

Keywords: service deployment, hypergraph partition, multi-tenant, hierarchical services, SOA.

1   Introduction

Service-Oriented architecture (SOA) has become the standard for enterprise application development and integration. In SOA model, many kinds of computing resources (e.g, applications, services, and servers) are provided as services [1]. It has been considered as an effective solution for enterprise users because of its low cost and rapid reuse [2]. SaaS (Software as a Service) providers usually develop and acquire software applications and host them as services to serve specific requests of their clients.

In service component based SaaS applications, each multi-tenant application consists of a series of services while services are shared by multiple tenants. The multi-tenant applications improve profit margin for both service providers and enterprise users through reducing delivery costs and decreasing service subscription. However, it also introduces a noticeable problem that how to guarantee the quality of service (QoS) for multiple tenants who share applications. If the server that services deploy on is overloaded, the QoS for tenants will be sharply down. In the global

---

* Corresponding author.

The original version of this chapter was revised: The copyright line was incorrect. This has been corrected. The Erratum to this chapter is available at DOI: 10.1007/978-3-642-33068-1_20

M. van Sinderen et al. (Eds.): IWEI 2012, LNBIP 122, pp. 185–192, 2012.

consideration, the QoS for each tenant can be mapped to the loads of services that consist the multi-tenant application, that is to say, we should keep the server balance in order to meet the Qos for tenants. Additionally, the server load changes with user requests dynamically.

Therefore, in this paper we propose an approach based on hypergraph partition to solve the problem of dynamic service deployment under the premise of load balance. The approach is designed to ensure that SaaS providers can deploy and manage the service instances with the dynamic change of multiple tenants' service requests. A hypergraph-based service model is used to represent hierarchical services and these services are divided into several partitions. We propose algorithms that map each hypergraph partition to a server to deploy and balance each partition according to user requests change.

The structure of our paper is organized as follows. In section 2, we outline hypergraph partition-based service deployment. This is followed by section 3 that describes our algorithms for dynamic service deployment. We give some discussions about the overall performance of the approach according to experiments in section 4. Finally, conclusions and future work directions will be shown in the last section.

2   Hypergraph Partition Based Service Deployment for Multi-tenant SaaS Applications

2.1   Hypergraph-Based Service Deployment Model

We consider various business requirements and the dependencies that exist in multi-tenant applications and services, thus services are divided into three levels in our research [8]: business-independent level, business-dependent level and composite business level. There are two kinds of dependences between the services, including functional dependency and business dependency. Such dependences widely exist in tenant applications and services, services in different and identical levels. But traditional DAG is hardly able to represent such structure and dynamic change of hierarchical services. Therefore, we introduce hypergraph partition theory into the service deployment. We establish directed hypergraph-based service deployment model to map servers.

Definition 1 (service): A service is a tuple S = (sId, subServices, sDes, sLevel), where: sId is the identifier of service; subServices is a finite set of services that the service depends on; subServices = { s_1, s_2, ... , s_m }, where each s_i = (target, tRefType), target∈S, tRefTye is the type of dependence which including functional dependency and business dependency; sDes is the description of service; sLevel is the level of service, including business-independent level, business-dependent level and composite business level.

Definition 2 (tenant application): A tenant application is a tuple T = (tInfo, Services, tQos, tNonFun), where: tInfo is the basic information of tenant application, including the tenant information and so on; Services = { S_1, S_2,..., S_n} is a finite set of services; tQos is the QoS for the tenant; tNonFun is non-functional properties of the tenant.

Definition 3: A service deployment directed hypergraph is denoted as SDDG = <V, E>, where:

1) V = {v_1, v_2, ..., v_n} is a finite set, where: each v_i ($i \in [1,n]$) corresponds to a service s_i, while v_i = {S, sR, sG, sQos, sGain, sType}.
  * S is a service which is rented by multi-tenants.
  * sR = {sr_1, sr_2, ..., sr_k} is a finite set of resources that the service need.
  * sG = {sg_1, sg_2, ..., sg_k} is a finite set of resource quantities which sg_i corresponds to sr_i ($i \in [1,k]$).
  * sQos is the quality of service.
  * sGain is the gain value of service. It is the important basis for vertex movement in hypergraph partition. In this paper, sGain represents comprehensive value of resource consumption computed by the resource consumption estimation model. The higher the value, the greater it impacts the partition. It indicates that the vertex has higher priority during the current partition adjustment.
  * sType is the type of vertex, including BV and FV. BV is a base vertex, which is chosen to move to another partition. FV is a free vertex except to base vertexes.

2) E = {e_1, e_2, ..., e_m} is a finite set of hyperedges, m = |E| is the number of hyperedges, eq = { sPre, v_i},($q \in [1,m]$)
  * sPre is a non-empty subset of vertices v_j, which $v_j \in V$. It indicates that the vertex v_i depends on its predecessor vertexes set, that is, the service can be deployed only after the services in its sPre are deployed. sPre = { sv_1, sv_2, ..., sv_k}, k = |sPre| is the number of vertexes which belong to sPre.
  * eType is the type of hyperedge, including CH and NCH. CH is a critical hyperedge. It indicates that current hypergragh partitions will be changed if one vertex that belongs to it moves from one partition to another. NCH is a non critical hyperedge except to CH.

Definition 4: FB and TB, FB is From Block. FB (v_i, e_j) is the source partition that v_i which is connected by hyperedge e_j belongs to. TB (v_i, e_j) is the destination partition.

2.2   Hypergraph Partition for Service Deployment

The services are represented by a hypergraph-based model, and we use the properties of hypergraph partition to solve the problem of dynamic service deployment. We divide vertexes in the hypergraph into different partitions on the basis of the balance formulas and map the hypergraph partitions to the servers.

Definition 5 (Hypergraph Partition): Hypergraph Partition for Service Deployment PS = {P_1, P_2,..., P_k}(as shown in Figure 1) is a final set which includes k subsets of the vertex set V of service deployment directed hypergraph SDDG = <V, E>, where: each $P_i \in PS$ ($i \in [1,k]$) is a non-empty, pairwise-disjoint subset of V; Pw = {pw_1, pw_2,..., pw_k} is the weight set which pw_i corresponds to P_i , where pw_i is the weight of partition P_i ($i \in [1,k]$), k = |PS| is the order of the partitions. Function F(P_i): P_i->S_j

$(i \in [1,k], j \in [1,m])$ represents the mapping relation between hypergraph partition P_i and server j. PS must meet the following conditions:

- $\sum P_i \cup P_j = V, P_i \cap P_j = \varnothing (i, j = 1, 2, ..., k, i \neq j)$
- $pw_i = \sum\limits_{v_j \in P_i} CA_j$, $pw_{avg} = \sum\limits_{p_i \in PS} pw_i / \sum RC_m$ where pw_{avg} is the average of all

  weight pw_i
- For each $e_i \in E(i \in [1,m])$, service i can be deployed only after the services in its source set sPre have been deployed.
- For each $v_i \in V(i \in [1,n])$, the quality of service i should be guaranteed.
- Each partition p_i is balanced only if it meet the balance formula below:

$$pw_i \leq (1+\partial) pw_{avg}, \partial > 0 \qquad (1)$$

∂ is a predetermined maximum load parameters of imbalance deviation.

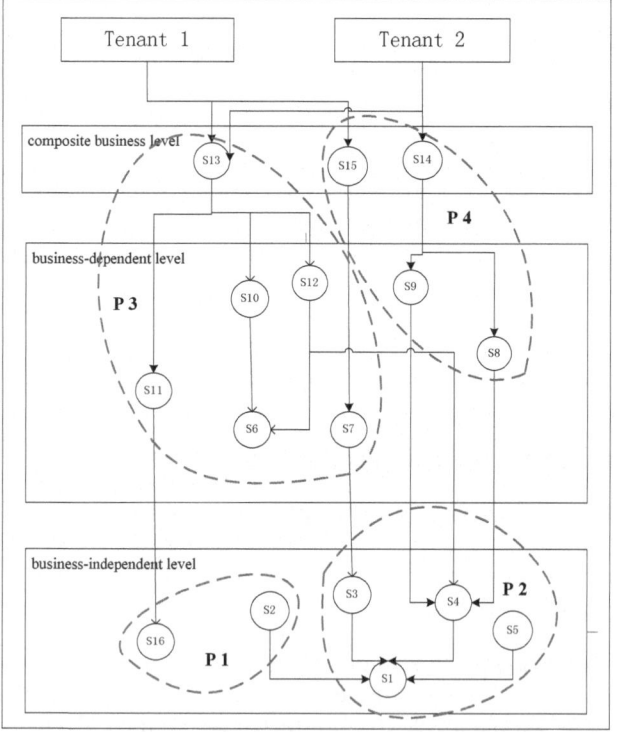

Fig. 1. There are two tenants and fifteen services in the hypergraph model. Hypergraph partition for service deployment PS = {P_1, P_2, P_3, P_4,} has four subsets.

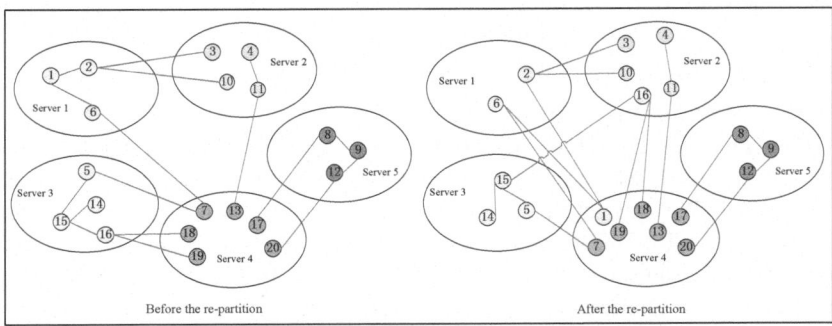

Fig. 2. The left part is the twenty service deployment before the hypergraph re-partition while the right part is the deployment after that

3   Algorithms for Hypergraph-Partition-Based Service Deployment

The algorithms proposed in our paper are based on the hypergraph partition for service deployment. The main idea of the algorithms: Firstly, we initialize the service deployment directed hypergraph SDDG according to parameters. Then, we get the partitions of SDDG on the basis of balance formula. Finally, we map each partition to servers and adjust the hypergraph partitions to keep balance constantly. It mainly includes two parts: First Deployment and Re-partition.

The structure of the main algorithm described as below:

In First Deployment, we initialize the SDDG, get hypergragh partitions of service deployment and deploy the corresponding services on servers.

In Re-partition, we first get actual resource consumptions of every server from the system at regular intervals. Then we adjust the current partitions to keep load balance according to the actual resource consumptions. The resources that are considered include CPU, memory and I/O.

STEP 1 Initialization
We initialize the service deployment directed hypergraph SDDG on the basis of parameters such as tenants and services. The hypergraph partition is based on the SDDG.

STEP 2 First Deployment
When the so-called "first deployment", we can't get real-time resource consumptions of services, so we use the multi-tenant resource consumption model to estimate comprehensive resource consumption CA_i of each service s_i in SDDG. Then we call the function One Partition recursively until each hypergraph partition is balanced according to balance formula (1). Finally, we map each partition to a server, that is to say, we deploy the services that belong to each partition to the corresponding server.

One partition is a recursive function that belongs to First Deployment. Once called, it will check whether the current partitions are balanced. If they are balanced, function returns. If they are not, it divides the current partitions into two parts and calculates the weight set of new partitions because estimated resource consumptions of services change with the dependence relation among them.

STEP 3 Re-partition Deployment
The actual resource consumptions of servers change with user requests. When a server is overloaded, we should adjust current hypergraph partitions in order to re-deploy services. We can get the actual resource consumptions from server system. If the server s_i is overloaded, we select service s_i which is deployed on server s_i and has the highest sGain and move it t into the server whose load is lowest. Only when the current partitions get balance again, we stop the re-partition.

The main algorithm includes three sub-algorithms: Initialization, First Deployment and Re-partition. There are n services and m servers. The time complexity of algorithm Initialization is $O(n)$ which has a linear relationship with the size of services. The algorithm First Deployment calls algorithm One Partition recursively and its time complexity is $O(nlogn)$. The algorithm Re-partition is related to the size of services and servers and its complexity is $O(nm)$. To sum up, the time complexity of whole algorithm is $O(nm)+ O(nlogn)+ O(n)$ which is service quantity and server number related.

4   Performance Evaluation

In this section, we present the performance based on an extensive set of experiments to verify the correctness and effectiveness of our algorithms. The experiments are based on the following scene: Twenty services are deployed on five servers. The servers in our experiments are the same. The resource they provide is one unit while the limited load is 0.7 units. We consider three kinds of resource which include CPU, memory and I/O in the experiments of our paper.

Experiment 1: To verify whether the algorithm First Deployment can get the hypergraph partitions that ensure balance conditions, we list the weight of P_i after first partition of 20 services.

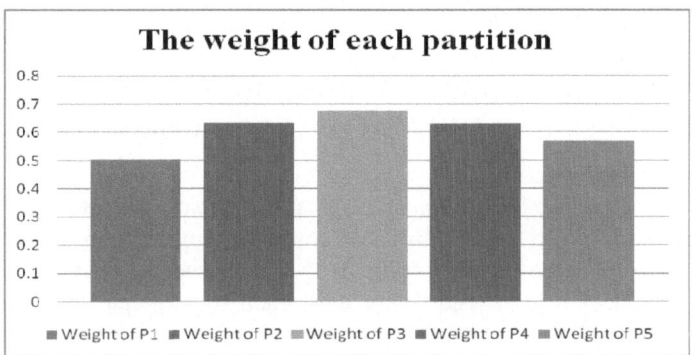

Fig. 3. We get the first partitions after the algorithm First Deployment. The weights of every P_i ($P_i \in PS$) are similar and each partition keeps balance on the basis of balance formula (1). It indicates that the algorithm can get the reasonable hypergraph partitions.

Experiment 2: The system gets the actual loads of 5 servers every day. If servers are overloaded, the system re-partitions the hypergraph according to our algorithm. Then, we adjust the deployment of services to keep server load balance. We compare the actual load of 5 servers before the re-partition with that after the re-partition.

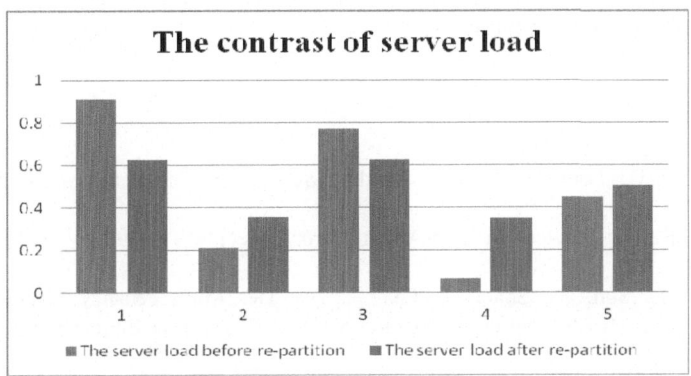

Fig. 4. The blue blocks represent the server loads before the re-partition while the red ones represent the server loads after that. The loads of 5 servers are not balanced before the re-partition deployment. Server 1 and server 3 are overloaded. After the adjustment, the loads of 5 servers are balanced again and none of them is overloaded. It indicates that our algorithm is correct and effective. Figure 2 shows the hypergraph partitions before and after the adjustment.

5   Conclusion and Future Work

In this paper, we study the dynamic deployment with the change of user requests for service-oriented multi-tenant SaaS application. We propose an approach based on hypergraph partition to solve it. The hypergraph partition is used to divide the services into several subsets while each partition is mapped to a server. If the services of every partition are satisfied to the balance formula, it means the corresponding server is not overload, that is, the servers keep balance. From the experiment results, we can conclude that our algorithm works well when we deploy services on the first time and re-deploy them when servers are overloaded.

Although the current approach is good, there are several that need to be improved in future. We plan future work to address the following considerations:

1) We consider the servers are identical and the resources that they provide are equal. In more cases, the servers are different and the resources are not equal. We will consider the differences among them.

2) Sometimes, the loads of some servers are too low, and we can combine the services deployed on them to get more value.

The two points above are not researched deeply in this paper and our future work will be developed around them.

Acknowledgment. The authors would like to acknowledge the support provided by the National High Technology Research and Development Program of China (2011AA040603, 2012AA040904), the National Key Technologies R&D Program of China (2012BAF12B07), the Natural Science Foundation of Shandong Province (ZR2009GM028, ZR2011FQ031) and Independent Innovation Foundation of Shandong University (IIFSDU).

References

1. Newcomer, E., Lomow, G.: Understanding SOA with Web Services. Addison-Wesley (2005)
2. Thomas, E.R.L.: Service-Oriented Architecture: Concepts, Technology, and Design, New York (2005)
3. Tsai, W.-T., Sun, X., Shao, Q., Qi, G.: Two-Tier Multi-Tenancy Scaling and Load Balancing. In: IEEE International Conference on E-Business Engineering, pp. 484–489 (2010)
4. Wang D.-S., Zhang Y.-C., Zhang B., Liu Y.: Load Balancing Strategy for Multi-tenancy SaaS Applications Supporting Service on Demand. Journal of Northeastern University (Natural Science) 32(3), (March 2011)
5. Wang, J., Zhang, D., Wu, Q.-Y., Guan, Y.-A.: Research of a Machine-Learning Based Load Prediction Approach for the Service-oriented Computing Environment. Computer Science 34(9) (2007)
6. Wang, Q., He, X.-H., Zhao, Y.-K., Hu, R.-L.: Load Balancing Algorithm Based on Access Characters load Prediction. Journal of Academy of Armored Force Engineering 23(5) (October 2009)
7. Liu, B., Yang, J., Zhao, Y.: Dynamic Cluster Configuration Strategy for Energy Conservation Based on Online Load Prediction. Computer Engineering 36(24) (December 2010)
8. Wang, R., Zhang, Y., Liu, S., Wu, L., Meng, X.: A Dependency-aware Hierarchical Service Model for SaaS and Cloud Services. In: 2011 IEEE International Conference on Services Computing (SCC 2011), July 4-9, pp. 480–487 (2011)
9. Catalyurek, U.V., Boman, E.G., Devine, K.D., Bozda, D., Heaphy, R.T., Riesen, L.A.: A repartitioning hypergraph model for dynamic load balancing. J. Parallel Distrib. Comput. 69, 711–724 (2009)
10. Kwok, T., Mohindra, A.: Resource Calculations with Constraints, and Placement of Tenants and Instances for Multi-tenant SaaS Applications. In: Bouguettaya, A., Krueger, I., Margaria, T. (eds.) ICSOC 2008. LNCS, vol. 5364, pp. 633–648. Springer, Heidelberg (2008)

Service-Oriented Digital Identity-Related Privacy Interoperability: Implementation Framework of Privacy-as-a-Set-of-Services (PaaSS)

Ghazi Ben Ayed and Solange Ghernaouti-Hélie

Information Systems Institute, Faculty of Business and Economics,
University of Lausanne, CH-1015, Lausanne, Switzerland
{Ghazi.Benayed,Sgh}@unil.ch

Abstract. Protecting digital identity is crucial aspect in order to successfully enable collaboration between heterogeneous and distributed information systems. In this context, privacy could play a key role for digital identity protection and security. Thus, an identity layer in which interoperable privacy is delivered in the shape of a set of services, rather than monolithic applications, would be inevitably responding to the need of collaboration. In this article, we suggest a novel layered service-oriented implementation framework that information systems security projects' members could borrow to successfully turn digital identity-related privacy requirements into a set of services. Several blocks are distributed amongst five layers and three mapping gateways determine the roadmap of the implementation effort governance. Seven loosely coupled, publicly hosted and available to on-demand calls services are specified to accommodate service-oriented architectures. OMG SoaML diagrams, BPMN process descriptions and SOA-artifacts specifications are provided and explained.

Keywords: Digital identity, privacy, interoperability, implementation framework, SOA.

1 Introduction

Recent years have seen the trend of business globalization which urgently requires dynamical collaboration among organizations. The business processes and organizations' information systems need to be integrated seamlessly to adapt the continuously changing business conditions and to stay competitive in the global market. Collaborative environments present major challenges to privacy since there is an exchange of digital identities between collaborators [1]. Moreover, privacy is a critical right and a protection to enforce, if we wish to provide to individuals with the means to protect digital identities. When privacy is compromised, security of the individual, the organization or the country could be threatened [2-10]. Thus, there is a need to establish a balance between the benefits of collaborative environments, which provide knowledge discovery and sharing against the protection of individual and organizational privacy needs [11].

The original version of this chapter was revised: The copyright line was incorrect. This has been corrected. The Erratum to this chapter is available at DOI: 10.1007/978-3-642-33068-1_20

M. van Sinderen et al. (Eds.): IWEI 2012, LNBIP 122, pp. 193–200, 2012.
© IFIP International Federation for Information Processing 2012

A technical approach is not sufficient enough to tackle privacy issues and Privacy-enhanced Technologies (PET) is an example of technical initiative failure [7]. We promote a multidisciplinary and integrated approach, which dictates that law, policies, regulations and technologies are to be crafted together. Moreover, digital identity management functionalities are increasingly delivered as sets of services, rather than monolithic applications. So, an identity layer in which identity and privacy management are interoperable could respond to the need of distributed environments. Such interoperability could be offered through design of a set of loosely coupled, publicly hosted and available to on-demand calls services and implementations on open standards.

In this article, we aim to respond to the following main questions: how we could implement interoperable digital identity-related privacy (DigIdeRP) system? Narrowly, how to disassemble digital identity-related privacy business interoperability into a technical interoperability in the shape of set of services: Privacy-as-a-Set-of-Services (PaaSS) system? The research is information system design-type in the field of security and its outcome is to suggest a layered service-oriented implementation governance framework that could help information system's security designers, architects, and developers to turn DigIdeRP requirements into a set of services that can domicile a service-oriented architecture (SOA). The framework relays on the idea that privacy is to be engineered to integrate identity from the start, rather than attaching it to identity after the fact. The implementation governance framework helps to align DigIdeRP initiatives with organization's business goals and security strategy. Such initiative requires an engagement from top level security management throughout the project. This article is organized as follows. In section 2, we explain the need of interoperable privacy within federated digital identity systems and we describe the target PaaSS system. In section 3, we describe each block of the implementation governance framework that could help information system's security implementation team to successfully conduct DigIdeRP interoperability initiatives in the shape of PaaSS system. We identify seven services through the use of OMG SoaML modeling language from DigIdeRP requirements and we describe services' consumption with BPMN flow-chart based notation. We provide a range of SoaML diagrams to illustrate the design and pre-implementation steps. Finally, we conclude and present future work in section 4.

2   Layered SO-DigIdeRP Implementation Framework

Oracle suggested best practices within SOA governance framework [12] to help guide SOA implementation projects. In general, a framework can help to better manage implementation risks and encourage stakeholders work together, collaboratively throughout the process as a team. In addition, it allows people, processes, and technology to be collaboratively integrated [13]. The framework serves as a basis for vital understanding between business and technical managers on how to collaborate in order to conduct such initiatives. In earlier work [14] , we presented an overview of the framework but here we suggest various blocks that we dispatch over five layers and three mapping gateways, see figure 1. The blocks in the Service-Oriented Digital Identity-related Privacy (SO-DigIdeRP) framework determines a roadmap that security team could follow to successfully implement interoperability.

2.1   Layer1, Layer2 and Mapping Gateway

In the purpose-level SOA layer, we articulate the need of implementing DigIdeRP initiatives, which are to be approached from a strategic point of view with a high level of clarity on objectives. In the purpose-business mapping gateway, we identify the privacy requirements sources related to digital identity such as policies, fair information practices, laws and procedures. In business-level SOA layer, we specify four blocks: 1) functional requirements' specification. Ten DigIdeRP requirements [15] are already specified and detailed; 2) digital identity management (DigIdM) technical model specification. Technical models are already been covered and compared in [16] in which digital identity federation is elected because it secures distributed systems and allows better privacy protection; 3) specification of DigIdM deployment perspective. ITU report [17] classifies DigIdM systems' works and projects into a landscape of three perspectives: a) network operator centric perspective in which capabilities that maximize and protect network assets are sought; b) application service provider centric perspectives in which capabilities that maximize and protect application assets are sought; and c) user-centric perspective in which capabilities that allow privacy protection and user control over digital identity are sought. Considered as a derivate of digital identity federation, user-centric digital identity federation is a novel and promising approach that provides more control over digital identity [18]. That's why user-centric approach is adopted. DigIdM technical model and DigIdM deployment perspective blocks are grouped into DigIdM architectural model envelope; and 4) the business process portray deals with providing process-based view of DigIdeRP requirements. Six DigIdeRP processes are identified and described in flow-chart Business Process Modeling Notation (BPMN 2.0). The processes are: a) ServiceRequest process; b) ProfileToChallenge process: the subject sends a profile-to-challenge-request to the SP in order to be able to access his profile, check its validity and have the capability to change it. The SP sends the possessed profile that is drawn from digital identity attributes aggregation. The subject may send a change, update or modify profile request to the SP, which confirms the update operation. However, no action will be undertaken if the subject is in agreement with his profile, see figure 2; c) EnrollmentRequest process; d) DigitalIdentityToUpdate process; e) PeriodicDigitalIdentityToUpdate process; and f) EditDigitalIdentity process.

2.2   Layer3 and Service Design Approach

SoaML is an OMG specification, which describes a UML profile and metamodel for designing services within a service-oriented architecture. SoaML is chosen for two major reasons: 1) SoaML is a modeling language that helps to ensure an easy understanding and validation by the project members since SoaML permits a technology-neutral representation of the services; 2) SoaML supports the activities for modeling service that could be accommodated by service oriented architecture. SoaML permits to identify service candidates and to design services for SOA and not SOA itself [19].

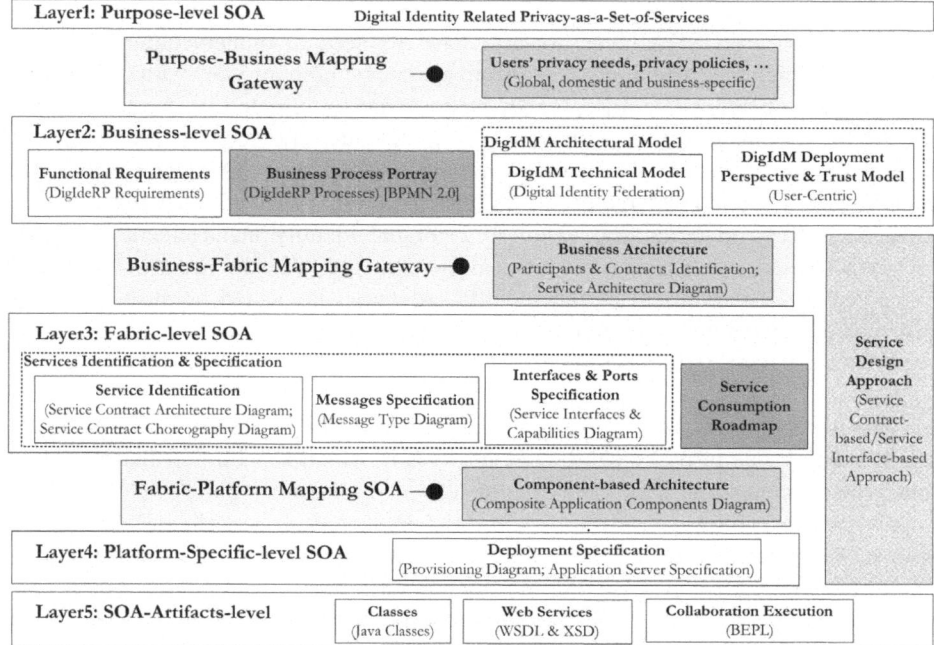

Fig. 1. Layers and blocks of SO-DigIdeRP implementation framework

Service design approach is an inter-layers block. SoaML modeling capabilities support the service "contract-based" and "interface-based" approaches [20]. We had to choose between the two approaches before undertaking activities in the business-fabric mapping gateway, fabric-platform mapping gateway, layer 3, and layer 4.The service-contract approach requires an already established business and collaboration agreement between parties. In the adopted DigIdM identity federation technical model, circle-of-trust sets the agreement between parties of the identity federation, thus, service-contract approach is the best-fit.

In the business-fabric mapping gateway, we set the SoaML service architecture diagram to define participants and service contracts. We define seven service contracts, which would be later on seven services. We identify participants (subject, IdP, SP) that participates in a service contract with either a "sender" or "receiver" role, which may change when participants participate in other service contracts. For instance, in the ProfileToChallenge service contract, the Subject plays the role of a sender and the SP as a receiver and in DigitalIdentityRequest service contract the senders are the Subject and IdP; and the receiver is SP. In the fabric-level SOA, we define seven services without regard for their implementations: 1) ContractAgreement service;

2) DigitalIdentityRequest service; 3) DigitalIdentityToUpdate service; 4) PeriodicDigitalIdentityToUpdate service; 5) Enrollment service; 6) ProfileToChallenge service; and 7) EditDigitalIdentity service. For each service, we provide details through establishment of SoaML service contract architecture diagram, service contract choreography diagram, and message type diagram. Each service contract diagram shows though a connector that an interaction is established between two roles stereotyped "consumer" and "provider". Methods are available either in consumer service interface or provider service interface. The latter can invoke methods that are available through consumer service interface and vice-versa. The service choreography diagram highlights the negotiation and communication process between service interfaces in term of calls of methods. Moreover, different inputs of the methods are messages that are described in messages diagrams.

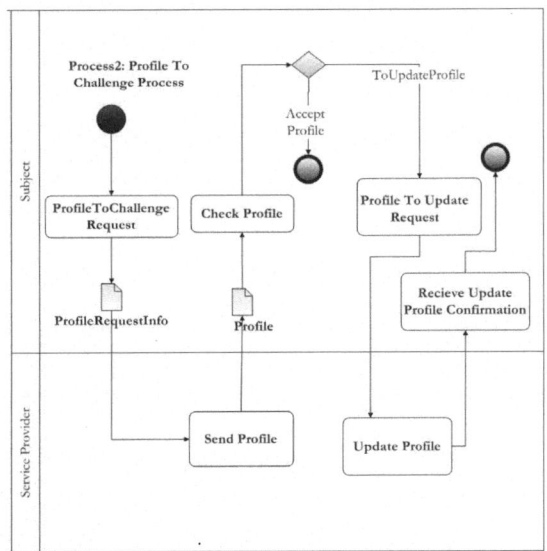

Fig. 2. BPMN Description of ProfileToChallenge Process

In figure 3, the service contract is established between the consumer ProfileToChallengeReceiver and the provider ProfileToChallengeSender. Each role is represented by an interface. The consumer invokes ProfileRequest with profileProperties message type, which encloses subjectRef information. The provider invokes sendProfile method with profile message type. The consumer is able to send a request for a profile change by invoking profileToUpdateRequest method with profile properties message type. The provider receives a profile change acknowledgement as a result of consumer's invocation of updateProfileConfirmation method with UpdatedProfileConfirmation message type.

In the service consumption roadmap, we combine BPMN process description with SoaML service identification and specification in order to define how services are consumed to execute processes. To execute ProfileToChallenge process, the service

ProfileToChallenge is consumed four times with different methods and following this order: 1) (Service Name: ProfileToChallenge Service, Requester: Subject, Recipient: SP, Method: ProfileRequest); 2) (Service Name: ProfileToChallenge Service, Requester: SP, Recipient: Subject, Method: SendProfile); 3) (Service Name: ProfileToChallenge Service, Requester: Subject, Recipient: SP, Method: ProfileToUpdateRequest); and 4) (Service Name: ProfileToChallenge Service, Requester: SP, Recipient: Subject, Method: UpdateProfileConfirmation).

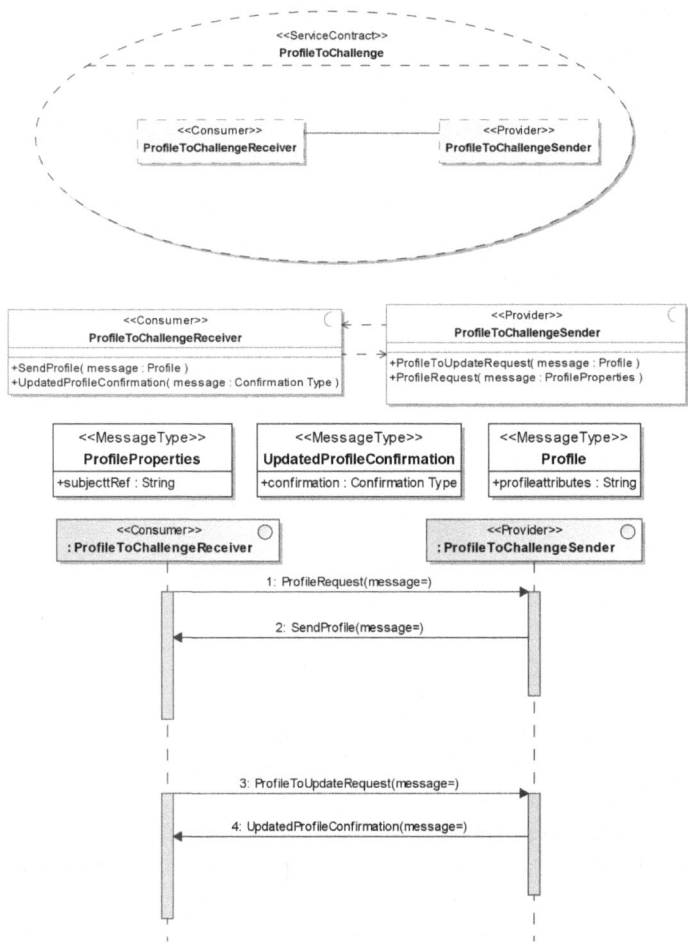

Fig. 3. ProfileToChallenge service contract, message type and choreography diagrams

2.3   Layer 4, Layer5 and Mapping Gateway

In the fabric-platform mapping, we describe, through SoaML composite application component diagram, different components to be implemented. The composite application component diagram is a platform-independent diagram; however, the provision diagram, in layer 4, is a platform-dependent one. We implement in Java Enterprise Edition, the provision diagram. We integrated Eclipse IDE (version 3.4) with ModelPro SDK (version 1.1) in order to generate the code of SOA-related artifacts, layer5, including Java code for service interfaces and SCA components, and XSD, WSDL, SCA Composite files.

3   Conclusion and Outlooks

SO-DigIdeRP framework blocks descriptions are based on OMG SoaML, which helps to systemically choose and identify services on the basis of service contracts specifications. We intend to explore the existence and applicability of other service modeling languages on SO-DigIdeRP framework and to compare framework outputs. While SoaML service contracts has provided a major contribution to model DigIdeRP requirements, but we find that it also interesting to explore the development of DigIdeRP requirements with RuleML and to evaluate benefits and inconveniences against possibilities that are offered by SoaML. We intend also to implement services from network operator centric perspective and application service provider centric perspective based on the description of each DigIdM deployment perspective requirements. Moreover, we will adopt service interface based approach instead of service contract based approach and we'll explore differences. The major limit of the framework is services longevity issue. When DigIdeRP requirements, DigIdM technical models, deployment or trust models changes, impacts of the changes affect the design and implementation of all services at a risk of existing services reutilization. This is due to the tightly-coupled nature of DigIdeRP requirements. Metamodel for privacy policies within SOA of [21-23] in which researchers have made a decomposition of privacy policies, and it is inspiring us to conduct future research to explore whether the service identification starts from requirements disassembling rather than from service design.

References

[1] Duan, Y., Canny, J.: Protecting User Data in Ubiquitous Computing: Towards Trustworthy Environments. In: Martin, D., Serjantov, A. (eds.) PET 2004. LNCS, vol. 3424, pp. 167–185. Springer, Heidelberg (2005)
[2] Philippsohn, S.: ID and the Law. In: Birch, D.G.W. (ed.) Digital Identity Management: Perspectives on the Technological, Business and Social Implications, pp. 193–203. Gower Publishing Limited (2007)
[3] Cochrane, P.: Forward of the Book. In: Birch, D.G.W. (ed.) Digital Identity Management: Perspectives on the Technological, Business and Social Implications. Gower Publishing Limited (2007)
[4] Cameron, K.: The Laws of Identity. ed: Microsoft Corporation (2005)
[5] Hansen, M., et al.: Privacy and Identity Management. IEEE Security & Privacy (2008)
[6] Bell, G., Gemmel, J.: A Digital Life. Scientific American Magazine, 58–65 (2007)
[7] International Telecommunication Union, Digital Life. ITU Internet Report (2006)

 [8] Windley, P.J.: Digital Identity: Unmasking identity management architecture (IMA). O'Reilly Media (2005)
 [9] Cukier, K.: A special report on managing information. The Economist February 23-March 5 (2010)
[10] Organizing Committee of Digital Identity & Privacy (Human Capital & Social Innovation Technology Summit), Call for Controbution to Managing Digital Identities for Education, Employment and Business Development (2007)
[11] Bellotti, V.: What You Don't Know Can Hurt You: Privacy in Collaborative Computing. In: British Computer Society Conference on Human-Computer Interaction, pp. 241–261 (1996)
[12] Afshar, M., et al.: SOA Governance: Framework and Best Practices (2007)
[13] Kelley, D.: Practical Approaches for Securing Web Applications across the Software Delivery Lifecycle (2009)
[14] Ben Ayed, G., Ghernaouti-Hélie, S.: Architecting Interoperable Privacy within User-Centric Federated Digital Identity Systems: Overview of a Service-Oriented Implementation Framework. In: Benlamri, R. (ed.) NDT 2012, Part II. CCIS, vol. 294, pp. 165–177. Springer, Heidelberg (2012)
[15] Ben Ayed, G., Ghernaouti-Hélie, S.: Privacy Requirements Specification for Digital Identity Management Systems Implementation: Towards a digital society of privacy. In: 6th International Conference for Internet Technology and Secured Transactions, ICITST 2011, Abu Dhabi, UAE (2011)
[16] Ben Ayed, G.: Consolidating Fragmented Identity: Attributes Aggregation to Secure Information Systems. IADIS International Journal on Computer Science and Information Systems 4, 1–12 (2009)
[17] ITU Focus Group on Identity Management (FG IdM), Report on Identity Management Use Cases and Gap Analysis (2007)
[18] Jøsang, A., Pope, S.: User-Centric Identity Management. In: Proceedings of the AusCERT Asia Pacific Information Technology Security Conference, pp. 1–6 (2005)
[19] OMG. Service oriented architecture Modeling Language (SoaML) - Specification for the UML Profile and Metamodel for Services (UPMS) (2009)
[20] Elvesæter, B., et al.: Specifying Services Using the Service Oriented Architecture Modeling Language (SoaML): A baseline for specification of cloud-based services. In: The 1st International Conference on Cloud Computing and Services Science (CLOSER 2011), Noordwijkerhout, The Netherlands (2011)
[21] Allison, D.S., et al.: Privacy and trust policies within SOA. In: International Conference for Internet Technology and Secured Transactions, ICITST 2009 (2009)
[22] Allison, D.S., et al.: Metamodel for privacy policies within SOA. In: The 2009 ICSE Workshop on Software Engineering for Secure Systems, IWSESS 2009 (2009)
[23] Garcia, D., et al.: An Electronic Contract Model for Privacy Protection in Service-Oriented Architecture. In: Fifth International Conference on Digital Information Management (ICDIM 2010), Thunder Bay, Canada (2010)

Research on Semantic Interoperability for Business Collaboration

Zhan Jiang, Lanfen Lin, and Fei Xie

College of Computer Science
Zhejiang University
Hangzhou, China
{jiangzhan,llf,skyfire_xiefei}@zju.edu.cn

Abstract. In order to deal with the heterogeneous systems and variety of business data, business model and description of different enterprises in the interoperation process, a semantic interoperability framework for business collaboration is proposed in this paper. In the framework, a multi-facet ontology system supporting business collaboration is introduced to give unified understanding throughout interoperation process. Based on the framework, a method to extract ontologies from multi sources quickly and to realize semantic mapping based on mixed ontologies is utilized to resolve the semantic conflicts. Web service is employed to eliminate the system-level heterogeneity and is semantically enhanced to meet the requirements of service discovery. After that, the on-demand business construction is achieved through services dynamic combination. Finally, a prototype platform is developed and the feasibility of our framework was verified. Our proposed framework provides beneficial references for SMEs to realize inter-enterprise business collaboration in China.

Keywords: semantic interoperability (SI), ontology, Web service, business collaboration (BC).

1 Introduction

Software systems introduced by enterprises during the construction of enterprise informatization improve business efficiency. However, due to the heterogeneity caused by different software vendors and programming language, the business collaboration via system interoperation is hard to run smoothly. Web Service adopts a serial of standard technologies and protocols such as WSDL, UDDI, XML and SOAP [1]. Relevant business functions of enterprise systems are encapsulated into well-defined web services and invoked to shield system-level heterogeneity. Besides, it breaks through the restriction of territory and becomes a convenient and effective method to achieve long-distance business collaboration. Since enterprises differ in management pattern, business process and product model and so on, and employees in different departments or enterprises describe the business concept, data and model in dissimilar ways, semantic conflicts emerge throughout the process of business collaboration, it's necessary to find a method to resolve the semantic-level conflicts.

The original version of this chapter was revised: The copyright line was incorrect. This has been corrected. The Erratum to this chapter is available at DOI: 10.1007/978-3-642-33068-1_20

M. van Sinderen et al. (Eds.): IWEI 2012, LNBIP 122, pp. 201–208, 2012.
© IFIP International Federation for Information Processing 2012

The emergence of ontology technology provides a new method for solving semantic problems of system interoperability. Ontology, as "an explicit specification of a conceptualization" [2], is able to represent the knowledge of specific domain in semantic level. It has been widely applied in many fields of computer science, such as knowledge sharing, software reusing and information retrieval. In order to achieve system interoperability among enterprises, ontology has been introduced by researchers to model heterogeneous systems to maintain semantic consistency among different systems. Bichindaritz proposes an ontology-based framework for semantic interoperability of case-based reasoning systems in biology and medicine [3]. Hu and Li etc. presents an ontology-based method of semantic interoperability to solve the interoperability problems in CAD and GIS [4]. Yang and Zhang gives a method of construction models interoperability by building construction domain ontology and modeling CAD models [5]. Park and Ram develop a comprehensive framework and methodology to facilitate semantic interoperability among distributed and heterogeneous information systems [6]. And lots of projects, likes STASIS, ONTOGOV, TERREGOV [7] also achieve semantic business collaboration in specific domain. Some researches concentrate in certain field and have domain limitations, and some are proposed in the general perspective and testified effectiveness. But it's hard to apply them to the SMEs collaborations in China. The informatization level of SMEs in China is backward, and there exists no available business model in these SMEs, not to mention ontology construction and maintenance. In this paper, taking SMEs in China as subject, considering the real situation encountered throughout business collaboration, a practical framework of semantic interoperability (SI) is proposed to realize business collaboration (BC).

The rest of the paper is organized as follows. Section 2 describes the characteristics and obstacles of SMEs cooperation. The semantic interoperability framework is given in section 3. Section 4 elaborates on the key technologies involved during the process of business collaboration. Section 5 discusses the enterprise interoperation process and the implementation of the framework. Finally, section 6 concludes the paper and discusses some future work.

2   Analysis of SMEs Collaboration

There are five typical characteristics in the industry cluster of SMEs: 1)the large number of enterprises in the region, more than 90 percent of them are small and medium-sized enterprise(SME) . 2) The business collaboration in this area is extreme complex because of the large number of enterprises and the frequent business cooperation among them. The multiple collaborations among the enterprises include supply, manufacture, sales, logistics and service. 3) Among these SMEs, disparities of levels of IT are extraordinary. Not only the various software vendors, but also the incompatibility of information technologies like system architecture, infrastructure, programming languages and so on, leads to the high heterogeneity of systems, which means it is infeasible to realize system interaction by means of point-to-point system interface. 4) Enterprises benefit from the variety of product range but suffer from various product naming and coding rules. 5) The business process and marketing strategy are often changed to response to market fleetly.

Every enterprise cooperates with elses in one or more business fields by means of particular system. In the region, usually more than two enterprises participate in inter-collaboration process. Taking account of product performance, price and delivery, the manufacturer could spill the order and purchase from a variety of sources. In this situation these systems of enterprises involved co-operate with others to realize the procurement. There are three obstacles existing in the business collaboration between enterprises:1) the business object model differs from system to system, and employee of different enterprises and departments differs in many aspects, like domain engaged, post occupied, education level, expression ability and so on, contributing to the different understanding and description of single concept. When enterprise cooperates with others, there might exist something ambiguous or even conflicting. 2) service adopts an open and standard method to shield the system-level heterogeneity, but the method only stipulate the specific grammar format of the interface, like service operations, inputs and outputs, lacking of semantic description of service features and functionality. Since the services aren't described accurately, it's difficult to meet the requirements of service discovery and combination. 3) the cooperative enterprise is chosen until the business collaboration begins, thus the inter-enterprise business process can't be preset. And enterprises differ in many aspects like business processes, organizations and management decisions, endowing business collaboration with the characteristics of high dynamic and randomness.

3   The Framework of SI for BC

In order to solve the problems of semantic inconsistency throughout the process of system interoperation, a multi-facet ontology system supporting business collaboration is introduced. The ontology system consists of shared top-level ontology, domain ontology, local ontology and service ontology. Shared top-level ontology, describing the general concept and the relationship between concepts, is domain-independent. It coordinates the relationship among else ontologies to maintain the concept consistency. Domain ontology and local ontology are both introduced to express the business concepts and relationships between concepts related in business collaboration. They differ in different objects, one for a specific domain and the other for concrete enterprise application. Service ontology is used to describe the concepts related with service and relationships. It gives the description of service attribute, functionality and interactive information. OWL-S [8] is adopted to describe the ontology information, since the model OWL-S of semantic description mainly focuses on the service functionality and is lack of service non-functional description. So the ServiceProfile ontoloty model of OWL-S is extended to express non-functional features like quality, expense, valuation. ServiceModel and ServiceGrouding are inherited to express basic attribute set and interface set.

Based on the building of ontology system, a framework of semantic interoperability for business collaboration is proposed, as shown in Fig. 1. There are three parts in the framework: the ontology system and the rules used for semantic conflicts resolution, the service repository based on the encapsulation of enterprise system and semantic enhancement, the dynamic combination of inter-enterprise process and the rules used for enterprise process conflicts resolution. The three parts dissolve the semantic inconsistency gradually in data level, system level and business process level corresponding to the obstacles met in the process of system interoperation. The three levels are progressive and the lower level of interoperability is the foundation of the upper level.

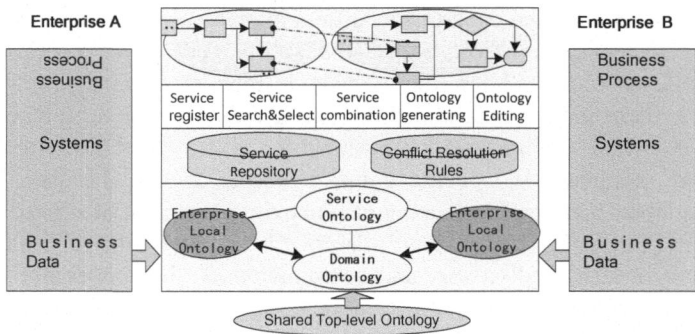

Fig. 1. The framework of semantic interoperability for business collaboration

4   The Key Technologies of SI for BC

4.1   The Construction of Ontology for Business Collaboration

The common method of building ontology [11] theoretically is correct, but the heavy workload and long cycle become prohibitive to SMEs in China, and it requires the ontology constructors having a good understanding of this domain. Consequently, a practical method for quickly building ontology is necessary.

(1) Local Ontology Construction

In the process of ontology construction on basis of structured data, the relational model (such as ER chart) can be obtained from database structure. The concepts, relationship, attributes, attribute type, primary key and foreign key can be extracted from the relational model and be transformed into corresponding rules, such as relationship are mapped to concept in the ontology, namely owl:Class, attribute are mapping to owl:Datatypeproperty, etc. These mapping rules are stored in the database for each enterprise. Under the guidance of the mapping rules, local ontology can be quickly built from databases of every enterprise.

Since there are a great number Semi-structured data, like XML files, which can be obtained from enterprise systems. Considering the regular corresponding relations between XML Schema and the description language of OWL [10,13], utilizing these XML files to construct local ontology appears feasible. Firstly, by parsing the XML document, extracting structural information and its data content, the corresponding XML Schema and XML Data files are generated respectively. Based on the detailed mapping relations between the elements of XML Schema and OWL [13], XSLT template is defined to transform the XML Schema elements to OWL elements. After the XML Data file is transformed to ontology instances, the ontology model and ontology instances are merged together to generate final ontology files.

Unstructured data is data without fixed structure and the method is similar with the common ontology construction method, it's too time-consuming and workload-heavy to build a local ontology in this way for an enterprise.

(2) Domain Ontology Building

Since the creation of domain ontology demands a mass of workload, and it's practically impossible for domain experts to finish it solely. The essence of Web 2.0 is using the internet to publish and share the information. Inspired by this, we utilize Web 2.0 technology to realize self-building of domain knowledge, only if a valid mechanism for information organization and management is adopted. In such case, the domain ontology is more effectual because it comes from the public and takes full advantage of the wisdom of them. This paper introduces a mature business domain-independent ontology as the basis, and the users in various regions can create and maintain the domain ontology by extending ontology content continuously, then domain experts or professionals review and normalize the concepts and knowledge enriched by different enterprise users, consequently forming a domain ontology shared by all users building.

4.2   The Resolution of Semantic Conflicts in Enterprise Interoperability

Semantic conflict can be divided into data-layer conflict and scheme-layer conflict. The former is caused by the different perception of the same concept and data value by different people, such as in naming, precision and representation, while the latter is caused by the differences of logic structure employed to express a same concept and data, including attribute set conflict, summarized conflict, polymerization conflict, associated conflict, etc. The process of semantic conflicts resolution is described below. First, the conflict list is generated by judging whether there are semantic conflicts exists between the collaborators. Then the mapping rules between the domain ontology and local ontologies are established for every collaborator respectively. After connecting the mapping rules of two collaborators together, the mapping specification is obtained. Thus, after the completion of the enterprise local ontology and domain ontology construction, how to establish the mapping between enterprise local ontology and domain ontology became a critical problem for the semantic conflicts resolution.

The multi-strategy mapping method first uses the enterprise local ontology and domain ontology as well as their respective data instances to train the learning classifier. According to classification results, a similarity measure algorithm is used to calculate the similarity of each pair of concept nodes, to determine the relative position of the concept in the other ontology. Then, based on HowNet, after using the method proposed by Ni, Wang etc. [12] to calculate the similarity of concept definition and utilizing similarity evaluation function and to assess the similarity, the similarity matrix is gained. Finally knowledge of domain axiomatic constraints is applied to assess the similarity and the mapping rules are generated. The mapping relations, higher than threshold value settled are stored in the mapping rules library. Most of the data-layer and scheme-layer conflicts can be resolved through the mapping rules, also permitted to be created manually for others conflicts.

4.3   On-Demand Inter-enterprise Business Processes Construction

Since the inter-enterprise business process has the characteristics of high dynamic and randomness, service engine and service mediation are put forward to realize the service combination in two steps. First, requirements are annotated and divided into several structural sub-needs, describing detailed contents like product category, product name, quantity, delivery. The logic and constraint relations among the sub-needs are recorded. Secondly, based on the description of sub-need, the service engine searches service repository to generate candidate services sets and evaluates the services combination. A multi-object genetic algorithm is employed to meet specific goals such as quality-preferred or delivery-preferred. After the optimal services portfolio are chosen, the relationship between requirements and service set is established. This process only concentrates on the temporal and logical relationships, hierarchical constraint of services from the functional and non-functional requirements of service, without considering the service provider, the actual business process. Next, service mediation analyze the actual process of every business interactions to generate the inter-enterprise business process. Finally, based on the relationship between requirements and service set and the inter-enterprise business process for each interaction, the on-demand inter-enterprise business processes is constructed by service mediations, as depicted in Fig. 2.

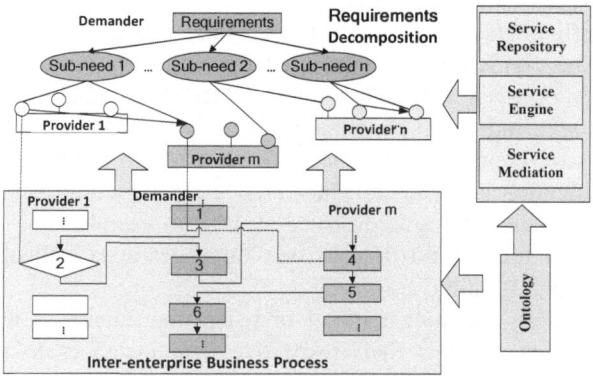

Fig. 2. On-demand inter-enterprise business processes construction

Every enterprise needs to define its business processes, and the platform attempts to link the business processes of collaborative enterprise up to detect whether conflict exists. Once conflict is found, it implies related enterprises to resolve the conflicts by creating mapping rules or collaborative business process building. During the process of generating the inter-enterprise business process for each service interaction, owing to the different business process model and the description, the inter-enterprise business process should be constructed based on the business process mapping specification to resolve the inconsistency of business process. Based above, after dividing the requirements into sub-needs and mapping the sub-needs into service sets, the dynamic inter-enterprise business process is achieved by the combination of enterprise business process according to every service interaction of the service set.

5   Application and Conclusion

Based on the research contents, a platform based on J2EE framework, Web Services and OWL-S 1.1 specification is developed. The system mainly includes modules of ontology building and maintenance, service register center, business process model editing, conflict mapping rules management, workflow engine and so on. Table 1 shows the auto-generated mapping specification between the two enterprises' local ontologies. Fig. 3 shows an instantiation of the cross-enterprise business processes constructed. When manufacturer A publishes the demand as "products X5000 in 2-3 days" and chooses its suppliers, the platform detects the business process conflicts. Based on the mapping rules, both the supplier B and logistics services providers C add a new process as "send order confirmation" in order to comply with the process of A.

Table 1. The mapping specification between local ontologies

Local Ontology A	Domain general ontology	Local Ontology B
Category: low-voltage apparatus	Category: low-voltage apparatus	Category: low-voltage apparatus
Attribute :Pro-duct name	Attribute :Product name	Attribute :Prod-uct description
Attribute: Product code	Attribute: Product model	Attribute: Product NO.
Attribute: cost per unit	Attribute: unit cost	Attribute: unit price
Attribute: number	Attribute: number	Attribute: quantity

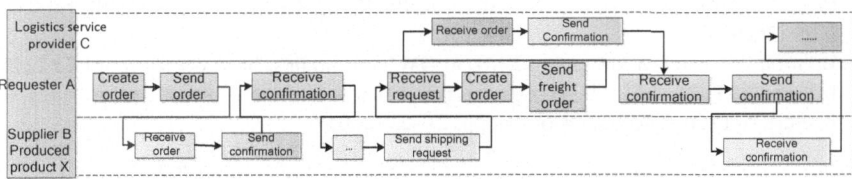

Fig. 3. Instantiation of inter-enterprise business process construction

This platform has been partly applied to the representative Liushi low-voltage apparatus industry cluster in Zhejiang Province of China and proved to be workable. Through this platform, systems of different enterprises can interoperate with others and promote the efficiency of the business cooperation, especially among the core enterprise of the supply chain and the upstream and downstream enterprises surrounding it. But it still needs lots of related prerequisite work and manual intervention during the process of business collaboration, like business process model building, local ontology building, leading to the restriction of the application scope. The future work is to increase automation and reduce the workloads of enterprises.

References

1. Van Der Alsta, W.M.P., Benatallah, B., Casati, F., Curbera, F., et al.: Business process management: where business processes and web services meet. Data &Knowledge Engineering 61(1), 1–5 (2007)
2. Uschold, M., King, M.: Towards a Methodology for Building Ontologies. In: Workshop on Basic Ontologies Issues in Knowledge Sharing (1995)
3. Bichindaritz, I.: Mémoire: A framework for semantic interoperability of case-based reasoning systems in biology and medicine. Artificial Intelligence in Medicine 36(2), 177–192 (2006)
4. Hu, Y.-J., Li, S.-P., Guo, M.: Ontology-based product knowledge representation. Journal of Computer-Aided Design & Computer Graphics 15(12), 1531–1637 (2003) (in Chinese)
5. Yang, Q.Z., Zhang, Y.: Semantic interoperability in building design: methods and tools. Computer-Aided Design 38(10), 1099–1112 (2006)
6. Park, J., Ram, S.: Information systems interoperability: What lies beneath? ACM Transactions on Information Systems 22(4), 595–632 (2004)
7. Guglielmina, C.: The COIN Project – Vision, Objectives, Results. In: COIN IP Workshop. Enterprise Interoperability & Collaboration in China: Barriers and Challenges, 20th Anniversary of the Cooperation between China and Europe in ICT for Enterprise
8. Jiang, Z., Wang, M., Lin, L.-F.: Research on service-oriented reconfigurable business collaboration platform for cluster supply chain. In: International Conference on Manufacturing Automation, ICMA (2010)
9. W3C. Team comment on the OWL-S submission[EB/OL] (September 12, 2007), http://www.w3.org/Submission/2004/07/Comment
10. Rahm, E., Bernstein, P.A.: A survey of approaches to automatic schema matching. The VLDB Journal 10(4), 334–350 (2001)
11. Noy, N.F., McGuinness, D.L.: Ontology development 101: A guide to creating your first ontology. Technical Report SMI-2001-0880, Stanford Medical Informatics (2001)
12. Ni, Y., Wang, H., Huang, N., Lu, Y., et al.: A Heterogeneous System Integration Framework for Business Collaboration. In: Intelligent Computing and Intelligent Systems, ICIS (2009)
13. Bohring, H., Auer, S.: Mapping XML to OWL ontologies. In: Proceedings of 13 Leipziger Informatik-Tage (LIT 2005) Leipziger Germany. Lecture Notes in Informatics (LNI), Lecture Notes in Informatics (r2qi), pp. 21–23 (2005)

Erratum to: Enterprise Interoperability

Marten van Sinderen[1], Pontus Johnson[2], Xiaofei Xu[3], and Guy Doumeingts[4]

[1] University of Twente, The Netherlands
m.j.vansinderen@utwente.nl
[2] KTH Royal Institute of Technology, Stockholm, Sweden
pontus@ics.kth.se
[3] Harbin Institute of Technology, China
xiaofei@hit.edu.cn
[4] Université Bordeaux1, Talence Cedex, France
guy.doumeingts@interop-vlab.eu

Erratum to:
M. van Sinderen et al. (Eds.)
Enterprise Interoperability
DOI: 10.1007/978-3-642-33068-1

The book was inadvertently published with an incorrect name of the copyright holder. The name of the copyright holder for this book is: © IFIP International Federation for Information Processing. The book has been updated with the changes.

The updated original online version for this book can be found at
DOI: 10.1007/978-3-642-33068-1

M. van Sinderen et al. (Eds.): IWEI 2012, LNBIP 122, p. E1, 2012.
© IFIP International Federation for Information Processing 2017

Author Index